CHINA IS NOT OUR ENEMY

UNDERSTANDING CHINA IN CONTEXT TO CREATE A MORE HARMONIOUS WORLD

Tai P. Ng, Ph.D with Wah-Won Ng

 FriesenPress

One Printers Way
Altona, MB, ROG OBO
Canada

www.friesenpress.com

ISBN
978-1-03-912538-4 (Hardcover)
978-1-03-912537-7 (Paperback)
978-1-03-912539-1 (eBook)

1. *HISTORY, ASIA, CHINA*

Distributed to the trade by The Ingram Book Company

TABLE OF CONTENTS

INTRODUCTION

Dr. Tai P. Ng

I am a Chinese Canadian, a proud citizen of the world, and a concerned member of humanity. I was born in the former British colony of Hong Kong in 1939, when Nazi Germany invaded Poland, kicking off World War II (WWII) in Europe. Two years later, Japan attacked Pearl Harbor, and the US entered WWII by declaring war on Japan, Germany, and Italy. The Battle of Midway in the Pacific in 1942 and the D-Day landing at Normandy in 1944 marked the beginning of the Allies' victories in the war. When I started school in 1945, the atomic bomb was dropped on Hiroshima and Nagasaki, after which both Germany and Japan surrendered, and WWII finally ended. During those first few years of my life, humanity lost millions of precious lives, and many homes, families, cities, and even countries were destroyed and needed to be rebuilt. The memories I still retain from that war showcase its destructive power, from horrific Japanese atrocities to the endless stories of suffering in my family and among the Chinese people. Such reminiscences and sentiments have been difficult to share with North American friends because WWII was fought across the ocean millions of miles away from our homes. Most younger generations only read about the crimes of Nazi Germany and the Holocaust in Europe, the atomic bomb, or Japanese internment camps in North America. Innocent Japanese people did suffer heavily from the horror of the atomic bomb, but unfortunately, in the minds of many Canadians and Americans, that final act to end the war mistakenly turned all Japanese into victims rather than aggressors. And sadly, the real culprits of Japanese militarism and WWII in Asia were never truly persecuted for their crimes, which were just as horrific as those of the Nazis. This irony demonstrates the determinant power of the dominant Western narrative in this world. Despite all this, I am very proud to be a Canadian and love my chosen home country because of its peace-loving efforts; Canada is also the first country in the world to adopt an official multiculturalism policy, which helped create the culturally-inclusive environment I feel privileged to live in. Like many other Asians who have made North America their home for many years, I sincerely hope this doesn't change drastically because of increasing US and Canadian hostility toward China, Chinese people, and their businesses.

In 1956, I left my family in Hong Kong to study at Hampton High School in Melbourne, Australia, when I was only sixteen. Since then, I have lived, studied, worked, and retired as a geophysicist in Australia, Canada, and the United States for over sixty years. Having spent the most valuable period of my productive life in the Western world, and as a keen observer of global mega-events, I've been feeling a great urge to share what I have been living and thinking through, witnessing, and interpreting during my short tenure on planet Earth. Through the years, my personal interests have centered around traditional Chinese cultural heritage, which I've treasured because of its humanistic caring tenets, but in fact, both Chinese and Western cultures have nurtured me through the years, and been vital to me growing up and becoming who I am today. Writing is my way of repayment. As an avid student of the histories of these two civilizations in both the Chinese and English languages, even into my eighties, I still maintain great enthusiasm towards global events and affairs, continuously and dutifully observing, learning, interpreting, comparing, discovering, hypothesizing, and even debunking many of the trends and interpretations.

Serious global watching is a dynamic and engaging undertaking. In our present interconnected world, it should also be done holistically and contextually, with an open mind, maximum objectivity, and political impartiality in order to minimize distortion. This is not easy even for professionals or experts, since institutional biases limit their stance. It is even more dif-ficult because every one of us has our own biases based on our cultural identity and life experiences. But as a concerned member of humanity, whenever in doubt I always try to peel away the layers of labels, not think-ing as a Chinese, Canadian, Asian, or American, but instead focusing my moral judgment on what would best benefit humanity. Therein lies my dream of human solidarity, social harmony, and universal peace regardless of culture or belief. I dream of a world where we can live in harmony and unity, embracing rather than fearing our differences. I believe the first step towards that is a willingness to have an open mind and assume positive intent, followed by building empathy and living Stephen Covey's famous fifth habit of highly effective people—seeking first to understand, then to be understood.

Why this book?

It has been over thirteen years since the publication of my last book, *Chinese Culture, Western Culture*, which has given me time to reflect, remi-nisce, and learn more about our world. Before 2007, I was highly appre-hensive at the lack of good information in the West, and the unhealthy amount of misinformation causing misunderstandings concerning China almost daily in North American media. At the time, my book was an early attempt to provide some basic historical information and context, since there were very few good English resources available. I did not write about events after the Opium War, though, because at the time of publishing, China was early in a key juncture in its history, and I was not sure how the mega-trend of contemporary China was going to develop. Since then, both China and the world have undergone rapid transformations that affected each other, but especially since the financial crisis of 2008. As China's direction has become more clearly defined in the last two decades, and it has successfully demonstrated its ability to follow and deliver on its devel-opment plans, its actions and future are also becoming easier to interpret, giving me renewed enthusiasm and impetus to share some of my perspec-tives on what is happening. All the assumptions and directional insights I offered in my last book still hold, but the pace of change has definitely quickened. Regardless of what the future holds, China is really starting to carry its weight, the impact of which is being felt in many ways around our increasingly interconnected world.

With its current population of over 1.4 billion people living across a continental-scale territory, contemporary China consists of one majority Han race and fifty-five official minority races. China has widely diverse cultural and economic conditions, and many varieties of local dialects, customs, foods, and historical stories have been preserved and co-exist within China to this very day. This diversity has been sustainable throughout its long history because of the many tolerant and inclusive tenets and virtues embedded in Chinese culture. Many are natural human values, commonly found in other human cultures and societies, but in China's case, they have been reinforced through Confucian narratives, generation after generation, continuously evolving to this day. This makes China so much more complex and organic than outsiders can possibly imagine. Many experts in Western social sciences often misinterpret China simply because their expertise does not include first-hand domestic Chinese experience. Even for foreigners living inside China, it is not easy to discern the complex network of organic social and political development if their observations are too narrowly focused.

With a mindset that China is our enemy, Western biases tend to focus on specific individuals and institutions, ignoring the main trends of development, which are clearer in direction and intent, but could easily be dismissed over ideological or political differences as authoritarian communist propaganda. To be newsworthy, Western media often focuses on events of rare occurrence or extraordinary issues, especially regarding human rights or other governmental violations. With its size, diversity, complexity, and cultural intricacy however, one can inevitably find the best and worst of anything, and everything in-between, happening somewhere in China if you look hard enough. Unfortunately, by emphasizing the most sensational stories, Western news tends to represent the edges of society and the extremely small percentiles of a normal distribution which may not be statistically significant. This may be one of the key reasons that I and many others find Western news and reporting to have such strong negative biases against China and its people. China seems to always be either on the verge of a catastrophic collapse, or being painted as an enemy seriously threatening the established order of the free world.

My interest, on the other hand, is to discern the macroscopic trends from the long history of China in order to study where the country and its civilization is heading, especially in contrast to its Western counterparts. To properly extrapolate the two trajectories requires understanding of so many different fields in science, humanities, and social sciences, including but not limited to geography, sociology, political science, economics, comparative philosophy, brain studies, organizational behavior, mass socio-psychology, and many more, while mapping them to history and global context. The scale and scope of this endeavor is infinite, which can be daunting to many. It is much more ideally suited to generalists like me rather than the specialists that typically write about specific topics regarding China and global affairs. Even then, the depth and breadth required is so overwhelmingly large that I can only hope to scratch some of the surfaces and inspire other generalists with similar macroscopic interest and focus, but ideally with stronger and different backgrounds or experiences, both culturally and professionally, to carry this forward. Understanding the macroscopic situation and seeing the bigger picture from different perspectives is important for our collective future and global development, but has mostly been ignored by global citizens and even academic communities, as they tend to focus and train in highly specialized fields. A more holistic and contextual understanding of humanity and its multifaceted cultures is becoming critical to our survival as a species because of our strong influence on each other, and on our planet, due to increasing global connectivity.

To keep my writing grounded in facts and statistics to maximize objectivity, I've tried to ignore simplistic political or ideological labels that may be mainstream, avoid getting lost in the rabbit hole of explaining specific situations that critics are vocally monitoring regarding Chinese governmental actions and policies, and misinformation often generated for political purposes, and instead focus solely on statistically significant mega events, as well as conditions of the general populace in China, which represents that vast majority living in the 95th percentile of a normal distribution. It is almost impossible not to make over-generalized statements or sound like a naive idealist. Hence, I fervently hope our dear readers can rise up with us to see the forest instead of getting lost in the trees, and be patient and understanding of the limitations this endeavor naturally brings.

Long term central planning from five to twenty-five years is a hallmark of the Chinese government, both central and provincial, and something you rarely see in the West because of its short election cycle. While the longer-term plans are definitely more of a directional guideline, their Five-Year Plans are all available to the public in great detail, and they have built enough momentum, experience, and consistency now to hit or even exceed most of those milestones, even in a fast changing world. Following the pragmatism and flexibility of the Chinese tradition, the Chinese government is designed to be very adaptive to rapid changes in local, national, and global conditions, thereby making serious China watching both interesting and demanding. Unfortunately, with the rapid pace of organic change, misinterpretation and misunderstanding are also becoming more frequent, even with up-to-date information, because so many people lack the historical context—this includes Western-educated Chinese people, and even some of the specialists in the relevant fields of interest. My hope is to provide readers with an appropriate amount of historical context and systematic thinking so they can better understand and interpret Chinese decision-making processes and situations.

Different paths of civilizational development

I find both Chinese and Western cultures to be fascinating because of how different they are, and yet, if you look closely, they are also very complementary to each other. This is not to say they are the only cultures in the world, obviously, but because both have led the world at various times in history and many others have sprouted from the origins of these two, they are arguably the most consequential and influential to humanity. Over the years, I have been intrigued by what, how, and why there are such disparities, and consequently studied a wide range of aspects throughout the history of both cultures, looking at thinking as well as diverse philosophical, cultural, social, economic, and political human experience. These disparities influence people's attitudes and behaviors in life, and social and political aptitudes, resulting in very different communities and ultimately civilizations. Each culture was primarily local in its early days of development and unique in a broad sense. Each had its own advantages and disadvantages in order to adapt to its different environments, but neither was consistently better than the other. One's advantage can easily become a disadvantage and vice versa when the situation or context changes. Just as for individual humans, self-awareness is key to knowing when to apply your strengths and when to make up for your shortcomings.

China has come a long way economically since 2007, but is getting even more difficult for outsiders to understand because it is developing along a very different trajectory, and is dealing with more diverse and complex problems in its modernization than any other country has experienced, because of its scale, socio-political values, and long-spanning history. It is also trying to return closer to its own roots and re-embrace some of the ancient ways, which makes it even more incomprehensible to Westerners. Increasingly, however, many Chinese people and even some non-Chinese are realizing the profoundness of traditional Chinese culture and civilization in term of its contribution to humanity and how it should be more appreciated and treasured. The large scale in terms of land mass and population, its long history—persisting continuously for thousands of years—the tenets of harmony in diversity and broadminded inclusiveness, the resourcefulness of its people, its secular, humanistic, and pragmatic culture—these and many more make the Chinese experience uniquely complex, unrivaled by any other civilization in history, and completely incomprehensible without proper context. Coupled with so much misinformation and misunderstanding propagated by English media, any efforts that can result in a better understanding of China in the Western world will enable the two civilizations to co-exist more harmoniously, thereby contributing to world peace.

Written Chinese history dates back continuously for three thousand years. For environmental and geographical reasons, the primarily agrarian Chinese civilization developed in isolation and very early on grew to be large-scale in terms of people and territory, diverse in population, and possessing a maturity in governance unmatched by others. The vastness and scale of China cannot be overemphasized in contrast with other cradles of civilization at the time such as Greece and Mesopotamia. All of the Greek city-states would have fit into the smallest of the Chinese kingdoms in the fifth century BC. The Yangtze and Yellow Rivers were two of the world's ten largest. Many of the larger plains, plateaus, and provinces in China exceeded the size of an average-sized country in Europe. With such a drastic contrast in scale, the challenges encountered were also very different, resulting in very different sociopolitical thinking, ideals, and interpretations of leadership and "state governance." Such disparity persisted throughout history and is easily observable even today, though pundits with different cultural backgrounds may offer varying interpretations of why.

Throughout its long history, Chinese people have been challenged and suffered, generation after generation, through countless natural and human calamities, persevering like none other and developing a resiliency to difficult conditions. Through these, they learned that leadership capability, moral governance, and social harmony are key to their happiness. I believe a key reason behind the tenacity and durability of this culture is its rootedness and embeddedness—its philosophy of viewing humanity as an integral part of Nature, knowingly controlling our own desires and greed, and working within constraints instead of battling against them. Practicing self-restraint during good times, saving and conserving for the bad times. To the Chinese, all social relationships are modelled after the family, the most basic reverent relationship produced by Nature, which is considered moral and just. Ethics and morality, not religion, are at the core of Chinese civilization.

Both the Chinese people and their government continuously learn from the many lessons of history (both their own and others) and have developed an aptitude for human organization and collaboration, knowing that humans are weak if isolated and can only survive when grouped together in families and communities. Confucian heritage taught Chinese people to be humble, tolerant, benevolent, and altruistic to fellow humans, especially to weaker ones. Because of their past suffering, Chinese people hate conflict and war of any kind, and always aspire for peace. Attainment of balance in life and social harmony are their core cultural objectives. They constantly strive to establish a uniquely competitive form of governance which selects capable and ethical leaders through examination, experience, and meritocratic promotion, and build a hierarchical bureaucratic system of government which, when it works, is effective, stable, and trustworthy for the majority of its people. Emphasizing introspection and education, the Chinese system today trains professional party cadres and politicians to behave morally and serve the people. This has also led to many corrupted officials being purged and convicted. The efficacy of the current Chinese system was demonstrated during the pandemic of 2020, even though some Westerners kept blaming China for it and focusing on human rights rather than the number of lives saved. To many Chinese, however, social harmony and security with good governance is the best kind of human right, a form of positive freedom.

Before the communists came to power in 1949, Chinese people were vividly described as being like a pot of loose sand. Many of the people living in China now understand the organizational and protective function of their government, recognizing that their wellbeing in life and that of their family members relies heavily on its integrity and capability. They know a good government when they see one, as they still remember how much they suffered under the bad ones in the past. When they find a government they can trust, however, nobody works as hard to willingly to follow its leadership. Contrary to common Western expectations about an "authoritarian communist regime," 800 million Chinese were lifted out of extreme poverty over the past four decades. In November of 2020, China announced that it had attained its goal to eradicate extreme poverty, despite the pandemic that year—a tremendous achievement unmatched anywhere in the world or in history. But even more importantly, if one travels to China and interacts with the locals, it is obvious that the Chinese people are generally more free, richer, and happier than any other time in their history, and even compared to many others in the world today. China is following its own path of modernization and rejuvenation and even the most powerful country in the world cannot stop its progress. But beyond acknowledging this fact, we should make the time to truly understand why.

To most Westerners, China is a black box with total lack of transparency. I believe that is because a strong historical and cultural context is crucial to any understanding and interpretation of China and its people due to its uniquely large scale, culture, complexity, and extensive historical experience. In the United States, in particular, after four years of feeding public misinformation concerning China under the Trump administration, people can no longer tell facts from lies, both domestically and internationally. American top officials persistently demonize China to divert attention from other problems within its own borders, creating hostility towards China and Chinese people for many Americans. The wars waged against China by the US government on multiple fronts such as trade, Intellectual Property (IP), and others, will take many years of focused time and effort before it can be undone. Yet our world increasingly needs to have the two top countries working together to solve many of our global problems rather than competing for dominance. My hope is that more people will be willing to be objective and open minded to a different perspective and culture, and that this book will help bridge that contextual gap through an increase in mutual understanding, appreciation, empathy, and trust.

Reducing misunderstandings

In the September/October 2020 issue of *Foreign Affairs*, strategist Aaron Friedberg[1] argued that the United States and its allies and partners should use aggressive policies to contain China. He was not alone in taking that stance—there are easily thousands of similar articles and speeches from various renowned professors and politicians. The author of this particular article is a Professor of Politics and International Affairs at Princeton University. Immediately after its publication, a group of eight top American foreign affairs experts, including Michael D. Swaine, Ezra F. Vogel, et al.[2] responded by pointing out that Friedberg's hawkish position on China was based on a flawed presumption that the bulk of Beijing's policy disagreements with the West arose from its authoritarian political system. They point to the fact that many of China's international concerns have grown out of long-standing nationalist beliefs and cultural attitudes that long predate communist rule. These include the resentment caused by over a century of predatory Western behavior in East Asia, a profound, and at times bristling, pride in China's rise, and deep-seated fears that a more freewheeling domestic political process could jeopardize the stability that has facilitated greater prosperity. Such nationalist attitudes and concerns

---

1 Aaron L. Friedberg, "An Answer to Aggression: How to Push Back Against Beijing," *Foreign Affairs*, Volume 99, Number 5 (September/October 2020).

2 Michael D. Swaine, et al., "The Overreach of the China Hawks: Aggression Is the Wrong Response to Beijing," *Foreign Affairs*, October 23, 2020, https://www.foreignaffairs.com/articles/china/2020-10-23/overreach-china-hawks

would prevail even in a democratic China—there is no reason to believe that China's system of government is what makes Beijing eager to protect what it regards as its territory and reestablish itself as a major power in Asia and the world.

I tend to concur that Friedberg's interpretation of China is purely dualistic, based on a false Cold War mentality of capitalism versus communism, which is typical of Eurocentric thinking. I was also encouraged to see so many of his peers recognize the long historical and cultural context so they could interpret China more holistically, organically, and contextually, something I hope all our readers will be able to do after reading this book. China will continue to pursue, and likely succeed, at its long-term strategy, despite antagonistic American attitudes. But cooperation and win-win are a better strategy for both countries and the world. Depending on which expert's strategic advice the US government decides to follow, the outcome can be as drastically different as war or peace for the world. There is a lot riding on getting it right.

I have personally experienced both cultures for decades and witnessed how particular situations, thinking, and actions can be influenced by these cultural and historical differences, as well as how the fortune of each civilization has changed during my lifetime. It has been even more fascinating as I've aged to realize that once you can truly understand both the historical trajectory and background context of a given culture, events start to become predictable on a macroscopic scale. At the end of the day, countries behave relatively consistently based on their worldview, history, and values. Though leaders may differ in their own thinking and values, very rarely do they significantly deviate from their country's historical trajectory. This is why it's so important to build contextual understanding of each other, to continuously keep in mind the historical background and context that guides every decision. Through mutual trust and empathy, the result of a deeper understanding, we can get to better know each other, and maybe even ourselves. It took China over 200 years to realize that the Western scientific method, thinking, and spirit are excellent ways to understand and work with Nature, something the ancient Chinese did not know. But once they understood the capabilities of science, it became a powerful tool for innovation and improvement to our quality of life, as we are witnessing today. Similarly, it will take time for Westerners to realize that the traditional Chinese ways of balance, inclusiveness, humility, tolerance, win-win, conservation, and sustainability are important to social harmony and human solidarity in our interrelated world. Our world will be a better place if everyone can work more collaboratively.

Understanding China is complex but not impossible. I believe that properly interpreting any situation requires an open mind and knowledge of three vectors applied to the main players in that situation—thinking preferences, historical trajectory, and situational context. When one of the players is China or traditional Chinese, my hope is that this book can provide you with the background needed to better interpret the situation and get a better outcome for all involved. But please keep in mind that people are unique and ever changing as they grow, so no book or knowledge gained should ever be treated as a substitute for taking the time to get to know the other person and trying to walk a mile in their shoes.

How to use this book

This book is divided into three main parts. Part One focuses on Chinese thinking preferences, and hence worldviews, looking briefly at how they diverged to be so different from Western thinking preferences, but also how they are complementary. How we think influences our attitudes and approaches to life, which in turn influences our worldviews and how we interact with others, and then how we build communities and ultimately civilizations. Chinese civilization has endured for over 5000 years, and I believe many of the traditional tenets that trace back to Confucius and influence many Asian cultures even today are an enduring reminder to humanity on how to behave and how to treat others. Holistic and correlative thinking, belief in an inherently good human nature, and the ability for self-cultivation to restore the good in people, learning and practicing good virtues and striving for self-transcendence, the importance of social responsibility, recognizing harmony in diversity, and following "the Way"—these are all concepts that are experiencing a rebirth because they are natural concepts that resonate with most of humanity and provide an important balance to much of Western society and thinking.

Part Two begins by providing a brief mega-historical account of the development of Chinese civilization essential for understanding China and the Chinese people. Chinese intellectuals always pride themselves on taking responsibility for the well-being of the whole world (*Tianxia*) and its people, which is a significant part of Chinese heritage. One cannot understand China without understanding its intellectual heritage, socio-political aspirations, and commitments, which are by-products of its large-scale development. The evolution of the Chinese Communist Party, the traditional secular and humanitarian political tenets and ideals, the building of a bureaucratic and meritocratic hierarchy, the precept of benevolent governance, the precept of a shared future destiny, and even the development of a modern Silk Road—all are intricately related to traditional thinking, worldviews, and philosophy. This is completely different from the West, where everything is viewed through a lens of theistic rationalism over the last two millennia.

Part Three speculates on how the paradigmatic differences between China and the West could affect our future, and some concepts and lessons we should leverage more. With a goal of crafting a better future for humanity, we need to collectively think bigger in order to solve the problems facing our world in the future. Globalization is forcing us all to become intricately connected, whether we want to or not. Historically we have relied on our governments and a handful of global institutions to solve the world's problems, but increasingly the problems are becoming too large for any one country or any one institution to properly solve—problems like climate change have shown how vulnerable humanity really is if we don't live in harmony with Nature and within the limits of what the Earth provides for us. We are also learning how urgent and necessary it is for us to work together if we are to craft a peaceful future for humanity. This is where the Chinese tenets and experience around human collaboration and solidarity, as well as the Confucian narrative on how to be human, become relevant and important.

The COVID-19 pandemic of 2020 was a strong reminder of the powerful laws of Nature within which humanity should operate. We are more connected and more reliant on Nature than ever before. The Chinese Confucian Way, which was derived through centuries of living in accordance with Nature, has a strong emphasis on human relations, which requires tolerance, mutual respect, social harmony, win-win thinking, and balance in order to achieve universal peace. This way of thinking is experiencing a rejuvenation, as many believe it may well be the right pre-scription of universal values and principles to guide humanity to a peace-ful shared destiny in the future. Unfortunately, even China today needs to return to its own cultural roots and heritage after centuries of civiliza-tion decay and corruption, plus foreign incursion. People need to be re-educated, and at the same time, they need to renew and modernize their nation. Progress has been made, even though it takes time and there is still a long way to go, especially when so much effort is wasted counteract-ing misinformation and hostile politics. Throughout 2020, politics aside, the Chinese were able to demonstrate to the world their unique cultural efficacy in handling the pandemic, and that through traditional Chinese Confucian tenets and effective benevolent governance, they can protect their people and even defeat a pandemic.

There are a lot of irrational fears about China—its people, its foreign policy, its politics. People fear what they cannot understand, and when that fear becomes prevalent in people with power, it can lead us to war. While America has led our world since the end of World War II, and will con-tinue to for some time to come, it is more divided now than ever before. It has become skeptical and pessimistic, and has started closing its doors to the outside world. I am comforted that the new Biden presidency is bring-ing the US back into key global commitments like the Paris Accord and the WHO. With global risks like climate change facing us, we need the commitment and the leadership of the US to make meaningful change. Our democratic system of government is based on partisan competition which follows the paradigm of a zero-sum game where gaining a seat in Congress for a Democrat means a corresponding loss for a Republican. Such a paradigm can be toxic when applied to global affairs, especially for a superpower. We all want world peace and to do the right thing, but the US has turned that into a crusade for democracy instead of world harmony. That must change because we don't need another Cold War. Until they can allow room for other systems in the world and to stop assuming all non-democratic nations are naturally flawed, there can be no true peace. When we can all accept that there are other ways of thinking about things, other worldviews, other ways to run a country, then we can start to truly embrace our differences rather than fighting or fearing them. And taking it a step further, we can start to leverage the strengths of each to build a stronger, more harmonious, and more peaceful humanity on Earth.

We must see the urgency now and take every shortcut available to us, including learning from our collective histories and purposefully building our empathy and tolerance towards each other rather than standing our ground confrontationally. We must work together to craft a new world order that combines the best of humanity's experiences and values. We must seek harmony in diversity, leveraging each other's strengths and learning from each other continuously to get stronger faster. The time is now, and each of us can make a change, however small. I long for the day when humanity of all races, religions, and creeds can collaboratively work together, building harmony and peace for our future generations. I am so proud you have chosen this book as a step on your journey towards a better us, and a better world. Let's stop with the "us versus them," and instead, let's all encourage the empathy and tolerance in ourselves and each other that will save the future of humanity and bring us through this challenge together.

Part I:
A Different Way of Thinking

Anyone who has interfaced with both Chinese and Westerners can attest that people traditionally ingrained in the two cultures often think quite differently. But as anyone brought up in a hybrid of both cultures can attest, they can be very complementary and it is possible, even beneficial, to live and breathe as a mix of the two. They may seem opposite at times, but we prefer to think of them as your right brain and left brain. Everyone has both, but typically a tendency to use one more than the other. If we hone our ability to flex both sides of the brain, we become intellectually capable of dealing effectively with more situations. As our world merges into a more global society with a shared future, the ability to understand both Chinese and Western thinking is becoming a necessary skill for all of humankind.

ONE: THE EVOLUTION OF THOUGHT

Jean Piaget's theory of cognitive development is an interesting model for how humans develop knowledge. Piaget observed children playing and noted that infants used two innate reflexes, assimilation and accommodation, interchangeably in an attempt to adapt to their environment. As their experience in any given environment increases, these two reflexes get replaced with constructed, rather than innate, schemas and then structures. As a person's structures become more complex, they are organized in a hierarchical manner from general to specific. Within this hierarchy, Piaget identified multiple stages of cognitive development from infancy to adulthood. The first is experience itself; that is, the repetition of observations and motor actions in the context of interacting with the environment. Knowledge is then developed as experiences accumulate. Finally, the ability to think results from the accumulation of knowledge. This process of observation, interaction, experience, knowledge, and thinking is a dynamic feedback system, a self-reinforcing process.

This evolutionary process should be equally applicable to the development of a culture as it is to human growth. A culture in its infancy is shaped by observations and interactions between individuals and their environment. Over time, those experiences turn into knowledge represented by preferences, customs, and traditions, and even rituals that get passed down from generation to generation. Hence, in order to truly understand how and why people in a specific culture thinks, it is important to examine the environments that incubated those cultures and people's interactions with those environments in order to understand how their knowledge and thinking was cultivated.

TWO VERY DIFFERENT HUMAN EVOLUTIONS

The reality is that the differences in Chinese and Western thinking go much deeper than most of us realize. In fact, we asserted in our last book[3] that the differences go back as far as the Ice Ages approximately two million years ago. Apart from genetic considerations, environmental and evolutionary differences such as natural milieu, climatic conditions, and geographic location all played an important role. Pre-humans and early humans were closely integrated with their natural environment because of their total dependence on Nature for food, water, clothing, and shelter. Since most of China was situated in much lower latitudes relative to Europe, it was never covered in ice sheets like Europe was. This is apparently the most important factor in the abundance of fauna and flora observed in China. In contrast, there was a scarcity of plant life and small animals in Europe, which suffered heavily from the severity of the Ice Ages, and was left mainly with large animals that had to be hunted as a source of food. We believe this major difference had profound consequences on the development of our brains and thinking processes during the Paleolithic Era in both China and Europe (including the Near East). In addition, China was developed in relative geographic isolation compared with the open, active, seafaring heritages around the Mediterranean.

Steven Mithen[4] and others studied prehistoric evolutionary thought development, outlining elements, timelines, and causative factors in the evolution of the human mind by integrating evolutionary psychology, developmental psychology, brain study, and cognitive archaeology, and

---

3 Tai P. Ng and Wah-Won Ng, *Chinese Culture, Western Culture: How Cross-Cultural Views of History, Philosophy, and Human Relationships Will Change Modern Global Society* (iUniverse Inc, 2007).

4 Steven Mithen, *The Prehistory of the Mind: The Cognitive Origins of Art, Religion and Science* (Thames and Hudson, 1996).

compiled a systematic account. Mithen identified three distinct phases in the development of intelligence. The first phase, occurring in both infants and early hominids, involved mostly processing of information, making connections, and solving problems. The second phase, exemplified by young children and hominids of the middle period, involved building functional structure or specialized modules that functioned mostly independently of each other—for social understanding (how to behave in a group setting), natural environment (sensitivity to plants, animals, and surroundings), language (to communicate with others), and technology (development of tools). The third phase is where humans finally begin to use language, but almost exclusively for social interchanges, developing improved cognitive fluidity over time. They were able to prove that for various reasons, humans from different historical or environmental settings established different sets of connections of intelligence, faculties, and skills through prehistory and history. This contributed to the formation of different cultural preferences, traditions, and sensibilities. For example, after the Ice Ages, European ancestors needed to focus on big game hunting to survive. Hunting animals much bigger than themselves required not only knowledge of the animals, but also skills, tools, teamwork, tactics, and workable strategies. As Mithen postulated, humans needed social skills to perform effectively as a group and share the fruits of their labor. This led to a focus on the development of rational and analytical thinking.

The Greeks, with their insistence on seeking truth through explicit knowledge, ultimately adopted idealistic dualism as a major life philosophy that endured for many years in the Western world. It is widely accepted that the patterns set by the Greeks and Romans permeate Western civilization and have produced many brilliant thinkers throughout history. They are almost all deep thinkers, experts in their specific fields of interest. Modern English derives well over half of its vocabulary from Latin and Greek. Philosophy, politics, religion, science, art, music, and athletics are all words whose etymology can be traced back to the Greeks and Romans. The ideas expressed by these seven words are highly significant because they represent the essence of Western heritage. Western civilization, which inherited the Greco-Roman culture, was able to eventually create science, from which we are still benefiting today.

Ancient Greek contributions to philosophy were not an accident. Greek art is intellectual art, the art of men who were clear and lucid thinkers. It is therefore rather plain and simple. It is axiomatic that Greek art is the dictum of men who wished to brush aside all obscurity, superfluity, and entanglement in order to see clearly, plainly, and unadorned that which they wished to express. Classical sculpture focused mostly on the human figure. Depicted in moments of supreme poise or captured in athletic acts, the human body was apotheosized in stone. Artists sought to express the body as a perfect organic unity, an unassailable, archetypal form, with its shape and figure clearly embodying Platonic ideals. Gods and goddesses were imagined in human form, but they were ideal in proportion, and without imperfection. The unclothed human figure in its most perfect manifestation was admired for its harmonious beauty. The Greek's early commitment to rational, logical, analytical thinking, and perfection as depicted in Greek art is astonishing. Classical Greek scholars' obsession with ontology and the development of causal thinking follows from this tradition. And the simplistic and dualistic preference of the Greco-Roman heritage had a strong influence on the subsequent development of Western values, philosophy, worldviews, religion, and sociopolitical ideals.

The Chinese, on the other hand, survived the Ice Ages much more easily. Because most of low-latitude China escaped the spread of the ice sheet, the plants and animals in the environment were abundant and diversified, and the people had neither the time nor the need to study any one species of prey or forage extensively. By the late Pleistocene period, the brain size was fully developed, so they had the potential intelligence of a modern human. Their survival was not threatened, and they were content to live as a part of Nature, which provided in abundance. Because the inhabitable areas of China were also much bigger than those in Europe, population growth was proportionally larger and more dense, which drove early development in Neolithic agriculture on a scale larger than that seen anywhere else in the world, as well as a need for humans to learn how to live in harmony with themselves, other humans, and with Nature.

The early Chinese were keen observers of Nature. Many classical Chinese sages spent a lifetime essentially categorizing and recording their surroundings and observing patterns in the sky. Over generations they sorted many species of animals and plants according to their similarities and differences using specific characteristics such as overall shape, texture, color, sound, specific posture, personality, and habits. With the abundance of Nature, they became quite practical and utilitarian, trying to utilize as much of their surroundings as possible to enhance their lives, and often characterizing objects in terms of their usefulness and application. This tendency carried over to Chinese philosophy, legends, and even religions, all of which are practical, moral, or contain an important lesson to learn. It was the different Chinese sages in Chinese legends who taught people how to use fire to cook, build shelters for protection, and who tasted one hundred plants in a day to sort out the ones safe for human consumption. This is in stark contrast to Greek or Roman mythology which typically showcased gods and goddesses with the power to bend Nature to their will.

VIEWS ON NATURE AND REALITY

Human conceptualizations of Nature underpin our views of the world and, consequently, influence our thinking. The ancient Greeks asked many questions and thought deeply about thinking itself.[5] They pondered the "what" questions—What is truth? What is real? What is the world made of? Or at times, what am I? Consequently, Western truth is based upon the knowledge of what is real and what represents that reality. It seeks permanence and substance in things and an ontological understanding of knowledge. It is not accidental that Western civilization ultimately became dominated by Christianity, a monotheistic religion. The Greeks prided themselves on objectivity, universality, causality, and deductive principle-based thinking. Yet the early Greeks' rejection of empirical and sensory experience as well as any non-causal or less than rational, analytical, or explicit ways of thinking has had enduring dire consequences to the Western world. Only after the Renaissance and Enlightenment were more inclusive perspectives on thought recovered. But even then, dualistic thinking continued. The Western inclination for seeing the world as black and white, right or wrong, and in terms of zero-sum games where the winner takes all still persists today. Consciously or not, Eurocentric thinking still dominates in the Western world.

---

5 David L. Hall and Roger T. Ames, *Anticipating China: Thinking Through the Narratives of Chinese and Western Culture* (State University of New York Press, 1995).

Instead of asking the "what" question as the ancient Greeks did, the Chinese tended to ask "where." Where did I go wrong? Where can I improve? Where have we been? Where is the Way? The Chinese have long accepted the fact that change and motion are an integral part of life, so they sought "the Way" to accommodate this phenomenon, or apparent reality. Chinese thinkers were not preoccupied with rationalizing why everything changes and instead sought to experience the world rather than understand it. For Chinese people, thinking is actualizing or realizing the meaningfulness of the world, a process that engages the whole person. If we can look at events from every possible perspective, the whole picture of the truth will come out, just as a prism can take a rainbow of colors and recompose white light from it. Being tolerant and inclusive of differences in order to illuminate a more beautiful whole is the way of Nature.

The ancient Chinese were too pragmatic in their thinking to be concerned with epistemology and ontology. For Confucius (551–479 BC) and the Chinese tradition, thinking was not about abstract reasoning or objectivity. Rather, it was an activity intended to lead to the achievement of a practical result. It sought to maximize the potential of the existing possibilities and contributing conditions. The Chinese generally make no distinction between reality and actuality because they believe the validity of principles can be tested only through actual events. Reality is a tacit concept grounded in concrete observation and experience. So rather than using norms to evoke a behavioral response, they prefer to use images, models, analogies, and metaphors to communicate and cultivate relationships.

The Chinese approach to thinking also follows a pattern of polar oscillation or cyclical return. The world is envisioned as a theatre with a limited playbill of tragedies and comedies running in repertory. The Chinese believe in infinity and the cyclical nature of time. History, whether personal, societal, national, global, or cosmological, repeats itself in many different ways. Thus, if we are attuned to the lessons of history, we can see the future through both the present and the past.

The world, as a part of the universe, is a dynamic organism in which every element and every event is interrelated. The Chinese believe that even our bodies, as microcosms of Nature, are all mimicking in miniature the functioning of the universe, and each person is a unified continuum of body and soul. The Chinese approach to solving problems, whether personal, social, or political, is to strike a dynamic balance between the extremes and look at it holistically. This is the rule of the golden mean. It is therefore natural that humanly personal, familial, social, and world orders, not the supernatural, are what constituted Chinese morality and ethicality. As holistic and practical thinkers, the Chinese people, and Chinese intellectuals in particular, have always been concerned with the destiny and future of humankind, a topic traditionally less of interest to more individualistic Western thinkers.

CORRELATIVE VS. DUALISTIC THINKING

Chinese thinking often depends on a type of analogy or metaphor, which may be called correlative thinking. Some of the earliest Chinese documentation in existence contains observations that their world and the plants they gathered for food came and went in cyclical patterns, according to the changing weather of the four seasons. They also became aware that the two extremes, which they called yin and yang, were complementary. Any single polarity alone lacked meaning in the absence of the other. As they saw it, the elements and events of the world always appear in pairs. Cold and hot, low and high, moon and sun, night and day, left and right, give and take, complete and one-sided, genial and overbearing, all are symmetrically related and reliant upon their complement for meaning. Yin does not transcend yang, just as night does not transcend day. Every element in the world is simply relative to every other. More significantly, in Nature's order, night always turns into day, and day always turns back to night. The extreme yin will become the opposite yang; such is the rule of Nature.

The concept of polarity, which is key to understanding Chinese thinking, contrasts with the concept of dualism which is not relative, as well as the ideological and religious universalism that has long occupied Western thought. Traditional Western ways of thinking look at polar extremes as conflicting or differentiating, a process of synthesis and antithesis, being and non-being, as opposed to the more Chinese concept of complementarity and wholeness. It is easy for Westerners or Arabs to think they have mastered the only "Truth" in the world, and to seek global domination through a mission to spread the Word. And if their faith is ever threatened, they are willing to become martyrs.

In contrast, the Chinese are indifferent to the notion of a final end, and literally live the mantra of "change is the only constant." They seek to interpret reality as a combination of all its manifestations, which itself is an interrelated continuum. Reality consists of a myriad of things that can be viewed in multiple ways, including ourselves, similar to the way a prism can diffract white light into a rainbow of colors. The world is ever changing, and we must literally "go with the flow" and adapt ourselves to the change. History is a time record of such changes, and we can all learn from it. Both space and time are interrelated continuums. Since the Chinese are not committed to principle-based deductive reasoning, they use both inductive and deductive reasoning in the process. This is why contextual and historical understanding of our world is so important, especially for how the Chinese view the world. While recognizing that so much of reality is tacit, indeterminate, and unpredictable, they nevertheless work to keep it grounded with concrete observation and experience. If we cannot change others or the circumstances, we can always change ourselves by learning from others, our past experiences, and from Nature, and better ourselves to contribute to our shared future reality. By extension, it is our duty to accommodate each other since we are all related, even though in certain respects, we are different. This process should always begin from the inside of our hearts, introspecting to elucidate our own moral selves, and asking ourselves, "how can I do more to collectively better myself, my family, and our world?" It is with this culture and thinking that China has persevered continuously for millennia. This collectivistic attitude is one of the key differentiators between traditional Chinese thinking and the individualism of Westerners.

HOLISTIC VS. ANALYTICAL THINKING

Western thinking is strongly analytical. Concepts, rules, and ideologies all need to be well-defined—logical, rational, and explicit. For this reason, Westerners excel in the world of classical science. Ambiguities are to be avoided wherever possible. They use abstraction to isolate one aspect from all others (and from its context) so they can focus attention solely upon one object or aspect. This type of isolation of an aspect is useful when you wish to study a particular aspect, and discover the laws that govern it, free from other influences. This is a key concept of the scientific method, so it is not accidental that Westerners brought the world modern science. Western logic, when applied to the experience of humanity, has resulted in a dichotomy of man and Nature, body and soul, individual and society, individual and state, space and time, and so forth. Separate, independent, individual parts comprise the whole, creating a single-ordered world.

Western culture seeks rational or logical order that is inclined toward universality, generality, and absolute substitutability, which in principle is indifferent to the elements that comprise the order. As such, it is natural for the Western world to develop a monotheistic civilization with universal political ideologies around individualism, democracy, liberalism, and rule of law for every man and woman, all created equal with inalienable rights.

In contrast, Chinese thinking is weak on the analytical side but tends to be more holistic, integrative, and inclusive. They dislike definitions and are more comfortable with ambiguity. Concepts, rules, and ideologies are often tacit and implicit, and allow plenty of room for interpretation and spontaneity. The universe is a dynamic organism with humanity, society, earth, and Nature fully integrated in dynamic equilibrium. It is open, with no ends and no clear marked boundaries between things. Every element of the universe is interrelated to every other element. Space-time is a wavelike continuum with every moment of existence and every process or phenomenon constantly recreated and renewed, novel and spontaneous each time. The ideal world order is multifaceted, harmonious, and aesthetically pleasing.

An aesthetic order begins with the uniqueness of each thing, assessing whether and how each element contributes to the balanced complexity of its context. Aesthetic order focuses on the way in which a single, specific detail contributes to a harmony comprised of many individual details acting in relationship to one another. Aesthetic order presses in the direction of particularity and uniqueness, and away from universality. So it is equally natural for the Chinese to develop an aesthetic civilization with a hierarchical social and political order, and a bureaucracy of government reliant on strong, virtuous, and capable leaders with humility to serve for the collective benefit of the common people.

The concepts of aesthetic and logical order are inversely related. A complex of elements reaches the maximum of aesthetic disorder with the realization of absolute uniformity. But this is the highest degree of rational order. Each is powerful and brings order to their world. Yet each has its advantages, disadvantages, and applicability dependent on the situation and context, which changes rapidly as a function of time.

TWO: ATTITUDES AND APPROACHES TO LIFE

How one perceives oneself is probably one of the most important issues in modern psychology because it ultimately affects all other relationships. Self-perception also determines one's temperament, attitudes, and approaches to life, which in turn influences our value systems and worldviews.

VIEWS ON HUMAN NATURE

A major Chinese classic *Zhongyong*, or *The Doctrine of the Mean*, opens with this verse:

> What *Tian* (Nature or macrocosmos) imparts to man is
> called *Xing*, human nature.
> To follow one's nature is called *Dao*, the way.
> To cultivate the way is called education.

Since the time of Confucius in fifth century BC, and in the Warring States period that followed, also known as "the Hundred Schools of Thought," Chinese philosophers of all schools have debated the notion of human nature. The Xunzi (~310–220 BC) believed human nature was essentially bad. The Gaozi believed human nature was neither good nor bad. Mengzi, or Mencius (~372-289 BC), the dominant school of Confucianism, believed in the innate goodness of all humans. Mencius held that human nature is good because, when guided by innate feelings, a person will do what is good and develop into a full moral being. According to Mencius, there are four nascent moral senses: the feeling of compassion (benevolence), shame (righteousness or a failure in one's desire for goodness), reverence (respect or deference), and discrimination (judgment) between right and wrong. One of his examples was imagining the feeling of compassion that would be instinctively aroused if one were to see a child about to fall into a well. We react spontaneously because we are endowed with a heart that cannot endure the suffering of fellow human beings, especially the suffering of an innocent child.

Even though Xunzi believed human nature was inherently bad, he believed it could be taught, which was in agreement with Mencius and Gaozi. Like many early Chinese thinkers, Mencius believed that to cultivate oneself according to one's true nature is to follow the Way, which fulfills a design inscribed by Nature upon our human hearts. The microcosmos of our own heart-mind would naturally follow the laws of the macrocosmos, or Nature. Both Confucianism and Daoism, the two dominant schools in China, required an understanding of one's nature relative to one's context and a restructuring of one's values to accommodate the natural order of the universe, making one's own life significant at the same time. In both traditions, ego and human desire are the source of our disharmony with Nature and must be minimized through education and self-cultivation. The Legalist penal law and order is the last resort when all social efforts fail.

The Chinese notion of a good human nature and the need for self-cultivation and education is in sharp contrast with the traditional Western theological notion of original sin, which is the basis for all Abrahamic beliefs such as Christianity, Judaism, and Islam. The Chinese search for answers in life by looking inwards within one's self, while Western religious teachings encourage humans to seek redemption in the afterlife. If all humans are living in sin on Earth, then the establishment of codified laws and regulations with effective law and order enforcement are essential for protection, crime prevention, and the maintenance of social harmony in life. For the ancient Chinese however, moral commitment and responsibility should best be placed on oneself and their family, not on government or other authorities. Each person would do good if their ego and desires were in balance, which can only be achieved through self-cultivation and education. Governmental law and order are only necessary when society becomes morally bankrupt, and humane persuasion and moral education are no longer effective.

The Confucian notion of a good inherent human nature is now substantiated by recent results in multiple scientific disciplines including neuroscience, psychology, and evolutionary biology. A 2015 book by renowned neurobiologist Donald Pfaff[6] argues that the source of good human behavior—the benevolence that we associate with the highest religious teachings—emanates from our physical make-up. Our brains, hormones, and genes literally embody our social compasses. The author provides the latest, most far-reaching argument in support of this revelation, explaining in exquisite detail how our neuroanatomical structure favors kindness towards others. Unlike any other study in its field, Pfaff's book synthesizes all the most important research into how and why—at a purely physical level—humans empathize with one another and respond altruistically. It demonstrates that human beings are "wired" to behave altruistically from the beginning, such that unprompted, spontaneous kindness is our default behavior; such behavior comes naturally, irrespective of religious or cultural influences. Chinese traditional teachings over thousands of years keep reinforcing this, making belief in a naturally good human nature that will naturally follow virtuous ways an integral part of Chinese heritage.

TRANSCENDING THE SELF

Abraham Maslow, one of the founding fathers of modern psychology, introduced the well-known Maslow's Hierarchy of Needs in the early 1900s. Based mainly on Western experience, his system chronicled the progress of human self-consciousness in life through three stages: need-directed (survival and belonging), outer-directed (self-esteem), and inner-directed (self-actualization). Maslow pointed out that our first need and highest priority is survival, or basically, food and shelter. Once basic survival needs are met, people focus on belonging to a group, family, community, tribe, or country. After people attain the security of belonging, they aspire to stand out and become achievers. There is an urge towards individuality, but the

---

6 Donald W. Pfaff, *The Altruistic Brain: How We Are Naturally Good* (Oxford University Press, 2015).

prevailing values and acceptable behaviors of the group or community limit it. The highest level of conscious development is self-actualization, which is inner-directed. People at this level have already achieved self-esteem and typically also material success; therefore, they choose to shape their own destinies. By developing skills in critical thinking and introspection, they develop a deeper awareness of their own needs, strengths, and weaknesses. As a result, they become capable of setting their own direction for life and managing the development and learning needed to achieve it.

Notice there is no mention of morality or ethics in Maslow's model. As humans, the concepts behind Maslow's Hierarchy of Needs apply generally to everyone, including the Chinese. Basic human needs dictate how we interact with the outside world. However, there is a different twist at the second and third stage, if you factor in the Chinese cultural context with an emphasis on ethics. Traditional Chinese individuality and identity is relational, rather than personal. Further, self-cultivation of morality and ethicality is rooted in the cultural system of human relations. Traditionally raised Chinese children are more self-disciplined, and they are taught to keep their ego and self-esteem in check. They are required to show respect for others, particularly parents, the elderly, and teachers. Confucians learn the art of introspection much earlier in their childhood, not after they have achieved self-esteem and personal material success as Maslow suggested. In fact, instead of self-gratification, Confucian teachers emphasized ethics and a sense of responsibility towards your family, community, and country. Individuals were consistently taught to be compassionate, empathetic, even altruistic towards others, particularly to the weak and poor.

By being taught self-control and almost shunning self-gratification, Chinese children may develop critical thinking skills and understand their own needs later than their Western counterparts. They may be more reliant on others, particularly parents and their immediate families, for their own needs, and be comparatively late to recognize their own strengths and weaknesses. Having relied more on others for their basic needs, some Chinese children may mature and learn to be independent later than Western children. But by being firmly rooted in Chinese ethical traditions, they are also more conscientious, self-critical, flexible, socially sensitive, and arguably better team players. They learn early on how to collectively achieve as a team, even at the risk of some self-sacrifice on the part of an individual. On the flip-side, it is easier for some individuals to take advantage of others for personal gain, and the system appears to produce more introverts. In such cases, Daoism or Buddhist philosophy can be helpful to help humans psychologically return closer to Nature.

Ironically, very few people are aware that late in Maslow's life he wanted to add another level to the top of the pyramid called self-transcendence.[7] In some ways, it is similar to the Chinese emphasis on social ethics in that self-transcendence refers literally to transcending one's self. He said that ultimately, greater compassion for all of humanity requires self-transcendence to be separate from self-actualization and become a higher and final level at the top of his pyramid. To achieve self-transcendence he believed humans need to create peak experiences, which he defined as "feelings of limitless horizons opening up to the vision, the feeling of being simultaneously more powerful and also more helpless than one ever was before, the feeling of great ecstasy and wonder and awe, the loss of placement in time and space with, finally, the conviction that something extremely important and valuable had happened, so that the subject was to some extent transformed and strengthened even in his daily life by such experiences." By transcending the individual ego and focusing on things beyond the self, like altruism and spiritual awakening, humans can experience intense joy, peace, well-being, and an awareness of the unity of all things.

Taking self-transcendence one step further is a key Confucian precept called *Ren,* which is cultivated from a nascent sense of compassion, and if properly nurtured creates a person of *Ren* who has strong moral character and helps others to get there as well. There are a multitude of meanings within *Ren,* from a deep rooted ethical and spiritual introspection and cultivation of one's self and virtues, to self-realization, and all the way to an embodiment of humanity and universal love expressed as a genuine altruistic concern for the destiny of humankind. According to Wei-ming Tu[8]: "... from the substantial point of view, *Ren* is not only a personal virtue

---

7 Dr. John G. Messerly, "Summary of Maslow on Self-Transcendence," *Reason and Meaning,* January 18, 2017, https://reasonandmeaning.com/2017/01/18/summary-of-maslow-on-self-transcendence/

8 Wei-Ming Tu, *Humanity and Self-Cultivation: Essays in Confucian Thought* (Cheng & Tsui, 1998).

but also a metaphysical reality. In other words, not only psychologically has every human being the potentiality to embody *Ren*, but also metaphysically the moral mind, or the mind of *Ren*, is in essence identical with the cosmic mind. *Ren* is thus both the moral and ontological basis of self-cultivation ... *Ren* is morality ... not merely confined to the ethical stage; it also conveys religious significance."

It is worth noting quickly here that although Confucianism, by nature, is not a formal religion, and is often thought of more as a philosophy, it has played a similar role to many religions in guiding the behavior and ethics of Chinese society. Therefore, although Confucianism is not officially a religion, Tu concluded after life-long research on this topic that it is difficult to deny an element of religiousness, which some may choose to interpret more as spirituality.

It is interesting that there is no English equivalent for the word *Ren*. People have interpreted it as kindness, love, selflessness, benevolence, mercy, or humanity. It is all these things and more, encompassing something spiritual or mystical that English words cannot adequately express. *Ren* is not a quality you can easily acquire, learn, nor be born with. Instead, its roots are in our heart and mind, and a good Confucian needs to continuously cultivate it over their lifetime as one of the five key Confucian virtues. *Ren* is deeply connected with the self-reviving, self-perfecting, and self-fulfilling process of an individual as it grows. A person who has *Ren* is ethically and morally rooted in the deepest spiritual level of their selfhood, which provides an infinite resource of self-generating strength and energy to build relationships and help create a flourishing human community.

SOCIAL DARWINISM VS. SOCIAL RESPONSIBILITY

By the middle of the first millennium BC, all the great civilizations of the Eurasia continent had reached a point of maturity that allowed them to develop an objective view of their own beliefs, and to respond to the social and political changes that their societies were undergoing. What distinguished the Chinese from the others was that they looked at *Tianxia*, which can be described as all the lands and metaphysical realm where humanity lives together under the same sky (also referred to as Nature or Heaven, but with no religious connotations). It included Nature and human as an interrelated whole that came into being, and was maintained by its own forces of connection, without any supernatural explanation or divine creator. *Tianxia* was a world where both progress and backwardness were attributed to human decisions, not to gods or divinities. Chinese insisted on ethics rather than metaphysics, being the preeminent tool for organizing society, and on introspection, self-discipline, and education as the means to foster ethics. From this point onwards, the Chinese argued endlessly about how best to organize human societies. How to govern with justice and benevolence was the central issue in Chinese politics because of the large scale and complexity of encompassing everyone under this *Tianxia*.

This Chinese focus on issues that matter to the overall collective humanity differs strongly from the equally intensive focus on individual issues that characterizes the Western tradition and politics. As individuals with inalienable rights to life, liberty, and the pursuit of happiness, we need protection for our personal safety and for our property. Government and legal institutions provide protection, but there is deep rooted distrust of all institutions within Western society since the French and American Revolutions. Hence began the influence of social Darwinism, which has dominated Western thought for centuries, and still does today.

Social Darwinism is the concept that the strongest human groups and races will survive. It leaves people with no choice but to look out for themselves and their own kind in order to survive. Once started, such a process is self-serving and re-enforcing. Nationalism came into being after the French Revolution, and American exceptionalism naturally followed. These were a direct outcome of the age of Enlightenment, which saw the separation of church and state, and encouraged freedom of thought and individualism. Modern Western society is the manifestation of many Enlightenment ideals including rationalism, individualism, nationalism, universality, fraternity, liberty, equality, democracy, and capitalism. This Enlightenment mentality is still the most influential moral discourse in the political culture of the modern age. But similar to a pendulum swinging from one extreme to another, while the Christian faith totally dominated the Western world for a thousand years during the Dark Ages, it appears that the pendulum has swung to the opposite extreme of modern liberalism in the last thousand years, with repercussions we are seeing throughout the Western world today.

It's worth noting that besides social Darwinism, according to the writings by Daniel Bell and Hahm Chaibong,[9] other tenets from the Enlightenment also met with criticism after World War II, and especially during the Vietnam War in the mid-1960s, and lately the wars in Iraq, Libya, and Syria. The story of postwar ethics is one of accelerated disillusion, cynicism, and uncertainty. The efficient and rationally justified industrialized slaughter of millions of innocent civilians by a civilized Western nation hastened an erosion of belief in human potential and its ideological and ethical progress. As a result, a comprehensive understanding of the Enlightenment mentality requires a frank discussion of the dark side of the modern West as well.

Social Darwinism is one of the most misleading individual, social, and political doctrines, and is a major cause of extremist and confrontational Western emphases and attitudes. The paradox in the West is that our Enlightenment heritage has nudged us to the edge of a new abyss of postmodernism. Postmodern thinkers question all traditional values and commonly target universalist ideas such as objectivity, morality, reason, science, language, and social progress. They remind us how self-contained and fluid language and meanings are, and how dangerous this fluidity can be. Postmodernism, globalization, and rapid technological changes have combined to cause much uncertainty, insecurity, and social alienation while eroding feelings of group solidarity or community. Our present society is connected and characterized by multinational corporations, information superhighways, technology-driven science, mass-communication and social media, and conspicuous consumption. We are frequent conversational partners with associates thousands of miles away or on social media anywhere, but we are just as frequently strangers to our neighbors, colleagues, and relatives. As Bell and Chaibong put it, our global village exhibits "sharp difference, severe differentiation, drastic demarcation, thunderous dissonance, and outright discrimination. The

---

9 Daniel A. Bell and Hahm Chaibong, *Confucianism for the Modern World* (Cambridge University Press, 2003).

world, compressed into an interconnected ecological, financial, commercial, trading, and electronic system, has never been so divided in wealth, influence, and power." Even worse, we struggle to judge right or wrong, what is true or false, or carry an in-depth conversation with each other. We cannot even trust the media and our own governments.

Differences in cultural attitudes also affect our social and political emphases. Since Western society believes that all men are created equal because we are all children of God, individual human rights are of utmost importance. Social issues such as entitlement, illicit drugs, gun control, and even religious and racial intolerance and violence, are often defended in the name of individual rights and social and political liberty. Human rights and liberalism are sometimes even being used to justify obviously irresponsible actions of some citizens, and even governments. Internationally, they are also used to serve political purposes as demonstrated in Western attitudes towards civil disobedience and violence around the world.

If we look at the most respected political democracies like in the US, one may question whether it is really working as intended at scale. Democracy works well in small political entities such as city-states or in small countries in Europe with less-diverse communities where consensus can easily be obtained. The US federated states worked well when there was enough room in the new continent for expansion, allowing people to move around and find or build different communities. But recently, America's intricate government machine, built on checks and balances, has been all but paralyzed by partisanship. The three governing branches have been fighting instead of working, just when the country most needs leadership and change. Voter turnout for major US elections averages around 50-60%. Political party interests are often placed ahead of national interests, and parties seem to be doing their best to please voters in order to get their candidates elected. The four-year election cycle is also problematic—it is guaranteed that every four or eight years the entire leadership of the country will change with minimal contextual handoff. Can you imagine a company that changes leadership every couple of years? It would be challenging to any long-term planning or foreign relations for a company, not to mention a country.

With politics becoming ever more polarized, politicians are rapidly becoming one of the least trusted professions. Politicians are supposed to lead and provide direction for the wellbeing of their citizens, but instead, things like campaign financing have become a big issue. Money can control the outcome of elections, and sometimes the election seems to be a popularity contest at the party or individual level, rather than being based on how well a specific candidate can lead the country. Politicians basically start to appease voters with social benefits using borrowed money, and ultimately people are forced to vote for the less corrupt or less disliked candidates. It is a dangerous truth that if people feel helpless, politically alienated, and isolated from the decision-making process, they will not fulfill their roles as informed participants in a democratic process.

Even in the most economically advanced nations, the pervasive mood is one of discontent, anxiety, and frustration. For many, life generally loses its purpose. On the other hand, religious extremism, such as the Islamic and Christian fundamentalist movements, or racism such as white supremacy, grows at a rapid pace, threatening world peace. It is the greatest challenge of our time to redefine our own identity and relationship with others, seek new social and political meaning in our institutions, and reconstruct common ideals and traditions that will hopefully include all of humanity with which we have a shared destiny. The best first step in addressing such challenges may be to understand and learn from our own past and benefit from absorbing some of the thinking preferences, experiences, cultures, and traditions of other societies across the globe and throughout history.

We mentioned earlier that Chinese people adopt a more collectivistic attitude towards social and political matters. Since the very early days, they had to construct a society that functioned well across all of *Tianxia*, which at the time was probably similar in size and population to the US mainland today. That society was built on a foundation of broadminded inclusiveness and social responsibility in both individuals and government, which is still fundamental to what makes China the country we see today. Ever since the time of Confucius more than two thousand years ago, Chinese people have always been burdened with social responsibilities. Instead of the culture of "guilt" seen in Western society, where you are innocent until proven guilty by a legal system, Chinese has a culture of "shame," where you should feel ashamed of yourself if you did something immoral. You and your family are responsible and should have known better. Such rationale carries on to every level of society and government. It is the heart and mind of an individual, and the social and relational pressure on them, that keeps Chinese people moral and honest. This system works well for the majority, but even so, there are always a few rebellious characters or exceptions, like when people have a hard time fitting in, for example. Corruption is also difficult to avoid. There is much China can learn from the Western legal system and its experiences in order to avoid "the tyranny of the majority." To that end, China is in the process of developing a new legal system that combines social ethics with the rule of law.

With a culture strong on social responsibility, the downside is a lack of focus on rights. China has been in the news quite often of late due to human rights issues. Culturally, this may be because it has a different perception of what constitutes human rights. As a very pragmatic culture, many Chinese are most concerned with their right to life, which includes basic living needs such as food and shelter. Beyond that, they value security for individuals and their family. Regarding freedom, they tend to favor what Isaiah Berlin, in his famous 1958 speech, called "positive freedom," instead of the "negative freedom" which most of the Western world is more accustomed to. Negative freedom is freedom from interference, whereas positive freedom is freedom as self-mastery—the ability to ask not what we are free from, but what we are free to do. Positive freedom implies that the government should aim to actively create whatever conditions are necessary for individuals to be self-sufficient or achieve self-realization, and hence flourish. The alleviation of poverty is a good example of positive freedom, as people who escape poverty with the help of government are then better able to take control of their lives. In contrast, the Western world fears that kind of authoritarian intervention and hence is having a hard time alleviating homelessness. While each individual may be said to be free to choose their own destiny, including the freedom to bring harm to themselves, the absence of money, connections, or power in a capitalistic society is a major limiting factor on what choices each individual has, and hence why this is viewed more as negative freedom rather than a positive one.

In such a large country of over 1.4 billion people where the government's priority is to protect the masses, there are often times where they need to infringe on the rights of the few in the name of protecting the majority, for right or wrong. In China, there is no limit on the government's responsibility to the people. Because of this, the government can be perceived as taking a harder stance than others on extreme thought and restricting freedom of speech in order to keep the majority safe and happy. In such case, there must be established trust for people to believe the government is doing the right thing on their behalf. Building that trust takes time, and there are many within and outside of China that are skeptical of its intentions because of things like its propensity to lock down on any perceived negative information and only share what they view as a beneficial perspective on things, which affects its credibility over time. But it goes both ways—if people are willing to give China a chance and not misunderstand it at every turn by seeing it through a Western lens, or if the West could simply ease up on the political pressure, then perhaps China will gradually be more willing to be vulnerable and open to the world, thereby naturally building trust.

The COVID-19 pandemic of 2020 was an interesting showcase of the differences between a culture based on social Darwinism versus one based on social responsibility. In a study done on the American populace six months into the outbreak,[10] on average over 50% of Americans disapproved of the president's handling of the coronavirus outbreak. In contrast, a study of Chinese citizens about six months from the start of their outbreak[11] indicated that over 65% were satisfied with both their government's performance and protection during the outbreak, and it has been touted as a model for the world to follow. An October 2020 article in the Lancet,[12] a respected journal for infectious disease specialists, reported, "as of October 4, 2020, China had confirmed 90,604 cases of COVID-19 and 4,739 deaths, while the USA had registered 7,382,194 cases and 209,382

10 Aaron Bycoffe, Christopher Groskopf, and Dhrumil Mehta, "How Americans View The Coronavirus Crisis and Trump's Response," Oct 16, 2020, https://projects.fivethirtyeight.com/coronavirus-polls/

11 Cary Wu, "How Chinese citizens view their government's coronavirus response," The Conversation, June 4, 2020, https://theconversation.com/how-chinese-citizens-view-their-governments-coronavirus-response-139176

12 Talha Burki, "China's successful control of COVID-19," The Lancet, October 8, 2020, https://www.thelancet.com/journals/laninf/article/PIIS1473-3099(20)30800-8/fulltext

deaths. The UK has a population twenty (20) times smaller than China, yet it has seen five times as many cases of COVID-19 and almost ten times as many deaths." Why the huge difference?

Chinese people understand the protective function of their government, and as the pandemic impacted the health of individuals and their family, they were willing to go along with government efforts, including locking down whole cities and restricting public transportation to limit the spread of the virus, restrictions on gatherings for many months, and mandatory wearing of masks in public. They also had the benefit of experiencing a preview of this during the SARS epidemic in 2003, so many were able to take it seriously and act swiftly. The restrictions on their individual freedoms were deemed worthwhile and sensible as part of their social responsibility to the rest of society.

Americans however, had many individuals fighting against even the wearing of masks, including President Trump, who scorned others for wearing one. People claimed it was an infringement on their individual rights for government to mandate masks—they should have the freedom of choice. Each city or state could choose their own response to the pandemic, so after four months with consistently increasing numbers, only thirty-two states out of fifty had issued mandatory face covering regulations[13] and some cities were even fighting their states' decisions. When some states initiated a lockdown and quarantine, businesses and capitalism suffered so much that the public was in an uproar and they could not keep lockdown for long. In true social Darwinism fashion, many claimed it was their right to choose whether or not to wear a mask and go about their usual daily lives, even if the circumstances may be a danger to their health and others'.

This is not to say we didn't see heroes everywhere, regardless of country or culture. Chinese doctors and nurses flocked to Wuhan after the lockdown to assist with caring for the sick, risking their own lives in the

---

13 Lawrence O. Gostin, JD, I. Glenn Cohen, JD, and Jeffrey P. Koplan, MD, MPH, "Universal Masking in the United States: The Role of Mandates, Health Education, and the CDC," *JAMA*, August 10, 2020, https://jamanetwork.com/journals/jama/fullarticle/2769440

process. Similar stories were heard around the world as health care professionals stepped up to do what was necessary for their communities and families, even at the risk of their own health. If all of us would do our part to help others more often, just as those selfless volunteers did, we could strengthen our communities and in turn, the rest of the world. It is becoming increasingly important to work together instead of fighting each other and consuming valuable resources. The pandemic of 2020 was a stress test of how well we work cooperatively together. It reminded us how we should all work together for the betterment of each other and humankind, regardless of race, religion, ideology, or culture. We are all human beings that are susceptible to the same things when we are out of balance with Nature.

SPIRITUAL RESOURCES FOR OUR NEW WORLD

Coming back to the principle of self-actualization as conceptualized by Maslow, contemporary psychologist Scott Kaufman of Columbia University reported that, of the ten characteristics shared by a group of self-actualized people surveyed, most tended to agree on a feeling of oneness with the world, and the ability to merge with a common humanity while at the same time being able to maintain a strong identity and sense of self.[14] This supports our contention that these are not mutually exclusive, but instead mutually reinforcing. Further, regardless of what culture or set of thinking preferences you were brought up with, self-actualization can be learned and deliberately developed, just as the Chinese have for thousands of years. Successfully doing so can lead to greater well-being, including greater life satisfaction, self-acceptance, personal growth, autonomy, and self-transcendent experiences.

For the remainder of the 21st century, we need a new direction, a new paradigm, a new global conscience that every one of our global citizens can adapt to for the betterment of our future generations. Tu Wei-Ming[15] has

---

14 Scott Barry Kaufman, "Self-Actualizing People in the 21st Century: Integration With Contemporary Theory and Research on Personality and Well-Being," *Journal of Humanistic Psychology*, 1-33 (2018).

15 Tu Wei-Ming, *Centrality and Commonality: An Essay on Confucian Religiousness* (SUNY Press, 1989).

called on us to think beyond Enlightenment mentality and explore the spiritual resources that may help us to broaden the scope of the Enlightenment project, deepen its moral sensitivity, and if necessary, creatively transform its genetic constraints in order to fully realize its potential as a worldview for the human condition as a whole. In this age of globalization, humankind needs more than ever to find rootedness and localization. A renewed culture and tradition are enabling forces, which can create an even better future society and nationhood.

According to Tu, three kinds of spiritual resources are available to us, and a fourth is in the process of development. The first involves the ethico-religious traditions of the modern West, notably Greek philosophy, Judaism, and Christianity. Within these traditions, the exclusive dichotomies of matter/spirit, body/mind, sacred/profane, human/Nature, and creator/creature must be transcended to allow supreme values, such as the sanctity of the earth, the continuity of being, the beneficial interaction between the human community and Nature, and mutuality between humankind and heaven, to receive the importance they deserve in philosophy, religion, and theology. The second kind of spiritual resource is derived from non-Western, Axial Age civilizations, which include Hinduism, Jainism, and Buddhism in South and Southeast Asia, Daoism and Confucianism in East Asia, and Islam. These traditions provide sophisticated and practical resources in the form of worldviews, rituals, institutions, styles of education, and patterns of human relatedness. They can help to develop new ways of living that are an alternative to the Western European and North American exemplification of the Enlightenment mentality. We have already highlighted some aspects of Chinese and Confucian thinking, behavior, and worldviews, which we believe are complementary to their Western counterparts. The possibility of developing a better balanced, more humane, and sustainable environment, personality, communities, and nationhood based on these ideas and experiences should not be overly exaggerated, but neither should it be ignored.

Tu's third kind of spiritual resource involves the primal traditions, specifically Native American, Hawaiian, Maori, and numerous tribal indigenous religious traditions. These cultures have both physical strength, and even aesthetic elegance, and have sustained human life since Neolithic times. The implications for practical living are far-reaching. For example, their deep experience of rootedness, rituals of bonding in ordinary human interaction, emphasis on participation rather than control in motivation, empathic understanding rather than logical analysis in epistemology, worldviews based on respect for the transcendent rather than domination over Nature, and fulfillment rather than alienation in human experience, all still have direct relevance in our world today and into the future.

Finally, Tu suggested a fourth kind of spiritual resource that is emerging from the core of the Enlightenment project itself. Our disciplined reflection, as a communal act rather than an isolated struggle, is a first step towards the creative zone that religious leaders and teachers of ethics envision. The feminist critique of tradition, the concern for environment, and the persuasion of religious pluralism are examples of this new level of self-awareness. The development of new global civil societies will no doubt require reflection, along with leveraging the best and most applicable of all the spiritual resources listed above.

While all these diverse cultures and traditions have much to contribute, we will be focusing the next couple of chapters primarily on some key concepts and developments in Chinese culture and civilization, as contrasted to their Western counterparts. Over the last fifty years or more, many Chinese have been obsessed with learning about and adopting Western culture and thinking while shunning or even misunderstanding many of their Confucian Chinese roots. To that end, we contend that Chinese people generally know a lot more about Western history and culture than Western people know about Chinese history and culture. Due to current trends painting China as the #1 enemy of the West, our goal is to help level that playing field a bit. We believe these two cultures are complementary and there is much they can learn from each other if they are open-minded enough. If people of these two great countries and cultures can find ways to work cooperatively instead of competitively, the whole world will benefit from it. We need a new paradigm for global consciousness, institutions, and governance if our current technological, ethical, economical, environmental, and sociopolitical challenges are to be met. But before we can do that, we first need to understand each other better and reconcile our differences by building mutual trust. Our future generations and the future of humankind on Earth depend on it.

THREE: UNDERSTANDING CHINESE CONFUCIAN RELATIONSHIPS

Confucius lived from 551 to 479 BC, but his teachings and philosophy profoundly influenced the core of Chinese culture and how Chinese people think and act to this day. Unfortunately, over the last three dynasties of the imperial era, Confucian teachings turned dogmatic as authoritarian and despotic interpretations of Confucianism have resulted in widespread misinterpretation of the original intent, which has impeded progress and learning. Confucius's true original teachings, which are recorded mostly as case histories by his disciples, were intended to leave much to the imagination, encourage spontaneity, and require practice in the interpretation. In this particular respect, it is similar to the Old Testament, where you can revisit each story and saying a million times in the course of a lifetime and obtain a different meaning or a deeper insight each time. In an ideal Confucian society, morality and ethics serve as the foundation for building harmony, providing the ultimate guide for people in how to behave as humans. His ideas enabled the largest civilization in the world to flourish, generation after generation, for thousands of years. There is much we can learn from it and, in this chapter, we will introduce a few of the key precepts in his writing that we feel are still widely applicable today.

BASICS OF A HARMONIOUS SOCIETY

The Chinese word *xin* translates to both "heart" and "mind," so people often refer to it as the heart-mind. This implies there is no real difference between the functioning of the heart, which can feel and empathize, and the brain, which can think, in Chinese culture. The heart-mind is key to our self-awareness and is innately equipped with the basics of moral recognition. Our actions hence reflect our will or intention as a result of using both together. In a true Confucian-based Chinese culture, our heart-mind is the governor of the responsible self, so every relationship should start with the integrity and self-awareness of our heart-mind, basically introspection. One should examine their own intentions, rectify their heart-mind as needed, and make sure it is morally upright before sincerely going forth to establish relationships with others. In Confucian tradition, the concept of maturing the small self to a greater self is a process of self-fulfillment and actualization. Social harmony comes from every individual knowing his or her place in the natural order and playing his or her part well at every level of responsibility.

In physics, we often use the terms "particle" and "field" to describe an object and the force it exerts from a point across empty space. The concept of particle and field, and the focus of the field lines of force, is very useful in modern physics. We often hear references to quantum fields, gravity fields, or electromagnetic fields. All of these concepts are significant from the smallest scale of subatomic physics to the grand scale fields of astronomy and astrophysics.

Similarly the focus and field model can be used to describe the Chinese precept of relationships. Each individual possesses a force of morality that exerts influence upon his or her environment. Every person is a focus, having been born with innate goodness, although personal desires, excesses, and greed can mask some people. For those individuals, their innate goodness can be restored through introspection and moral education. A highly principled person, such as Confucius himself with impregnable virtues, exerts a powerful field of force, which can influence many people in their surrounding environment, and even through history. In this context, virtue and goodness means a person can exert a positive influence when their actions harmonize or resonate with the laws of Nature. In the absence of such harmony, he or she must contest against the laws of Nature, resulting in suffering. This is what contemporary Chinese philosopher Tu Wei-Ming called the "anthropocosmic" nature of Confucianism as an inclusive humanism rooted in the regenerative rhythms of the cosmos.

Everyone from individuals up to the rulers were expected to cultivate and practice five essential virtues in all their relationships, often referred to as the Five Constants. Like many Chinese tenets, there are no exact equivalents in English since they are mostly implicitly defined and achieved. In practice, a person who harmonizes and enacts one or two of these is good, while a person who embodies three or four is exceptionally virtuous. To err is human, so the intent and sincerity to act morally is more important than the actual achievement. Someone who can realize all five of these is a sage in accordance with Nature. Interconnected to each other are *Ren* (roughly representing benevolence and humanity), *Yi* (roughly representing righteousness), *Li* (roughly representing ritual propriety or morality), *Zhi* representing wisdom, and *Xin* representing fidelity, integrity, and trustworthiness. These virtues were used to determine who was a "true gentleman" in ancient Chinese society. Confucius valued the good man over the successful man, although he held that when things were right in the world, the good man would always be successful.

In a stable agrarian society, a person's initial sphere of influence is the family, where family ethics is the combined field of the individual family members. A family with strong, shared ethics would exert a strong field, first on the immediate community and then on the region, nation, world, and, ultimately, the universe. At each level of the sphere of influence, a member contributes as well as receives. The degree of his or her contribution and the degree of received influence depends on his or her own immanent moral suasion. Humanity's moral suasion is always grounded in behavior, expressed through principled actions, and viewable only in terms of recognized contributions to others. Thus in an ideal agrarian world, each hierarchy within this system, and, consequently, the overall whole of this perspective, embodies the ideals of a natural, ethical, and just cosmology in which everything and every person performs to his or her ultimate capacity for the harmony of the social environment.

The model society in the individualistic West is a civil society, where competing interests strive against one another under the rule of codified law, which administers justice with the goal of keeping the struggle within boundaries. The values of freedom and equality are central to this society. The traditional Chinese model society requires ethics, morality, and self-cultivation to be central to social relationships and responsibility. The ideal society is harmonious; the government looks after the people, the people respect the ruler, and at each level there is an unequal but reciprocal system of exchange that serves to maintain order, an aesthetic order.

THE WORLD AS AN EXTENDED FAMILY

The core unit in traditional Chinese society is the family, not an individual, as it is in the West. The Chinese word for family uses the same character as home, school, or linkage, suggesting that family was central to Chinese philosophical thinking about life, and serves as a model for understanding the nature of reality itself. In fact, all Chinese relationships are familial in the Chinese world. The state is modeled after the family, with the leader acting as a father, both caring for and responsible for their people. The first social objective of Confucianism is to achieve harmony in family relationships. For the Chinese, the family is the most important aspect of a person's life, the foundation of one's identity, one's morality, and the source of meaning in our life. Family is a product of Nature.

Traditional kin relations have been at the core of all social and political organization in China, predating the beginning of written history in 1612 BC. The family hearth has defined the basic dynamics of Chinese society up to the present day, especially in rural areas. The ideal family was a large group, primarily held together by filial piety (deep respect for one's parents, elders, and ancestors) and its expression through the religious sanctioning of ancestor worship, making the family an indefinitely perpetuated corporation whose living members were accountable both to forebears and descendants. In addition, the socioeconomics deriving from the fact that the family head controlled and was answerable for the activities of all family members also served to bind the family together. The traditional extended family consisted of a male head, his immediate family, and the families of all his male descendants, with several generations living together in a cooperative household. When the family head died and his property was divided, his sons became the heads of their own extended families. Thus the nuclear family—that is, a married couple and their children—were ideally part of a larger living and working unit, the extended family. Moreover, closely related extended families considered themselves related and obligated to all other clans sharing the same surname, who were thought to constitute a common descendant group.

Exogamy was practiced within the patrilineal lineage. A man might marry a first cousin on his mother's side because she bore a different surname, but he could not marry a woman of the same surname, even if the two families had lived at opposite ends of the country for centuries and had no traceable blood relationship. Indeed, such distinct differentiation between the father's side and the mother's side extends to the use of different titles for grandparents, uncles, aunts, and even cousins from maternal and paternal sides. The relation between any two members of the extended family is well-defined. Although increasing social complexity diluted blood bonds in later times, society continued to use real and fictitious kinship as fundamental building blocks for networking purposes. Each kinship role came with elaborate rules and expectations. By acting out these roles, individuals and families defined their identities and created opportunities for self-actualization and self-realization. This form of the family corporation persists up to the present and is commonly found in Hong Kong, Taiwan, the Chinese mainland, and countries of Chinese cultural heritage such as Singapore, Korea, and Vietnam. Just as individualism has created a vibrant Western society, traditional Confucianism created a stable Chinese society. Ideally, our future world can be both vibrant and stable.

From a family unit outwards, social harmony and cohesion are extended until they embrace all human relationships with the ideal of "bringing peace to all under heaven." The Chinese notion of interrelationship is comprised of all things that induce peace, including the spirit of self-cultivation, the ethic of responsibility, the value of family and social cohesiveness, reciprocity, human solidarity and inclusiveness, harmony within diversity, benevolent governance, harmony with Nature, and universal peace. Governance of the state follows the model of a family. The leader functions as the head of a family. The state takes responsibility in caring for its citizens. All citizens are their children. The emperor must cultivate and exhibit utmost moral supremacy and be a model of Confucian values. Political authority is judged and granted based on the mandate of *Tian*, the people's good will, and the ruler's virtue. Rulers should never rule by coercion. If a ruler is less than virtuous, *Tian* can withdraw their mandate.

Although Confucian ethics ensures that individuals understand their duties toward the family and community, they do not overemphasize the community to the detriment of the individual. In fact, Confucians regard individuals as the metaphorical root, comprising the foundation of society, while communities are the leaves that form a protective roof. They also often describe the relationship between people and state as akin to water and a boat. Water can float a boat, but it can just as easily sink that boat, depending on the water's turbulence and the boat's stability. Thus, while asserting the duties of an individual to the community, Confucian ethics stays contextual and not dogmatic.

Instead of an emphasis on the rights of an individual, which is prominent in Western literature about sociology and political science, the Confucian tradition of order stresses the obligations and duties of individuals to their family, community, and nation. In the Chinese community, kinship was formed through marriage relationships, clans were established through blood relationships, and villages were built through the regional relationships in which one was born and brought up—all of which evolved around the practice of filial piety. In Confucian ethics, the position of the tutor or teacher was particularly respected, ranking next to the father's position in every household. On a simple tablet in the family alcove, there were "*Tian* (Heaven or Nature), Earth (culture and history), Sovereign, Father, Teacher," listing the order of worship. Even though parents gave birth to the physical body of a child, the teacher had the most to do in formulating the pupil's spiritual and cultural life. By expanding the view that one must honor their physical life-giver, one must honor their cultural life-giver as well. Using the same reasoning, we must treat our close friends with high respect as well. Confucius's disciple Zengzi said, "The superior man on grounds of culture meets with his friends, and by their friendship helps to establish his virtue." Together with friends, the closely knit patterns of relatives, teachers, clansmen, and fellow countrymen were all interwoven around a filial axis in the Chinese community. Such a condition still prevails in rural China and in some conservative groups of overseas Chinese residents, even though much has changed in urban Chinese society.

The Chinese tend to see social relations in terms of networks rather than isolated boxes. The five ideal Confucian relations—between ruler/subject, parent/child, husband/wife, older/younger sibling, and between friends—are considered the basis of all social connections between people in traditional Chinese society. Sometimes, the additional relationship of teacher/student is included to make six. At least half of these relations are found within the family, a testament to the importance of family in China. Yet a relation to God is not considered here because Confucius felt one should not deal with God or any supernatural beings until one first learns to deal with human beings on earth. Theoretically at least, the notion of responsibility applies equally to both the ruler and the ruled. In an ideal situation, Confucian teaching holds that the superior member of each of the relationships (ruler, parent, husband, older sibling, older friends, or teacher) has the duty of benevolence and the role of providing guidance and loving care for the subordinate member (subject, child, wife, and so forth). The subordinate member, in turn, has the duty to obey and reciprocate, with not only loyalty and support, but love and respect. Under a Confucian social hierarchical order, everyone conducts themselves well within their appointed sphere and as a result, attains psychological and mental stability otherwise difficult to obtain in a competitive society.

HARMONY IN DIVERSITY AND *LI*

Harmony in diversity is one of the most important teachings of Confucian tradition. It helps to create an aesthetic order, as opposed to a rational or logical order. In the Western tradition, belief in a single-order world reinforces the search for natural and social uniformities which create a rational or logical order. In contrast, the aesthetic order that the Chinese sought is found in the harmony of the ten thousand things, the myriad unique particulars, including human beings themselves, that constitute the universe. The meaning of the word *he* (harmony) was originally applied to harmonizing in singing, but later extended to describe the unity of any non-identical objects. Harmony is depicted as the acceptance of diversity rather than a reduction to uniformity. Confucius repeatedly described social and political participation in terms of pursuing a harmony among diversities and differences. As David Hall and Roger Ames[16] explain: "The difference between *he* [和] translated here as "harmony" and *t'ung* [同], "agreement," is the difference between "attuning" and "tuning." Attuning is the combining and blending of two or more ingredients in a harmonious whole with benefit and enhancement that maximizes the possibilities of all without sacrificing their separate and particular identities. "Tuning" is finding agreement by bringing one ingredient into conformity and concurrence with an existing standard such that one ingredient is enhanced possibly at the expense of others."

Harmony in diversity is traditionally a Chinese political ideal. It is the essence of how a large-scale community or country should be organized and governed with minimum coercion. Diversity can be vertical—between levels of a governing bureaucracy—or horizontal—between different people, communities, and regions. In the *Analects*, Confucius specifically condemned factionalism in political service, such as that seen in the forming of political cliques, parties, or caucuses. He instead advocated a social and political harmony that can take the disparate opinions of its participants into account. Tolerance and humility are a necessity in this conception of sociopolitical order, which strives to allow the fullest possible disclosure of particularity. Supreme harmony is the state in which each thing abides in its correct place, but can also act free from interference. Harmony is thus a dynamic rather than static concept.

Diversity can easily cause human conflicts and hence there are numerous Chinese precepts aimed at reducing or handling conflicts in order to achieve harmony in diversity. Among them, *Li* is an important set of rites that defines how one should interact with humans, Nature, and even material objects. It defines a set of proper social norms and behavior that is intended to prevent human conflict. It includes things like the superior treating the inferior with propriety and respect, and having loyalty to superiors and respect for elders in the community. Given that Confucius's program for building character presumes the disciplining of oneself and the practice of ritual *Li*, attitudes such as respect, tolerance, and deference

---

16 David L. Hall and Roger T. Ames, *Thinking through Confucius* (State University of New York Press, 1987).

are preconditions required for the emergence of one's personhood within a community. The disposition of the society and the state accordingly unfolds in a dialogue between inherited tradition and present circumstance, and between inherited meaning preserved in ritual structures and the contribution of the present participants. The rituals and practices of *Li* are dynamic, intended to evolve over time to reflect changing views and beliefs in society, and all are aimed at preserving social harmony. Hall and Ames further stated[17]:

> Ritual action *Li* permits the spontaneous exercise of harmonizing actions. Law (*fa*) only controls external behavior. The existence of law, particularly penal law, however necessary it might be, suggests the failure of ritual action. Ritual actions (*Li*) are models for Confucius. They are objects of imitation… What is principally at issue here is the character of social harmony, and that leads us back to the contrast of aesthetic and rational order.

Confucians believed governments should place more emphasis on *Li* and rely less on penal punishment when they govern. Indeed, law becomes a coercive force when there is a loss of spontaneity in ritual action and the consequent substitution of dogma, as witnessed in the disorder of the late imperial era in China.

Masayuki Sato (2003)[18] studied the Confucian quest for order and ritual action (*Li*) by focusing on the origin and formation of the political thought of Xunzi, the founder of the naturalist and rationalist school of Confucianism. In a famous debate with Mencius, Xunzi maintained that humans are evil and the state needs to control and guide its populace in becoming good citizens. Xunzi argued that desire is the main cause of our evil nature. Unbounded desire is inimical to the state. Any person who follows his or her nature and indulges his or her emotions, such as

---

17 David L. Hall and Roger T. Ames, *Anticipating China: Thinking Through the Narratives of Chinese and Western Culture* (State University of New York Press, 1995).

18 Masayuki Sato, *The Confucian Quest for Order: The Origin and Formation of the Political Thought of Xun Zi* (Brill Academic Pub, 2003).

a fondness for profit or feelings of envy and hate, will inevitably violate the norms and rules of society and end up a criminal. Xunzi suggested we defer our desires via rituals. If people concentrate upon fulfilling ritual principles, they may satisfy both human desires and the demands of ritual. If people concentrate only upon fulfilling their desires, then they will end up satisfying neither. Thus, under proper government control and through moral education, desires can be channeled to the benefit of the state. For Xunzi, a successful state effectively controls human desire through the self-enforced mechanisms of morality and external pressure from those around them, which he refers to as their "environment."

According to Xunzi, humans differ from animals in their ability to form societies and the division of roles within that society. Through a sense of morality and justice, humans divide themselves and distribute resources to social constituents according to designated social roles. *Li* is the embodiment, or operation of morality, a prescription for self-controlling human desires. Sato attempted to elucidate various meanings and characteristics of the ritual principles of *Li* according to Xunzi, and claimed that Xunzi used the term *Li* to describe relatively concrete rituals and social norms, as opposed to the psychological or mental condition that Mencius seems to have envisaged. The practice of *Li* by all participants in a social structure would ultimately lead to social order and harmony, which could be associated with the providential process of heaven and earth. Therefore, *Li*, in the broadest sense, can be paraphrased as the manifestation of The Way, as well as a means for attaining order, Xunzi's highest theoretical goal. It has become a basic social norm in Chinese society.

CHINESE SOCIOLOGY TODAY

Ever since the Opium War (1839-1860), traditional Chinese civilization has collapsed under the onslaught of Western dominance. Traditional Chinese virtues and values came to be understood as flaws by some leading Chinese intellectuals and political leaders. The Confucian vision of the state as extended families was viewed as one of the reasons why Chinese people were unable to mobilize successful resistance to foreign invasions. The downward trend of Chinese civilization continued even after the demise of the imperial era and the establishment of the Chinese republic.

Deconstruction of traditional Chinese culture peaked during Mao's cultural revolution in the 1960s. But many key tenets of Chinese heritage still persist within the general populace, especially in rural regions, and are reappearing in different forms. With Deng Xiaoping's reform and opening, Chinese social relations again needed to take a new form, as many different traditions have had to be reconciled with modern sociopolitical concepts.

A relatively new Chinese term, *guanxi*, loosely translated as personal connections, relationships, or social networks has become important to Westerners doing business in China since Deng's Reform and Opening. It implies trust and mutual obligations between parties or within a social network, and it operates on personal, familial, social, business, and political levels. *Guanxi* is a neutral word, but the use or practice of *guanxi* can range from benign and neutral, to questionable and corruptive. The proper usage of *guanxi* has been crucial to the success of many foreign ventures in China, but has also opened the door to corruption and abuse for those Western companies and managers who do not take the time to understand Confucian-based culture and the proper use and role of *guanxi*.

Sociology ceased to exist in China from 1952 onwards as it was regarded as a part of the Western incursion in those days, but by 1980, China faced a number of challenges that required reliable data concerning population size and movement, among other things. The Ministry of Education was then tasked by the Party to reintroduce into China a sociology with American characteristics, technically sophisticated and teachable at both undergraduate and graduate levels. Yanjie Bian, who is concurrently Professor of Sociology at the University of Minnesota and Dean of Social Sciences at Xi'an Jiaotong University, was one of the students who went to the State University of New York at Albany in 1985 to undertake a PhD on social network analysis with Professor Nan Lin, who also taught at Nankai University. In 2019, Bian published a book titled *Guanxi: How China Works*.[19] The working definition of *guanxi* offered by Bian is that it is "a dyadic, particular, and sentimental tie that has the potential for facilitating the exchange of favors between the two parties connected by the tie." The theoretical models he outlined are *guanxi* as a social extension of familial

---

19 Yanjie Bian, *Guanxi: How China Works*, 1st edition (Polity Press, 2019).

ties, *guanxi* as instrumental particular ties, and *guanxi* as ties for asymmetric social exchange. Bian's background in both cultures becomes evident as he presents a balanced and qualified view on how delicately *guanxi* needs to be handled in order to be properly used in Chinese relationships.

In a review essay published in 2003, Bian[20] also reviewed post-1980, and especially post-1990, scholarship in the two interrelated fields of sociological study about reform-era China: sociology in the People's Republic of China (PRC) and Chinese studies in Western sociology. He found that since 1979, "sociology has been under the ideological and political influence of a durable communist party-state, but its development surely has been shaped by a persistent search for both a rooting in Chinese society and a recognition by and acceptance into the world community of sociology. Meanwhile, Chinese studies in Western and especially American sociology have moved into the mainstream of the discipline, benefiting from the adoption of standard survey methods to collect systematic data and from theoretical and substantive analyses about issues such as institutional change, changing patterns of social stratification, mechanisms of social mobility, and the centrality of social networks in social life." In a separate essay, he also observed that "Chinese class stratification has transformed from a rigid status hierarchy under Mao to an open evolving class system in the post-Mao period. Socioeconomic inequalities have also been altered. State redistributive inequalities are giving way to patterns increasingly generated by how individuals and groups succeed in a growing market-oriented economy... Finally, occupational mobility, a rare opportunity under Mao, is becoming a living experience for many Chinese in light of an emerging labor market. Scholarly works on status attainment, career mobility, and employment processes show both stability and change in the once politicized social mobility regime." Clearly, Post-Mao China is evolving to be vastly different from Mao's China in terms of social relations. It is no longer a simple model of authoritarianism nor is it the traditional Confucian model, but an evolving hybrid.

---

20 Yanjie Bian, "Sociological Research on Reform-Era China," *Issues and Studies*, Volume 39 Issue 1(2003): P139-174.

All complex and large-scale societies need to organize into hierarchy and stratification for specialization, efficiency, and order. State governance in China has always favored top-down hierarchical structure with virtuous and capable leaders and an effective governing bureaucracy accountable to the people. So politically, even though it has become a nation-state, it is still administered akin to an extended family of the past era. In its current form, it is organized close to a large modern corporation for efficiency and institutional policy focus. It is comprised of a governing board with a CEO in the head office (the central bureaucracy), with holding companies (provincial governments) working for the benefit of the shareholders (the people). As in a corporation, meritocracy is the most effective way to incentivize performance in the Chinese system. Corporations are non-democratic, but known for their high efficiency.

The social sciences discipline of sociology is a Western concept and is so new that it has seldom included the Chinese experience, but that is slowly changing. One interesting study by James H. Liu et al.[21] argues that the ethical and relational origins of traditional Chinese social identity enable culturally unique predictions about how Chinese people manage diversity and international relations today. Foremost among these are:

> (1) The Chinese identity is primarily defined by role-based social relations rather than clear category boundaries, so that,

> (2) Under conditions of low threat, traditional Chinese prescriptions for *guanxi* motivate "benevolent paternalism" rather than out-group derogation as the default script for dealings with out-group members, and

> (3) Under conditions of high threat, a defensive reaction in the form of nationalism fueled by a narrative of great civilization versus historical victimization is activated.

---

21 James H. Liu, Mei-Chih Li, and Xiao-Dong Yue, "Chinese social identity and inter-group relations: the influence of benevolent authority," *Oxford Handbook of Chinese Psychology*, ed. Michael Harris Bond (2010).

This theory explains why the modern US strategy of painting China as the enemy, imposing sanctions as pressure and using loud rhetoric in its press conferences, is triggering a strong defensive reaction from within China, and the Chinese are banding together stronger than ever to defend their homeland from baseless ideological claims. This type of confrontation is harmful, not just to the two countries involved, but to the rest of the world because of the stature and influence of these two countries.

FOUR: WORLDVIEWS, BELIEFS, ORDERS, AND CIVILIZATIONS

In the last three chapters, we explored possible environmental origins and factors contributing to the development of contrasting Chinese and Western thinking preferences. These different thinking preferences led to disparate attitudes and approaches in life, resulting in different approaches to human relationships. We believe thinking preferences and priorities are key because they affect both our conscious and subconscious minds, which in turn drive our value systems, worldviews, beliefs, and subsequently, our social orders and civilizations.

UNIVERSAL TRUTH VS. THE WAY

By simply asking the "what" and "why" questions, Greek philosophers believed in permanence, which is truth, true reality, and a unifying principle. Beginning in the sixth century BC, the central question for the early Greeks was how to reconcile the permanence (one, unity, being) required for a unifying explanation of the universe with the appearance of constant change (many, plurality, becoming). The Eleatics, and subsequently Xenophanes and then Parmenides reasoned logically that "it is" and "it is not" cannot be simultaneously true. What is not cannot enter our thoughts. Therefore, the existence of nonexistence is impossible because it is self-contradictory. By extension, that which exists, despite any contradictory sensory stimulus, must have always existed as a continuous, unchanging, timeless, indivisible unit, which is permanence behind apparent reality. "Change and becoming" and "diversity and plurality" require the acceptance of "it is not;" that is, the existence of nothingness, which is contradictory and hence, impossible. So Greek mathematics had no numeric zero. The denial of a void is still seen centuries later in the ideas of René Descartes (1596-1650).

As a consequence, traditional Westerners believe in a single order world, one unifying principle, and one universal truth that determine the reality of things in the world, an ontological understanding of knowledge. For reality to be unchanging, timeless, perfect, and complete, there is a need for a transcendent agency (the will of God) to reconcile the logical order of cosmos emerging out of an initial state of chaos. This Western dualism of "God the Creator" and "Man the Creation" is perhaps one of the most significant notions separating Western and Chinese views on the beginning of the universe and humanity. Based on this notion, the three Abrahamic religions—Islam, Christianity, and Judaism—were evolved as monotheistic religions. Religious belief is at the very core of both Western and Middle-Eastern cultures. Such faith and commitment can also be extended to Western partisan politics, dualistic thinking in international affairs, and many fields of social sciences—its resulting significance and consequence cannot be overstated. It is very different from the secular nature of Chinese thinking, worldviews, beliefs, and experiences.

According to contemporary Chinese philosopher Chen Chung-Ying,[22] the ancient search for cosmological becoming was presented in both Daoist and Confucian traditions from the classic *yijing (I Ching)*, also known as the *Book of Changes*, which centers on the harmonization of self and world. Chinese philosophy fosters a holistic outlook on both the universe and humanity within the universe, realizing the dynamic unity of all things and experiencing the dynamic source of all things. To use the term "dynamic" is to accentuate the importance of movement and creativity as

---

22 C. Y. Chen, in *Understand the Chinese Mind: The Philosophical Roots*, ed. Robert E. Allinson (Oxford University Press, 1991).

the universal nature of things (this is why it is called the Book of Changes). "Dynamic" implies getting behind the universal phenomenon and identifying the ultimate reality of all phenomena without denying the individual reality of a specific phenomenon. Concurrently, it is discerning the substance of things through the functioning of things. This insight into the nature of things led Cheng to call cosmological understanding of the world the "ontological" understanding of things. In order to distinguish it from how it is used in Western philosophy, he proposed the terms "cosmo-ontology" or "onto-cosmology" to represent the dynamic unity of cosmology and ontology reflected in the traditional Chinese Dao, or "The Way." Chinese people embrace the motto that "change is the only constant in the world," and finding "The Way" is how to deal with it.

Chinese Dao is radically different from one, unity, or *being* in the Western metaphysical tradition, as represented by Parmenides. In Western tradition, *being* is absolutely separated from the changing phenomenon of Nature, but the Dao never leaves things behind or aside. Instead, it always embraces them in change (many, plural, *becoming*). Whereas *being* denies reality to things in change and therefore condemns *becoming* to unreality, the Dao imparts both *being* and *becoming* to things. As such, it becomes the essence of both *being* and *becoming*, thus making *being* and *becoming* equivalent. Where *being* transcends the world by being self-identical, the Dao immerses itself in the world by producing difference and variety. Whereas *being* is the object of pure thinking, the Dao is the effect of a process of profound experiencing, including feeling and perception. Thus, *being* becomes the exclusive subject of ontology by excluding cosmology, whereas the Dao bridges the gap between ontology and cosmology by including both. The integration of *being* and *becoming*, the inclusion of cosmology and ontology, and the comprehension of both thinking and feeling, are all based on the comprehensive experience of things in the universe as a whole. The experience is one of unity in variety and variety in unity. It showcases the polarity of opposition and complementarity, and unity of oneness and difference, at the same time. In our contemporary world, there is always a Chinese Way in individual, social, political, and all other Chinese relationships that has no equivalence in Western thinking and culture. This is just one reason Westerners sometimes find it difficult to understand China and the Chinese people.

After contemplating this complex philosophical passage, we particularly enjoyed a simple description of Daoist aesthetic perspective cosmology by Ames and Hall[23]:

> There is no view from nowhere, no external perspective, no decontextualized vantage point. We are all in the soup. The intrinsic, constitutive relations that obtain among things make them reflexive and mutually implicating, residing together within the flux and flow. The mutuality does not in any way negate the uniqueness of particular perspective... A corollary to this radical perspectivism is that each particular element in our experience is holographic in the sense that it has implicated within the entire field of experience. The single flower has leaves and roots that take their nourishment from the environing soil and air. And the soil contains the distilled nutrients of past growth and decay that constitute the living ecological system in which all of its participants are organically interdependent. The sun enables the flower to process these nutrients, while the atmosphere that caresses the flower also nourishes and protects it. By the time we have "cashed out" the complex of conditions that conspire to produce and conserve this particular flower, one ripple after another in an ever-extending series of radial circles, we have implicated the entire cosmos within it without remainder. For the Daoist, there is an intoxicating bottomlessness to any particular event in our experience. The entire cosmos resides in the smile on the dirty face of this one little child.

Because of such disparities in the philosophical interpretation of reality and our world, the West has developed a monotheistic civilization while the Chinese world has always been following its own Way. Therefore, we really must understand the Chinese Way before we can properly understand and interpret China and its people.

---

23 Roger T. Ames, and David L. Hall, *Dao De Jing: Making This Life Significant, A Philosophical Translation* (Ballantine Books, 2003).

HISTORY AND SPACE-TIME

The Chinese characters for the universe are *yuzhou,* in which *yu* means space and *zhou* means time. When these terms are combined, they express the interdependence of time and space. The Chinese characters for the world are *shijie,* which combines the word *shi,* meaning "a generation" with the word jie, meaning "a boundary." Thus, shijie is literally "the present world," representing the fluid boundaries between past and future generations. For the Chinese, with their ready acceptance of change in the world, the concept of space and time is very real and distinct.

Sima Qian (145-86 BC), a renowned historian in the Han Dynasty and author of the monumental volume *Shiji* (also known as the *Records of the Grand Historian*), wrote "explore and understand the boundaries between man and heaven (sky), explain all transformations between the past and the present, so as to establish one school of thought." In a tradition that perceives a trinity of heaven, earth, and human conceptually, there are no fixed or discernible boundaries between any of the three. Heaven, earth, and human therefore encompass the totality of space, which is the universe. At the same time, because the past world continuously transforms into the present world, understanding and explaining the nature of such transformations, which depends on the interrelationships between heaven, earth, and human, can lead to the establishment of our own school of thought on space-time and human relationships.

Disparate philosophical traditions also perceive and interpret history and space-time differently. To the Chinese, space-time is a continuum of events or processes, and history is simply a time record of this continuum. This is in sharp contrast to the Western metaphysical tradition where our universe is a continuum of space created by God, made up of discrete planets and galaxies, and history is defined by key moments or key figures. As articulated by Hall and Ames,[24] in the development of Western thought, which is based on a strongly atomistic and essentialist commitment traceable to the early Greeks, the prominence of a historical figure is usually a function of the degree to which that figure reflects discontinuity with what

---

24 David L. Hall and Roger T. Ames, *Thinking through Confucius* (State University of New York Press, 1987).

has gone before. A Descartes, Newton, or Einstein is most visible because of the extent to which he challenges the status quo. Western historians perceive such figures as being responsible for setting their respective disciplines on a new track. This historical paradigm is reflective of the act/agent distinction usually presupposed in the Western interpretation of human experience. Moreover, it is consistent with a perception of historical research being primarily concerned with identifying agency and assigning responsibility for past events.

In contrast, the Chinese intellectual tradition is generally characterized by a commitment to continuity. It would be much easier for a philosopher to gain a hearing and win support for a new concept by reinterpreting the existing and popularly accepted vocabulary, than it would for him to advance his own original set of ideas. This same commitment to continuity meant that the authority one's ideas might gain by operating within the bounds of an existing tradition would far outweigh the pride of authorship. It is for this reason that most Chinese development of philosophical ideas tends to be expressed within a framework of organic growth, not through a dialectical process of thesis and antithesis. Thus, the difference between the Chinese and Western approaches seems to be evolutionary versus revolutionary, which is observable in every field of human experience.

The Chinese people often say, "history repeats itself." From this perspective, the Chinese understanding of time sounds cyclical. But Joseph Needham[25] proved that linearity of time has in fact dominated Chinese culture, even though elements of both linear and cyclical time were present. This emphasis on linearity of time in Chinese history does not imply a progressive world. Confucians insist on looking back with envy at the ideal societies of past times. Conversely, a vision of time as cyclical can be progressive. As contemporary philosopher Tang Junyi indicated, cosmology for the Chinese is not simply a linear zero-sum victory of order over chaos driven by some external cause. Rather, it is the holistic interpretation of the endless alternation between rising and falling, emerging and collapsing, and moving and attaining equilibrium occasioned by its own internal energy of transformation. This cosmic unfolding is not cyclical in

---

25 Joseph Needham, *Science in Traditional China* (Harvard University Press, 1981).

the sense of reversibility and replication. Instead, it is a continuing spiral that is both continually recursive and continually renewing. This process is analogous to the four seasons of Nature, in which spring returns every year but each spring season reveals itself uniquely. Humans in tune with Nature are an integral part of this process.

THE TRAJECTORY OF CIVILIZATIONS

In Newtonian physics, the trajectory of a given object can be determined by its mass, initial position, direction, and speed if it is in motion, and the sum of all the forces exerted on it. Likewise, we propose a similar framework in which our inner thinking preferences and the degree of our self-cultivation and education define our initial position, personality, or identity as an individual. Then we look at the circumstances, often influenced by various environmental, technological, cultural, sociological, economic, and political forces, and in many cases there is also a history behind it which drives it along a trajectory through time. If we understand the trajectory and then bring the thinking preferences and worldviews of the individuals involved to bear on it, we can start to see where and how things may change, allowing us to better predict the probable outcome of a given occurrence or event, or even the future trajectory of a civilization.

We used this framework to compare events that occurred both in China and Europe over six historical periods. The first and earliest period was during the Neolithic era. It was the age where many tenets of civilization such as basic thinking, language, art, ideology, customs, traditions, and worldview, were developed. Civilizations appeared when Neolithic villages merged to create cities, which then became larger as better technology, organization, and management became available. Urban communities that shared a common cultural heritage grouped themselves by assimilation or conquest into nations. Nations fused through further assimilation or conquest into empires. By tracing the progress and formation of the Roman and Qin/Han empires, we were able to see the beginnings of the cultural characteristics of Western and Chinese civilizations.

The Neolithic civilizations of Europe and the Near East were marked by fission, diffusion, expansion, conquest, counter-conquest, barbarian invasion, and colonization, culminating in the formation of the powerful Roman Empire in the first century BC. On the other hand, Chinese Neolithic civilizations were marked by economic, cultural, and political fusion, assimilation, kinship linkage, intermarriage, social stratification, and integration, which eventually formed the equally powerful Qin/Han Empires. Even in these early years, the differences were obvious, and we believe resulted from very different thinking preferences creating very different values, attitudes, and worldviews. Chinese civilization was a product of evolution as it interacted with other cultures, not the revolution that the West often experienced in military conquest or domination. The Chinese empire was also developed in geographic isolation over a longer time period, so it was focused on evolving its community and collective governance, in contrast to the openly competitive Mediterranean environment, which focused on individual freedom.

The Roman and Qin/Han Empires were broadly comparable in size, population, and historical time period. While they both benefitted from similar technological advancement, and both resulted from the military conquest of a powerful state, the two empires nevertheless developed very distinctive political, sociological, economic, and cultural characteristics. The resulting Chinese social and political entities were comparatively more stable because people were more tolerant and accommodative, generally appearing less fragmented and polarized. Europe, on the other hand, kept dividing for a long period of time until the recent formation of the European Union, which unfortunately is mostly an economic entity that is still struggling for survival. While it established a common currency, other areas such as political union were rejected in a referendum. The United States has been functioning well because of its federated constitution, rule of law, and the vastness of the New World. But more recently, American fragmentation and polarization is also becoming an increasing concern.

It should be emphasized here that it is not our intention to say any one civilization is comparatively superior or inferior. Each has its own strengths and weaknesses. The lessons we have learned from analyzing history indicate that if any civilization uses its strength to extremes, it will become their weakness, and vice versa. Even without going to extremes, a change in situation or condition can easily change our fortune. This is why contextual understanding of each other is so important, but especially for our leaders, policy creators, and decision makers. Unnecessary mistakes or tactical errors at the international level can have devastating consequences but can be avoided if the individuals running our nations can work towards building trust and empathy for each other.

The historical development of the other five periods were documented in our last book[26] so we will not repeat them here. But for every period we compared, we found similar patterns supporting the framework we put forth. The general rule seems to be that a civilization will thrive only if it can reinforce its own cultural strengths by continuously evolving and improving it, while at the same time learning from others' strengths to help or balance its own weaknesses. Stagnation causes decline. Europe learned from China during the Age of Enlightenment, and recently the Chinese have been learning science, technology, market economy, corporate management, financing, and more from the West. While the Chinese were accepting of Europe learning Chinese ways and knowledge in the past, the West has been less pleased about China leap-frogging it in recent years, although these are both examples of how civilizations can ride each other's coattails for progress, reflecting and learning from the other.

CHINESE AND WESTERN CIVILIZATION TODAY

Religion and science have always dominated Western thought. This is not surprising because the search for truth and transcendence has always underpinned Western history and philosophy. In recent years, the West has been increasingly accepting of secularization. Many postmodern Western philosophies no longer subscribe to traditional religious beliefs, but unfortunately that has led to a loss of values and morality leading to populism, relativism, anarchism, and factionalism all becoming increasingly problematic.

On the other hand, the Chinese worldview is neither supernatural nor preordained by principles. Westerners have religious unity, not national unity, while the Chinese are exactly the opposite, insisting on both national unity and religious plurality, simultaneously practicing Daoism,

---

26 Tai P. Ng and Wah-Won Ng, *Chinese Culture, Western Culture: How Cross-Cultural Views of History, Philosophy, and Human Relationships Will Change Modern Global Society* (iUniverse Inc, 2007).

Confucianism, and Zen Buddhism. Traditional Chinese people prefer ethics to religion, applied science over pure science, practical understanding of human relationships over metaphysics, and capable good government protection over uncontrolled personal freedom. Their worldview holds that humankind is simply an integral part of Nature and we must seek ways to live in harmony with it.

Some of the greatest strengths of Chinese civilization and its people include pragmatism, tolerance, harmony, adaptability, peace loving, and strong ethics. Chinese tend to emphasize similarities rather than differences in human relationships, and win-win instead of zero-sum games. Chinese society puts emphasis on duties and responsibilities rather than on rights. So in turn, its weaknesses include a lack of aggression, which often makes them appear weak and may invite aggression. In addition, they often choose to be practical rather than high principled, and sometimes seem undisciplined, drawing disdain from other elite cultures for doing things that seem uncultured.

In contrast, some of the greatest strengths of Western civilization and its people include progressiveness, competitiveness, high principles, rules and laws, faithfulness, adventurousness, and risk taking. They excel in innovating and enterprising activities. But conversely, its weaknesses can include inflexibility, a lack of tenacity and tolerance, and a passion for competition, winning, and domination that has unfortunately brought the destructiveness of imperialism, colonialism, and many wars to our world.

Because of the differences in thinking, history, and situational context, China and the US have created a very different set of political and social advantages and problems onto themselves. For example, Chinese emphasize the importance of human responsibility, which creates a relatively more harmonized and stable society, but also creates some problems with human rights. Americans emphasize the importance of human rights, which creates a relatively more liberal and free society but creates a totally different set of problems such as a lack of accountability and responsibility by some of its citizens and governments. What is most interesting, though, is that each side's strengths can help with the problems that the other side faces—they are, in fact, complementary in many ways. China has been learning from the West for the last few centuries and continues today, continuously experimenting and evolving, but conversely, the same cannot be said of the West yet, even though they could benefit from studying and learning about the Chinese ways.

Up until now, we have focused on the differences in thinking at civilizational and cultural levels that may affect national decision-making. But we are at an important juncture in global history where recent globalization has guaranteed that our future destinies will be intertwined. Better specialization, division of labor, and benefit sharing are all great developments for humanity. But some politicians still think in the Cold War mentality of zero-sum games and hegemonic interests, and intend to do their utmost to prevent further globalization. Such intentions can have dire consequences for the human race, as confrontational tactics may lead to wars with no winner. Worse, a nuclear war could lead to our ultimate demise as a species. At a time when humanity needs to band together and fight for our survival from large scale events such as pandemics and global warming, a "me first" Western attitude can be disastrous. We may already be too late to reverse the process of climatic destruction. But for the benefit of future generations, we must not think as Westerners or Chinese, but as humans, working together to effect the change we need for our species' survival on this earth. We must exert our democratic rights however we can, and make sure our voices are heard in governments around the world.

Our hope lies with the people. As intercultural communication improves as a result of globalization and technological advancement, some people have already begun to embrace the differences and gain a better appreciation of each other's culture. Social harmony is enjoyed in many socially and racially diverse communities. Many Chinese immigrants have been living in the Western world and regularly contribute to the cultural fabric of that society. Chinese festivals, such as the lunar new year and mid-autumn festival, are celebrated more and more in major North American metropolises such as Vancouver, Toronto, San Francisco, New York, and Chicago. Our communities are more harmonious as we get to know each other better. There are also more people than ever studying eastern thought such as Daoism, Confucianism, and Buddhism, practicing daily reflection and meditation, or believing in holistic prevention and healing, and seeking balance in their personal lives. As more people from both cultures understand the different ways of contextual thinking, they will become more empathetic towards each other, and we hope this book will help further that cause.

Part II:
Understanding China

To truly understand the Chinese perspective, we must not only recognize the differences in thinking and worldview, but also learn about the historical trajectory that China is on. Unfortunately, good information on Chinese history available to the Western world is either hard to find or extremely academic. In this section, we will quickly summarize some of the developments salient to understanding its historical trajectory, but focus mostly on changes in the last fifty years or so, as China has been working hard to come out of its own historical detour and get back on track, both internally and on the world stage. For those interested, our 2007 book, *Chinese Culture, Western Culture,* provides a more comprehensive history of both Chinese and Western civilizational development, and their impact on thinking preferences and worldviews.

China's transformation over the last fifty years has been nothing short of extraordinary, but it still has a long way to go. There are many reasons it will never be the democratic society that many in the Western world had hoped it would become. While some are discouraged by that thought, or even fearful of a so-called Communist country on the rise, we hope to help people to see beyond the labels. Understanding the context of what the country and its people have been through and the key narratives in play, is crucial to properly interpreting events as they unfold in our present day and moving forward.

FIVE: 10,000 YEARS OF CHINESE HISTORY IN A NUTSHELL

The southeastern quadrant of the Eurasian landmass, separated from other early civilizations by deserts, mountains, and seas, was the incubator of Chinese civilization. The region lies more than 4,500 miles from Asia Minor or southeastern Europe, the two cradles of Western civilization. There is evidence of intermittent communication between these ancient civilizations. However, because of the vast distances and difficult terrains that separated the cultures, early Chinese culture essentially developed in isolation. This isolation persisted until about two thousand years ago, ending with the opening of the Silk Road across the Pamir Mountain passes in Central Asia and the advent of sea trade. Even then, travel was hazardous and time-consuming. Hence, geographic confinement is one of the most important and unifying factors in early Chinese life and history. This is in sharp contrast to the development of ancient civilizations around the Mediterranean, where open communication and cross-cultural inter- actions were common.

As we know it today, China is about the same size as the United States, with almost 9,600 million square kilometers of territory. Its land abounds with diverse landforms, including many great river valleys and large river basins. The vastness and scale of China cannot be overemphasized in contrast with other cradles of civilization, particularly Greece and

Mesopotamia. All of the Greek city-states would fit into the smallest of the Chinese kingdoms in the fifth century BC. The Yangtze and Yellow Rivers were two of the world's ten largest rivers. The larger plains, plateaus, and provinces in China exceeded the size of an average-sized country in Europe. With such a drastic contrast in scale, the challenges encountered were also very different, resulting in disparate sociopolitical thinking, ideals, and in the meaning of leadership and "state governance." Such disparity persisted throughout history and is easily observable even today, although pundits of different cultural backgrounds may offer varying interpretations of why.

EARLY CIVILIZATION

The Pleistocene, otherwise known as the Ice Ages, was a geological epoch that began approximately two million years ago. During the Ice Age and the Paleolithic era, existential challenges and the use of tools led to the evolutional development of our human brain and culture. In the subsequent Neolithic era, progress in stone-working technology further precipitated the advancement and spread of agriculture around ten thousand years ago. During this era, our ancestors' means of survival slowly transformed from food gathering to food cultivation, leading to increased independence from Nature. Many of the foundational structures of civilization resulted from this important transition. Language, customs, traditions, forms of government, and many of our fundamental solutions to the uncertainties of the world respectively emerged during this period in China, the Near East, and Europe.

According to L. S. Stavrianos,[27] in the period between ten thousand and two thousand years ago, the global human population jumped from 5.22 to 133 million, a twenty-five-fold increase within just eight thousand years. Those groups who switched to agriculture the earliest grew the fastest. Those who remained food gatherers the longest were left behind. Chinese agriculture first developed around 10000-8000 BC. According to leading archaeologist Su Bingyee, there were six major regions of simultaneous cultural development in China, each progressing at its own speed and

27 L. S. Stavrianos, *A Global History: The Human Heritage*, 3rd Edition
(Prentice-Hall Inc., 1983).

with its own character, but they still managed to influence one another, even in prehistory. The warm, moist climate combined with the thick, loose layers of fertile loess soil in the North China Plain were two of the reasons for the early development of farming technology and farming in China. In the Near East, organized farming did not arise until the arrival of the iron plough at a much later time, and it spread to Europe even later. The Chinese actually domesticated millets in northern China and rice in southern China in the early Neolithic period.

China was heavily populated very early as a result of its success in agricultural development. But the Yellow River can be damaging as well as beneficial because of its capacity to carry large amounts of loess sediments, up to 46% by volume, in contrast to a great river like the Amazon, which carries only 10-12% sediment by volume. As a result, the Yellow River has changed course forty-one times throughout history.[28] Over thousands of years, it has created its own beds and channels on the accumulated loess, layers of which are often higher than the surrounding countryside. Thus, the safety of the countryside depended heavily on the security of the dikes constructed along the river. Yet these dikes were usually built with mud or sandbags and often broke under pressure. The resulting floodwaters inundated millions of acres of farmland, threatened lives, and precipitated significant homelessness in a pattern repeated over and over again since the beginning of Chinese civilization. A more recent official estimate suggests there were 1,590 breaches of dikes between 602 and 1938. During that time, the river changed course seven times. Large-scale famine and pestilence, faithfully documented and vividly described by historians and intellectuals alike, usually followed such natural catastrophes.

A large number of communities developed simultaneously in Neolithic China during the third millennium BC, and they interacted with each other whenever they occupied similar areas. In addition to expanding the communities, the hydraulic work required to tame the mighty rivers and allow human survival demanded effective leadership, social and resources organization, technological innovation, and genuine cooperation from all

---

28 Ray Huang, *Broadening the Horizons of Chinese History: Discourses, Synthesis, and Comparisons* (Routledge, 1999).

people. Engineers who were successful in building waterworks to alleviate flooding were worshipped as folk heroes. Traveling around China today, one can still see some of their water projects at work, and folk temples built for the engineers. One of the most impressive is the controlled water diversion project constructed around the third century BC by the father and son team of Li Bing in Sichuan Province. People today still benefit from their creation.

The scale of the challenges and the subsequent communities that were created pushed the Chinese government to become more mature and capable from very early in history. In fact, to this day, Chinese people often judge the competency of their government based on its effectiveness in fighting natural calamities like floods or droughts, or pandemics like COVID-19 in 2020. The competitive stimulus between communities enriched the quality of life for all and created conditions from which emerged an organized political entity, the state. With this evolution, China stepped into civilization.

The Three Dynasties Period—the Xia, Shang, and Zhou—began around 2083 BC. Archaeological data has confirmed literary sources that state that the legendary worlds of the Xia and later the Shang were multiracial alliances of many tribes. Many local cultures developed at that time into nations or groups of people with a defined identity. Interaction among them enabled the transfer and development of bronze technology, effective communication, and the organization and management of important large-scale projects. These frequent interactions signaled a change that finally pulled these local cultures, or nations, into a common area dominated by a single political entity, the Xia. Around 2082 BC, the Great Yu, a legendary hero whose successful waterworks tamed the flood of the mighty Yellow River, met with an assembly of ten thousand states, and was proclaimed the Overlord of Xia. The Xia people chose to support the son of the Great Yu as their leader after his death, creating a precedent for the first Chinese dynasty to transition from merit-based to inheritance succession.

Written history in China dates back to the Shang state around 1612 BC. The Shang, as a result of cultural and commercial exchange between the regions, cultivated both northern and southern crops, making significant advancements in agricultural production. Shang civilization developed well-documented large and multifunctional cities with populations that were differentiated and stratified by rank, status, and occupation. The Shang built cities and palaces, and were a regional power renowned for its architecture, oracle bone writings, and black ceramics, as well as bronze metallurgy, advanced in technology for its time. As Charles Hucker[29] summarized, large cities, horse-drawn chariots, a high-order bronze technology, and a fully mature version of the Chinese writing system are special developments differentiating Shang civilization from the preceding Neolithic cultures.

King Wen of the Zhou in Western China, who appeared in early writings as a paragon of benevolence and wisdom, made many alliances with neighboring chiefs. His son, King Wu, led a coalition that successfully overthrew the Shang state around 841 BC, even though armed with comparatively inferior technology. The Zhou justified the conquest by citing superior moral ground, first regarding the will of *Tian* (Nature or Heaven with no religious connotation), and subsequently the new ideology of the Mandate of *Tian* being reflected in the will of humanity legitimizing the rule. The Zhou eventually occupied about half of the area of present-day China, enduring almost 900 years.

The Zhou served as a guiding paradigm for governmental, intellectual, and social development throughout the length of Chinese history. From the time of the Zhou onward, the geographical Chinese world occupied the central plain, uniting the east and west and proclaiming itself as central with the name of "Middle Kingdom." The Chinese order was based on an agricultural economy in a single complex that encompassed a greater population and land area than any other civilization of ancient times. Because of its uniquely secular thinking and holistic worldview, its cultural coherence outlasted its political institutions. We talked earlier about the Chinese quality of broadminded inclusiveness and harmony in diversity. The universalism of the Zhou order made it receptive to foreign elements. From one generation to another, even though it was not without periods of serious setbacks, the Chinese nation and its people have demonstrated

29 Charles O. Hucker, *China's Imperial Past: An Introduction to Chinese History and Culture* (Stanford University Press, 1975).

its resilience and sustainability through its own self reform and evolution, learning from past mistakes and being receptive to outside influences.

Part of the great success of the Zhou was due to their ability to absorb divergent cultures and populations, and integrate multiple beliefs into a grand, centralized schema, which later generations of Chinese still share. This is the precursor of Confucianism, believing in moral self-cultivation, and in "things you don't want, don't give to others," which is a bit different than the more common Western phrase "do unto others as you would want them to do unto you." From that time forward, Chinese rate other people only by their degree of civilization and relationships with fellow human beings, and do not discriminate by race, creed, or religion. That is, you are one of us in the Middle Kingdom if you live and treat each other like us. This is core to the Chinese foundational precepts of diversity, tolerance, benevolence, inclusiveness, balance, harmony, flexibility, and long-term sustainability which define Chinese culture today, but which are in stark contrast to the religious foundation of Western culture.

By the middle of the first millennium BC, all the great civilizations of Eurasia had reached a point of maturity that allowed them to cast an objective view on their own beliefs, and to respond to the social and political changes that their societies were undergoing. It was then that the great central traditions of Greece, Persia, India, and China created highly elaborate systems of beliefs and values that gave coherence to their civilizations. And each of them was clearly distinct from the others. What distinguished the Chinese one was their view of humanity as an integral part of Nature without any supernatural explanation or divine creator. Theirs was a world in which both progress and backwardness were attributed to human decisions, not to gods or divinities.

The Spring and Autumn period (722-481 BC) of the Late Zhou was the time of Confucius (551-497 BC) and the beginning of Confucianism. Confucius was one of many private teachers of the day. He had three thousand student followers living and traveling with him, and he offered advice to rulers in various states. He taught only by example, both his own and those of other people, historical and contemporary. His focus was ethics, but his priority was instruction in the practice of becoming truly human. Confucianism involves the moral self-cultivation of humans in order to reveal our natural goodness through education, and to harmonize our relationships with others, Nature, and the universe. In fact, Confucius was the greatest humanitarian who ever lived. Confucius's students frequently asked him to define his virtues in the *Analects*. He repeatedly avoided doing so, focusing on specific situations and leaving ample room for spontaneity and creativity in their application and interpretation. When asked about serving spiritual beings and about death, he replied "If we are not yet able to serve man, how can we serve spiritual beings? ... If we do not yet know life, how can we know about death?"

The Warring States period (476-221 BC), also known as the One Hundred Schools period, followed what is considered the Classical Age of China. During this time Confucianism, Daoism, Legalism, Mo'ism, and many other different schools of philosophy, politics, and practical sciences, all developed along with the emergence of a large intellectual class. Fundamental changes in the arts, such as in the decorative designs of bronze, jade, and lacquered objects signaled a trend towards rationalization, eloquence, freshness, and worldliness instead of focusing entirely on ritual. Other advances included the transcription of laws, an increase in commercial activities seen in marketplaces functioning with a money economy, and an increase in social mobility.

Another significant development during the Classical Age of China was the formation of a new social class, the "*shi*," which consisted of scholars with high capability and great character who vowed to serve the country. This was the era in which the old nobility was losing its prestige, and they could no longer expect to automatically receive preference because of hereditary status. Some of the former elite became responsible for the dissemination of knowledge to the public. Armed with classical knowledge on benevolent governance and leadership with an altruistic spirit of providing service to people, the country, and *Tianxia*, this new elite group of *shi* later went on to become a privileged class of Confucian scholars throughout the Chinese imperial era. Even in China today, the spirit of *shi* lives on in the gentry of some modern institutions exerting strong influence on the government. In fact, there has always been a dichotomy of two Chinese cultures: one high culture belonging to the ruling elites, and a more common culture belonging to ordinary people. In order to belong to the ruling elite group one must, in principle if not in deed, share the altruistic spirit of *shi* and be able to shoulder the responsibility of the country and *Tianxia*, or the universe, being willing to sacrifice self-interest and if necessary, even life.

EMPIRES AND DYNASTIES

In 221 BC, King Zheng of the Qin proclaimed himself to be the first emperor. For the first time in history, China was a unified empire. The First Emperor's domestic programs emphasized unification, standardization, and centralization. King Zheng was best known for building the Great Wall to shut out the nomadic people; a giant tomb for himself, with its now-famous army of 7,500 terracotta warriors, each life-sized and distinctly individual; and artificial waterways that linked two tributaries in southern China, establishing a continuous transport route between the Yangtze and West river systems. Under Zheng's rule, irrigation networks were expanded, and canals funneled grain taxes to the capital. An efficient network of roads radiated out from the capital. More drastic domestic measures included the shifting of whole populations according to labor and military needs. State monopolies were imposed on salt and iron. The currencies were unified. Weights and measures were standardized. Axles on carts were also standardized, mainly to reduce ruts on the loess roads in northwestern China. Going to great lengths to organize routines and customs, the emperor also formalized written Chinese into a basic script, which has persisted to this day. Emperor Zheng defined and expanded China's frontiers, mobilizing large armies of conscripts. By 214 BC, his troops had reached the Vietnamese valleys in the northern and central regions, and the coastlines in the south.

Despite its many achievements, the Qin Dynasty only lasted for eighteen years. In 210 BC, the emperor died while on a trip away from the capital. Then in 202 BC, Liu Bang overthrew Zheng's heir to start the Han Dynasty. The brevity of Qin rule provided an objective lesson to the first sovereigns of Han, who anxiously recognized that while military force was important for conquering states, maintenance of power required ruling with virtue. Following the Legalist school of teaching, the Qin Dynasty had been extremely authoritarian. The Han Dynasty adopted the political structures that the Qin had erected, but did away with the terror and oppression of the former empire. They initially applied the Daoist philosophy of rule by non-action, gave people time to recuperate and adjust, and by doing so lasted for more than four centuries.

The Qin and Han empires were comparable to the mighty Roman empire, similar in population (about 60 million) and the size of their territories (more than three million square kilometers)[30]. Both empires were also great builders. But the similarities stopped there. The Latins and Greeks were mostly descendents of Indo-European nomadic conquerors from the steppes of Central Asia. They retained certain traits and characteristics of nomadic cultures, such as adaptability, bravery, and determination, but also aggressiveness, divisiveness, and destructiveness. The practical Romans, unlike the Greeks, achieved little in abstract science or philosophy, but they excelled in the building of aqueducts, sewer systems, bridges, and roads. The latter were so well-constructed that they continued to be used through the Middle Ages, and in some cases even today. Roman architecture focused around secular structures for gathering, such as baths, stadiums, amphitheaters, and triumphal arches. New building materials, such as concrete, brick, and mortar, made possible the type of grand scale vaulting necessary for many of these large buildings.

Culturally, the Romans, in a process of absorption and adoption as they built their empire, perpetuated the art, literature, and philosophy of the Greeks, the religious and ethical system of the Jews, the new religion of the Christians, astronomy and astrology from the Babylonians, and cultural elements from Persia, Egypt, and other Eastern civilizations. The Romans contributed their own talent in government, codified law, and architecture, and spread their Latin language around the Mediterranean. In this way, they created the Greco-Roman synthesis, a rich combination of cultural elements that has shaped what we call the "Western tradition" for two millennia.

While Rome's economy relied on slavery, Qin and Han prosperity rode mainly on the backs of free peasants. The Qin and Han empires were highly developed and much more culturally sophisticated political entities. Early development of a bureaucratic Chinese government and its centralization were major drivers of the textile industry, because silk was the main form of payment to both bureaucrats and nomadic people in the north and northwest. Chinese superiority in textile and metallurgical technology at the

---

30 Ray Huang, *China: A Macro History* (M.E. Sharpe Inc., 1988).

time is what helped them build relationships all along the Silk Road with urbanized states of the Eurasian continent, responding to the demands of central Asia, Persia, India, Rome, and other European centers. During four centuries of Han rule, the Chinese achieved political and cultural unity, albeit at the price of philosophical conformity. Nevertheless, Han society was relatively open and free. The Chinese way of life also radiated into the corners of both China proper and other peripheral areas.

All the empires were great builders, so infrastructure such as roads and water works were comparable both in scale and quality. They were all agricultural empires, but Chinese productivity was much higher. The fertility of the loess plateaus, the widespread use of cast-iron for agricultural tools, and the intensive use of irrigation allowed the Chinese to produce crops from the same piece of land every year without having to leave fields fallow, as was the case in Rome. You could say the Chinese were much better fed than the Romans.

Over the centuries, Chinese technology also advanced at a much quicker pace than the rest of Eurasia. The need for hydraulic engineering to tame the Chinese rivers was one major impetus, especially for advancing metallurgical technology. According to Milton Meyer,[31] the Han era made great strides in technology and science. The accomplishments of the time comprise a long list indeed. The Chinese first recorded sunspots in 28 BC while Galileo was the first European to discover sunspots, in 1613. They calculated a nine-year elliptical orbit of the moon around the earth, which was very close to the actual 8.85-year orbit. An early form of the seismograph was invented to record earthquakes. By 132 BC, its inventor, who was also an astronomer, had enumerated 11,520 different stars. The Chinese utilized sundials and water clocks divided into 100 or 120 equal parts. They continued to note solar and lunar eclipses and officially adopted the lunar calendar, in which the four seasons commenced in the first, fourth, seventh, and tenth moons, with the equinox noted in the second and eighth and the solstice in the fifth and eleventh. As advanced astronomers, they also created very accurate clocks.

---

31 Milton W. Meyer, *China: A Concise History*, 2nd edition (Rowman & Littlefield Publishers, 1994).

Han scientists wrote textbooks on subjects ranging from zoology to botany and chemistry. Scientists also invented the rudder for use on ships and created other useful devices like the fishing reel and wheelbarrow. The Eastern Han developed the water-powered mill and outfitted their horses with shoulder collars, which increased their efficiency as draft animals. Similar collars were not used in the West for another ten centuries. The Chinese experimented with problem-resistant rice strains, practiced crop rotation, and terraced slopes to grow fruits, vegetables, and bamboo. They also developed iron casting and steel fifteen centuries before Europe. In an epochal advance, the Western Han developed paper from rags, fibers, and the bark of trees, replacing the bulky and unwieldy wooden and bamboo slips in use until then. Pure paper, dated to around 100 AD, has been discovered in former Han outposts located in the dry, Central Asian deserts. In an early form of printing, classics engraved on stone were reproduced on paper by ink rubbing techniques. Unfortunately, because of natural disasters and civil strife, only fragments of the many Han books remain. Han physicians developed acupuncture to alleviate pain and treat various illnesses. The list goes on and on. In short, Han flourished for four centuries and is remembered for having a thriving and vibrant culture centered around human virtues.

As Joseph Strayer[32] explained, the Roman Empire was not a national state. It was a union of people who shared a common Mediterranean civilization under a single powerful ruler. As the empire declined, all those people broke loose. Revival and reconstitution took a new form at a much later date. In contrast, the Han Empire was a national state governed by an efficient and open bureaucracy and code of law with sustainable intensive agriculture within an efficient market network and economy, a common written language and cultural heritage, a shared ideology of Confucianism, and the apparent legitimacy of the mandate of heaven stipulating that the ruler must work for the benefit of the people. The Han Dynasty disintegrated about two centuries before the fall of the Roman Empire. Both collapsed under internal pressure from rebellion, corruption, and the

---

32 Joseph R. Strayer, *Western Europe in the Middle Ages: A Short History*, 3rd Ed. (Waveland Press Inc., 1991).

breakdown of social order as well as the invasion of barbarians. The twilight of the Roman Empire signaled a period of chaos and the beginning of a time in history now known as the Dark Ages, from which the Roman Empire never recovered as a political entity.

THE GOLDEN AGE OF CHINA DURING THE DARK AGES

Life in Europe during the Dark Ages was very hard. Very few people could read or write, and nobody expected conditions to improve. The only hope for most people during the Middle Ages was their strong belief in Christianity and the hope that life in heaven would be better than what they were experiencing on earth. As we now know, Christianity and the Church effectively dominated most of the cultural, political, and economic life of the people and history in Medieval Europe. Because the medieval church supported all of Europe's libraries and schools, and the only literate persons in early medieval society were churchmen of one kind or another, governments had no choice but to staff their bureaucracies with clergy.

While Europe began its Dark Ages, China was at the verge of another golden age—the Sui, Tang, and Song Dynasties. In 589, the Yang family, under the name of the Sui Dynasty, united China again. The Sui are known for building the impressive 1,200-mile Grand Canal that connects the drainage basins of the Yellow, Huai, and Yangtze rivers, enabling the resources of the productive south to be brought north. This national system laid the groundwork for the prosperity of the Tang Dynasty. Both the Sui and Tang advanced the bureaucratic civil service system that the Han established. Examination for civil service recruitment then broadened beyond Confucian topics to include history, law, poetry, mathematics, and even aspects of Daoism.

The Tang Dynasty lasted for almost three centuries, from 626 to 907, and was regarded as a golden era. Under the Tang Dynasty, according to Charles Hucker,[33] China combined prosperity, cultural grandeur, aristocratic sophistication, military power, and supremacy in foreign relations to achieve an age of greatness unseen since the Han. The capital, Chang'an,

---

33 Charles O. Hucker, *China's Imperial Past: An Introduction to Chinese History and Culture* (Stanford University Press, 1975).

with a population of two million people, became the world's largest and most brilliantly cosmopolitan city. One in six people was a foreigner. As one of the world's earliest planned urban complexes, the city, laid out in a rectangular grid, measured five by six miles and covered almost fifteen thousand acres. The Tang owed much of its early strength and prosperity to the maturing of institutions and its close communication with central and other regions in Asia.

It was the Tang that ensured a permanent Chinese presence in central Asia. All kinds of religions found their way to the Tang capital: Tibetan Buddhists, Persian Zoroastrians, Manicheans, Jews, Nestorian Christians, and Muslims. Many new crops from various regions added variety to Tang foods. In 801, a cartographer created a map, measuring thirty by thirty-three feet, which represented an area ten thousand by eleven thousand miles. On it, he noted seven major trade routes to the known Asian world. People from east Asian countries like Japan, Korea, and Vietnam stayed for months or years in China studying everything that could be learned: law, medicine, astronomy, Buddhism, and the great variety of techniques in which the Chinese excelled. The Japanese adopted whole aspects of Chinese civilization, as Korea and Vietnam had done before. For example, rice cultivation, Chinese script, the Tang code, bronze and iron metallurgy, city planning, Zen Buddhism, Confucianism, and Chinese aesthetics. The Japanese copied pretty much everything from China at the time, except for the Chinese bureaucratic system and Chinese meritocratic civil service, which was unacceptable to the feudal samurai world.

Cultural pursuits also flourished during the Tang era. Tang writers produced many scholarly works. Private and imperial libraries were extensive, and a special Tang archival bureau acquired and catalogued books. Printing advanced the compilation and availability of encyclopedias, which were particularly helpful to students preparing for examinations. Many local gazettes and collections of book excerpts were issued, supplementing the historical records as sources of topical information on Chinese politics, economics, and society. The flourishing genre of the short story dealt with both religious and everyday topics. Professional storytellers combined prose and verse. Even today, Chinese children can all recite famous poems from the Tang Dynasty, a true legacy of the time.

Chinese culture peaked during the Song Dynasty (960-1270), during which China experienced a commercial revolution fostered by growing urbanization and a cultural renaissance. One of the most significant cultural influences was the large influx of well-educated commoners into the ranks of officialdom by means of the national examination system. During the Tang, only a few dozen candidates had assumed this title each time the examinations were held. However, during the Song, the honor roll ran to several hundred annually. In the twenty years of Taizu's reign, there were nearly ten thousand new titles conferred. This expansion was partially because printing had developed rapidly, promoting literacy and education to the point that, for the first time in Chinese history, common people had realistic hopes that their sons might achieve status in the elite official class. The court of Emperor Taizu was composed of writers and scholars drawn from ordinary families rather than members of the ruling aristocracy, as had been the case under the Tang Dynasty.

This strong emphasis on civil accomplishment and a government operating in the interests of the common people set the tone for the Song. With cultivated people, *shi,* running the country, cultured thinking permeated society. There was a spontaneous flourishing of philosophy and new ideas. The Song refined many of the developments of the previous centuries. Included among these refinements were not only the Tang ideal of the universal man, who combined the qualities of scholar, poet, painter, and statesman, but also historical writings, paintings, calligraphy, and hard-glazed porcelain. Song intellectuals sought answers to philosophical and political questions in the Confucian classics; resulting in what is now called Neo-Confucianism.

In art, the bright color combinations of ink-and-wash painting gave way to mixed hues of gray with large areas of the surface left blank. Porcelain forms were simplified—becoming plainer and purer in coloration. Deeply introspective literary practitioners with lofty moral standards produced artistic achievements of the highest order, but they also seemed over-civilized, devoid of any streak of wildness or creativity, as if they were lacking part of what makes us human. This can be sensed in the contrast between the refined elegance of Song porcelain and the brash tricolor glaze pottery of the Tang Dynasty. By Song times, the technique of high-fired, hard-glazed porcelain was fully developed. Porcelain was produced in abundance for use in the imperial palace and commoners' homes alike, and increasingly for export throughout Asia and across the Indian Ocean to Africa and the Mediterranean world. Near the end of the Song Dynasty, the now-famous blue-and-white porcelain of China had emerged. In keeping with the simplicity of its designs, Song porcelain is characterized by a faint, incised motif, and often has no decoration at all.

Throughout Chinese history, there were agrarians living inside the Great Wall and nomadic people outside. Agrarians needed peace to grow and harvest their crops. Nomadic people, on the other hand, were hunters and fighters who followed their herds for a living. But their livelihoods still regularly needed supplies or products made from the Middle Kingdom. The Wall was the place where they met, traded, fought, and interacted with each other. Since China was very much geographically isolated at the time, there was limited interaction with the outside world. Hence most political and socio-economic interactions in Chinese history were between the agrarian and nomadic people on the two sides of the Great Wall (other than those found braving the four seas by sailing eastward). Agrarians usually suffered more in their encounters with the nomadic people because they were poor fighters, less aggressive, more tolerant, and hence appeared weak, which often invited further aggression. But once they decided their home base had been threatened and/or their basic moral principles violated, they always stood their ground and fought back fiercely and in no uncertain terms. Even today, stories of their bravery are still revered by the people, and Chinese are known to stand their ground to fight when they perceive their bottom line has been reached, or there is no other way out.

There were two events in Chinese history, during the Han and Tang Dynasties, when China was at its peak of civilization and was successful fighting against invading nomads. Emperor Wu of the Han fought the nomadic Huns around 130 BC; after their defeat they fled west which many believe subsequently caused the sacking of Rome by the Goths in 410 AD. Emperor Taizong of the Tang then allied with the Uyghur in central Asia and drove the Turks further west around 630 AD. In both cases, China was the dominant military power in central Asia, but still never sought hegemony or colonization because both Confucianism and Daoism was strongly against that, and as agrarians, they felt that there is no place like home. According to the ancient Chinese teaching, the more powerful you are, the humbler and more benevolent you should be in dealing with others, especially those who are weaker. So power was used instead to open up what is now known as the ancient Silk Road, a peaceful and enduring trading route between China, central Asia, and Europe, filling the immense appetite for silk, porcelain, sandalwood, and spices going west, and horses, ivory, incense, cotton, and gold heading back east.

There was also a marine route to Europe through the South China Sea and the Indian Ocean that was opened by the great Chinese admiral Zheng He of the Ming Dynasty in his seven expeditions of the early 1400s. His fleets consisted of as many as 317 ships and 27,870 men, with a nine-mast, 400-foot flagship that carried up to 500 troops. That was the largest naval expedition in history at that time. He eventually made it as far as Hormuz, the Red Sea, and the East African coast, sixty-five years before Vasco da Gama's pioneer journey for the Europeans coming from the west. The objective of Zheng He's expedition was not to expand the boundaries of China through conquest or colonization, as was the rationale on land. Rather, it was to explore cultural, political, and trade opportunities. It was the same Silk Road spirit whether camels or ships were involved, reflecting Chinese culture in practice. Such peaceful exploration is still being celebrated by people in various countries in Asia and Africa along these routes of friendship, once called the ancient Silk Road, or more contemporarily, "One Belt One Road."

These peaceful missions were in sharp contrast to the Mongolian conquest of Genghis Khan and his heirs through Europe at a later date. The Mongols were nomadic people, fierce fighters, and renowned for cruelty and destruction in their path of conquest. Some Europeans still vividly remember the horrific "yellow peril." Certain Western people are still fearful of the Chinese because they confuse the nomadic Mongol or earlier Hun fighters with peace loving agrarian Chinese. While they look similar, history tells us that the agrarian Chinese people also suffered from similar nomadic invasion and occupation for centuries throughout its history. Such a distinction is important for our understanding of present-day China and the Chinese people, the peace-loving descendants of Confucian, Daoist, and Buddhist agrarian believers.

According to Joseph Needham,[34] the Mongolian conquest brought Chinese inventions to Europe. These included gunpowder, the magnetic compass, printing, paper, the sternpost rudder, the foot stirrup, the breast strap harness, and many more advanced technological and cultural ideas. These all contributed to Europe staging the Age of Enlightenment and Exploration which eventually led to Columbus' discovery of America (using gunpowder and the marine compass) and the development of modernism (using printing, paper, and a new concept of civil governance). This stands as a testament of how cultures should learn from each other. Similarly, China is now building a new political and socio-economic culture based on the use of Western science, free market economy, global institutions, and management. Buddhism is another Chinese assimilation from afar—this time from India. It is only when we truly understand the historical, cultural, and thinking preferences driving people and their interactions that our impressions and understanding of each other will be more complete and balanced.

CHINA IN DECLINE

In the thirteenth century, we saw a reversal in the fortunes and paths of Europe and China. As Europe recovered from the Dark Ages, it accelerated through cultural, economic, and political development and modernization. Western thought preferences made the Scientific and Industrial Revolutions possible. During this time, Europe became open to new ideas and influences. On the other hand, China, after suffering much from the Mongolian military occupation, turned inwards during the Ming Dynasty and became closed to new ideas and influences. Traditional Chinese philosophy and thought preferences were weak against mighty military power. The Yuan Dynasty unsettled the dynamic balance previously in play and signaled the beginning of China's long decline.

The Mongolian dynasty of Yuan (1264-1368 AD) was a military occupation of China rather than a civil government. Kublai Khan and his nomadic Mongol masters adopted Chinese ceremonial and Confucian rites, and

---

34 Joseph Needham, *Within the Four Seas: The Dialogue of East and West* (University of Toronto Press, 1979).

even set up an office to collect materials for a history of the preceding dynasties. However, he refused to restore the government office examination system on the grounds that it might restrict his choice of officials to those who had knowledge of the Confucian classics. Although they relied on Chinese staff for administrative purposes, their deep distrust of their new subjects led to the decision that only Mongols could be appointed to high office roles and tax administration could only be entrusted to Muslims, who were allies of the Mongols. The population was classified based on a combination of ethnic and political considerations. The highest class was the Mongols, then their allies from Central Asia, then the inhabitants of northern China including the Khitans. The lowest class was the southern Chinese. This discrimination formed the basis for taxation and penal law. Mixed marriage was forbidden. This was all in stark contrast to traditional Chinese culture.

According to Stephen Haw,[35] the Mongol conquest was a turning point in Chinese history. There had been mostly continuous development of Chinese civilization up to and including the Song Dynasty. The Mongols subsequently destroyed many traditional Chinese cultural and political institutions but brought little to compensate. Chinese culture was by no means annihilated, but it became introverted. The Mongols also left a legacy of a more strongly centralized and autocratic system of government. The whole experience of being subjected to foreign rule was a deep shock to Chinese pride and contributed greatly to Chinese suspicion against outside sociopolitical influences even today.

If there is one lesson we have learned from Chinese history: whenever China is voluntarily open to foreign influences and ideas, it will flourish, such as in the Han, Sui, Tang, and Song periods, but conversely, it will decline when in self-isolation or under military occupation, such as in the Yuan, Ming, and Qing. One could argue that one peak of Chinese civilization was during the Sui and Tang Dynasties, when some members of the imperial family were from Siberia and many officers were members of different races from central Asia. The Tang capital, present-day Xian, was the most cosmopolitan multiracial city in the world. The most

---

35 Stephen G. Haw, *A Traveler's History of China* (Cassell Reference, 2002).

isolationist dynasty in Chinese history was the Ming (1368-1644), even though it finally managed to drive out the Mongols. But so much damage had already been done that traditional Chinese culture and institutions could not be fully restored. After the voyages of admiral Cheng He to East Africa, the emperor decided, since there was no threat from overseas, they could now burn all the ships and ban people from sailing. Afterwards the Ming collapsed inward and shrank, unable to even defend the country when another nomadic people, the Manchu, again threatened China from the northeast.

The Aisin-Gioro family of Manchu founded the subsequent Qing Dynasty (1644-1911). The Manchu conquered Inner Mongolia and temporarily subjugated Korea. Unlike the Mongols, they realized that to dominate the empire, they would have to do things the Chinese way. The first three emperors of the Qing were capable and renowned experts in traditional Chinese culture and classic scholarship. They retained many institutions of the Ming and even earlier Chinese derivations. However, this strategy proved unfortunate, considering the despotic nature of Ming institutions and bureaucracy. Superficially, the Manchu leaders continued Confucian court practices, temple rituals, and the Confucian civil service system. But racial distrust still carried on. The resulting Ming Neo-Confucian philosophy, emphasizing the obedience of subject to ruler, was enforced as the state creed. Manchu influence was so pervasive that their custom of braiding men's hair into pigtails was enforced on the Han population. After a brief initial recovery, China continued its decline. Unfortunately, such dogmatic Confucianism and its negative effects prevailed throughout the rest of the imperial period and into the Nationalist era.

When Westerners first came to China in the 18th century, they found a closed, backward, and despotic country with authoritarian and ignorant rulers, perfect for imperialist ambition and conquest. Before the Opium War, China's economy was still the largest in the world. China was a major exporter and had large trade surpluses with most Western countries. The First Opium War (1839-42) between the Qing and Britain, and the Second Opium War (1856-60) with Britain and France, were fought under the pretext of free trade, after which China lost its sovereignty and was forced to open up to Western domination. Chinese people suffered as the Western powers looted and humiliated the country. This humiliation is still remembered and negatively affects some of the Chinese psyche to this very day.

As Europe entered the Industrial Revolution, China's role in the global economy changed drastically. By 1913, its share of world manufacturing output had fallen from 33% to under 4%. In contrast, the West had risen from 18% to 82%.[36] With this dramatic change of fortune, the predominant image of China shifted to one of stagnant, impoverished despotism. Very few Chinese deny this reality of the past two hundred years. The establishment of the Chinese Republic in 1911 formally declared Chinese membership in the modern world. The Japanese invasion and civil war soon followed, sadly, continuing the plight of the Chinese people.

---

36 P. Bairoch, "International Industrialization Levels from 1750 to 1980," *Journal of European Economic History*, Volume 11, Issue 2 (Fall 1982).

SIX: FROM MAO TO NOW

Modern China began with the Nationalist Revolution of 1911 when Sun Yat-sen overthrew the Qing Dynasty and declared the establishment of the Republic of China in 1912. However, Sun Yat-sen, and subsequently Chiang Kai-shek, were not able to unify the country. Central authority waxed and waned in response to warlord-ism (1915-28), the Japanese invasion (1931-45), and a civil war with Chinese communists. Corruption, fragmentation, foreign concessions, and financial crises plagued the republic until 1949, when the nationalist government fled to Taiwan and the Chinese communists decisively won the civil war.

THE HISTORICAL ABERRATION OF CHINA AND THE BIRTH OF THE CCP

One cannot understand contemporary China without understanding the Chinese Communist Party (CCP), which has governed the People's Republic of China since the founding of the PRC in 1949 by Chairman Mao Zedong, father of the republic and a homegrown Chinese intellectual and revolutionary who led the party to victory. The nationalistic and pragmatic brand of communism we see today is totally different from the ideological brand of the USSR, who wanted to spread communism throughout the world. The current Chinese administration is mostly concerned with getting back to its traditional roots by working for the welfare of its own people, revitalizing rural China, and alleviating poverty, and this differs even from the revolutionary brand of its founder, Chairman Mao.

In getting to where it is today, the party has gone through many cycles of profound changes since 1949, moving from revolutionary back to evolutionary, with many successes and failures. It has gone through multiple leaders, each trying their best in their own way to solve the problems facing China during their tenure. Whether following or going against Chinese tradition, it has consistently demonstrated that the party is capable of learning, adjusting, evolving, and even transforming. The CCP today is not the CCP of 1949. As a member of the Communist International, Mao wanted to export revolution and the communist ideology, and stood against everything that defined traditional Chinese culture. The current President Xi Jinping wants to restore some traditional Chinese values and tenets, sharing prosperity, experience, and a future destiny with the world.

The founding of the CCP in 1921 was the combination of Marxist theory and the worker's movement in some cities of China by Chinese intellectuals who were inspired by the Russian Bolshevik revolution. They believed that imperialism, the subjugation and economic exploitation of weak nations by strong nations, was simply a result of capitalism that needed to be resisted. They were attracted by the other tenets of communism, which promised a new kind of society where class exploitation and oppression would disappear. There are certain similarities related to "sharing" between communism and the traditional Chinese ideal of *Tianxia*, where everybody in the universe lives like they are part of the same family. They vowed to free China and its people from imperialism and class oppression. With the founding of the People's Republic, Mao was credited with re-establishing Chinese sovereignty from imperialists. For the first time in many centuries, China was free from foreign domination, and again in control of its own destiny. Every Chinese leader since has vowed to protect each and every inch of Chinese territory from Western imperialist powers because the past humiliation is still fresh in people's minds, having occurred less than a century ago. China may seem territorial and unyielding in protecting what it views as its sovereignty interests in Taiwan, the islands in the South China Sea, and Tibet, but their extreme sensitivity is almost understandable when you consider that the Western powers previously took advantage, while China was weak, by inserting military presences into these areas, even arbitrarily claiming certain areas to be their own, and continuing to use them in an attempt to "keep China in check." In this sense, challenging sovereignty in areas that China views as its own is very much hitting their bottom line, and you can see them firmly standing their ground to fight back in the name of protecting China's good name, reputation, and people.

Mao was a charismatic and visionary leader and a scholar of Chinese history who knew the Chinese peasantry well, and understood its importance throughout Chinese history. Chinese peasantry is unique to China, different from European slavery or feudalism, and often misunderstood as in the orthodox classics of Marxism, which were based mainly on European experiences. China never had a slavery system comparable to that in Europe—there was never the concept of one person owning another in any sense. Mao organized land reforms in the rural areas and successfully mobilized the peasants to fight, first against the Japanese invasion in World War II, and later against the nationalist government, utilizing his skillful strategic adaptation of the classic *Art of War* by Sunzi. He was able to mobilize the masses to win decisive battles against much stronger adversaries, such as the well-documented battles during the Japanese and Korean Wars. However, his success in warfare did not translate well to economic management or nation building. Utilizing the people's devotion to him and the new republic, he created his own ideology, now known as Maoism, and started to build a utopian classless society and socialism through continuous revolution. Sadly, the Chinese people suffered greatly through these years.

Mao ran multiple social experiments that failed miserably. These included the Great Leap Forward where he tried to overtake the West simply with enthusiasm and determination, but little science. He destroyed any signs of elitism, but the communes he created were disastrous. Then with the Great Proletarian Cultural Revolution, he tried to destroy the powers of the elite class further by denouncing everything that defined traditional Chinese culture, persecuting any signs of class or wealth, and leveling everybody to be equal with the workers and peasants. He sent many students to the countryside to learn from the peasants, and then later as his power waned, he instigated the Red Guards to fight the revisionists within the government and safeguard his version of socialist ideals.

This was one of the darkest and most destructive periods in Chinese history, with the closest equivalent being the Dark Ages experienced in Europe. Red Guards across the country tortured and publicly humiliated their own parents, relatives, and loved ones in the public square. To destroy any visible signs of wealth or social corruption, they confiscated lands and persecuted scholars and intellectuals, as bourgeois, together with landowners. Education on anything but Mao's "Little Red Book" and his ideology was strictly forbidden, and hence whole libraries and piles of books were burned, cultural relics and historical artifacts were looted and destroyed. Any perceived religion wasn't tolerated, so Buddhists and Christians were forced to help burn and destroy their own temples and churches. His destructive efforts to equalize society produced social distrust which continues to have negative consequences to this very day. Even though the current government is trying to resurrect traditional Chinese culture and values, including social harmony and trust, balance, and the morality of Confucianism, it will take time to restore the nation and its people—this is not surprising when you consider that so many who lived through that period were never allowed to be properly educated. In this sense, some of the surrounding countries or regions like Korea, Japan, and Taiwan that absorbed early Confucian traditions and values, behave more like traditional Chinese than some people from China today.

There was only one silver lining from Mao's ideology and experimentation. Some of the students sent to the countryside learned a lot about surviving and advancing even under the harshest environments. The brightest of them learned many skills during their tenures with the peasants in the fields, such as agriculture, political science, economics, and even science and engineering. Many of them pursued a course of study and deep soul searching about China, its people, culture, and history, with all the time in the world at the farm. These individuals vowed to rebuild China and free its people from the poverty and hardship they personally witnessed and experienced. Their opportunity finally came when the universities reopened in 1977 after closing for ten years. The class of '77 was widely regarded as the best and brightest of their time, with a grit and determination like none other. This well-seasoned group of practical idealists subsequently led China to become the world's second largest economy today, well on its way to rejuvenation. Many of them, including President Xi, who worked on the farms for seven years in a remote village in the northwest, became top national leaders, party officials, specialists in many fields, university teachers, and corporate CEOs.

After the Korean War in the early 1950s, which we now know was started by North Korea, the United Nations put China under economic embargo, so Mao had no choice but to lean on and learn industrialization from the USSR. Under adverse conditions, he managed to build some heavy industries in northeastern China, forming a base for later industrialization. This lasted only a few years before the Sino-Soviet split in 1960. The split, combined with poor management, caused severe food shortages and wide-spread famine from 1959 till 1961. And the political turmoil continued until the end of the Cultural Revolution, when the plight of the Chinese people finally ended with Mao's death in 1976. The Chinese nation basically consumed itself for decades during Mao's reign, its people suffering continuously. But to his credit, some of the more innovative social programs and political structures he instituted are still in place, have continued to evolve, and have provided some stability for economic growth.

REVIVAL, REFORM, AND RE-OPENING

Shortly after, in 1978, Deng Xiaoping, one of Mao's revolutionary lieutenants and a visionary strategist, took over the helm of the party. Among the Chinese leaders, Deng was well respected and renowned for his pragmatism in sayings such as, "it doesn't matter whether a cat is black or white, if it catches mice it is a good cat." After decades of surviving Mao's revolution, he realized that China needed stability and peace in order to re-develop. He immediately instructed party members to end all ideological arguments, class struggles, and social experimentation, and instead "seek truth from facts" because "socialism does not mean sharing poverty." He sought ways to modernize China and revive the Chinese economy by making economic growth the core of his national strategy, a strategy that persists to this day.

To achieve economic growth, Deng developed a policy known as "Reform and Opening," which he drew from the experiences of the four Asian tigers (Singapore, Taiwan, Hong Kong, and South Korea), and his visit to the US in 1979. His idea of reform meant moving to a free market economy, opening China to the outside world at the same time. With no precedence in history of moving from a planned to a market economy, he started by opening certain regions of China to foreign investment as Special Economic Zones (SEZs) where industries could grow rapidly without affecting the rest of the country. By applying flexible and innovative Chinese governmental policies to help investors, then minimizing their taxes and providing cheap land, labor, and environmental resources (which unfortunately were viewed as expendable at the time), China was able to attract many investors from East Asia who brought with them much needed capital, technological know-how, production equipment, and knowledge and expertise in global politics, economies, financing, and trade. The resulting investment environment successfully generated growth and propelled Chinese urbanization and industrialization.

Deng's timing coincided with American corporations' search for cheaper manufacturing, also known as "outsourcing," providing a win-win situation for both countries. Manufactured products were exported back to the US and other countries as cheap imports, creating the US trade deficit problem that US President Trump and his advisors frequently blamed China for. This initial model worked well in the Pearl River delta because of its proximity to Hong Kong and Southeast Asia. Later on, the same model was successfully levelled up and applied to the Yangtze River delta close to Taiwan, thereby making Shanghai an international center for finance and technology for the nation. These SEZs became prototypes of supply chain economics, where a complete ecosystem of competitive producers, distributors, and vendors transform raw materials (whether natural resources or ideas) into goods and services deliverable to people anywhere at a minimum cost. Our current world is connected by many competitive supply chains and so far the Chinese have proven to excel at them.

While Deng was recognized as the architect of the Reform and Opening strategy, his ultimate achievement may have been restoring a sense of normalcy to China. Schools reopened and students studied abroad once again. Science and technology regained its importance. Businesses thrived. Economic and industrial growth accelerated. Global trade and investment flourished. Accumulating wealth was no longer an ideological or social sin. It was even acceptable to enjoy life and luxury. People were generally much freer, happier, and more optimistic about their future. Ultimately, Deng and his successors were able to transform the CCP from a revolutionary party to the governing elitist organization of China. Similar to the emperors and their governing bureaucracies in the past imperial eras, selection of leaders was once again based on high morality and ability, preferring social virtues over capability, merits over words, and the party's governing legitimacy came from meeting the needs of its people and leading them with a clear vision towards the future.

After years of intense negotiation with Britain, Deng was even able to reclaim Hong Kong back to China in 1997 with his "one country, multiple systems" scheme, which was later also applied to Macau in an agreement with Portugal. This scheme was actually quite original, and some people might be surprised to learn it was driven by traditional Chinese thinking. Because Chinese civilization is civilizational and not principle-based like it is in the West, China is not a nation-state in the conventional Western sense. For the Chinese, encompassing multiple religions is an acceptable and even common practice, so it is not too difficult to imagine a country with multiple systems of government working peacefully and collaboratively towards a shared objective. It is just another example of traditional harmony in diversity. It worked well in Macau, and continued working for twenty-three years in Hong Kong. Unfortunately, due to a variety of influences, this plan has been undergoing attacks from all sides, garnering quite a bit of international attention, with protests and unrest in Hong Kong in 2019. While we won't get into the details of that here, nonetheless the original intent was to allow different economic-political systems to work cooperatively together during a transition to bring a territory that traditionally has always been Chinese, back into China.

After Deng's death in 1997, he was succeeded by Jiang Zemin and Hu Jintao. Both Jiang and Hu were engineers by training. Both had led teams of engineers in the central committees and were part of helping to implement Deng's visions of transformation from a planned to market economy, building a prosperous China by letting some people get rich first. Under Jiang, more private small and medium businesses continued to diversify and grow. The Communist party started welcoming specialists, businessmen, and entrepreneurs into their ranks, in addition to the more classical communist doctrines of workers and peasants. By loosening the right governmental controls and adopting an open, pro-business, can-do cooperative attitude, Deng and subsequently, Jiang and Hu, empowered the people to experiment with innovative ideas, new approaches, new businesses, and new thoughts, while breaking the old political dogma. What resulted was an explosion of energy, innovation, and entrepreneurialism that had been suppressed for centuries. Rapid industrialization and urbanization took place, just in time for the information age of the twenty-first century.

Under Hu, China joined the World Trade Organization (WTO) in 2001. Despite initial fears that Chinese industries could not compete globally, the Chinese economy continued to thrive with close to double digit growth for three decades, even though it was still very labor intensive and export dependent. The increase in urbanization and industrialization helped hundreds of millions of people come out of poverty. But most Chinese continued to work as part of the lower supply chain in global manufacturing, earning a mere fraction of total sales as cheap labor. The per capita income of China is still low even today. But this period as a prime global supplier and manufacturer, even at the lowest levels, enabled China to collectively accumulate enough wealth to start investing billions in US treasury bills and start acquiring certain foreign enterprises critical to its own industrial development. Basically, China made its first pot of gold in a long time. In 2019, the Chinese share of the global GDP returned to over 18%, a massive increase from the 1.5% in 1978 when Deng first started his reform and opening. It may be a long time, though, if ever, before China returns from its historical aberration to its historic peak of well over 30% before the first Industrial Revolution in the 18th to 19th century.

THE DARK SIDE OF (TOO) RAPID GROWTH

China's first pot of gold was not made without heavy sacrifices. China is still in the process of cleaning up severe damage to the environment, both in the air and water. They are also cracking down on rampant corruption that resulted from rapid land, industrial, and commercial development, as well as the inadequacy of legal regulation and enforcement typically needed in a competitive free market society, especially for an underdeveloped country. Traditional ethics and values were destroyed by revolution and war and many Chinese were raised without a proper education. Allowing a few people to get rich first also created a powerful and connected wealthy class while the masses remained poor, encouraging even further corruption. If

China is not careful, this privileged class could easily become an oligarchy that will resist future reform, such as in some of the republics of the former Soviet Union. China has been fighting this corruption with rapid and continuous reforms, following a more socialist path that is lifting millions out of poverty and creating a sizable new middle class in major cities. In November of 2020, the government announced that they had eliminated all extreme poverty in China, as planned, a tremendous achievement on its path to restore hope to humanity. Yet rural China remains quite poor, so rural development will be a key factor in whether this modern Chinese experiment ultimately succeeds or not.

In 2008, the global economy was hit by the worst financial crisis since the depression of 1929. This financial tsunami started from Wall Street and quickly swept around the world due to global connectivity. The export-oriented Chinese economy could have suffered the most because of its heavy reliance on foreign trade, particularly American and European trade. But it turned out to be an opportunity for the Chinese leadership to demonstrate their resilience and agility. They immediately injected trillions of dollars of investment into infrastructure building. Projects of special significance to their future development included airport terminals, container fleets and ports, national high speed railway and freeway systems that connect every province, and later on, a high performance electrical power grid to connect most of the provinces and population centers, bringing electrical power and natural gas from the remote but energy rich west to the affluent but energy deficient industrial east. They also invested in building many farm roads to help connect rural producers to urban consumers. New subway systems and fiber-optic cables facilitated connectivity within cities and across towns. Despite the sluggish global economy, the Chinese economy miraculously continued to grow steadily at more than 8% per year. In addition, China made profound contributions to the global recovery—particularly beneficial to resource-rich countries such as Canada, Brazil, and Australia. Even today, China consistently contributes more than 30% of the total global economic growth and is a top leader in global trade and manufacturing.

But as we've seen time and again, rapid development is never without repercussions. When Xi Jinping took over the party leadership in 2012, he was challenged with national problems such as rapidly increasing provincial debt, rampant corruption, severe environmental concerns, worsening income and regional disparity, inefficient state-owned enterprises, overcapacity in many sectors of the manufacturing industry due to stagnant global economic growth after the financial crisis, overly expensive housing sectors, and overbuilt ghost towns. At the same time, exports continued to decline, and low domestic demand and the lack of a service industry meant the country could not replace it internally. People were reluctant to spend money for domestic consumption without a social security system in place. Stories of Chinese storing their life savings under their bed were true; on average, Chinese people were saving over 40% of their earnings, causing very different kinds of economic problems than we typically see in the West.

Many of these problems arose because of the unique Chinese situation and the history leading to it, and they must be solved in a way respectful of that context. For many years, the Chinese people followed Deng's approach of "crossing a river by feeling one stone at a time." This was an effective approach, taking many small steps towards progress, particularly when the Chinese economy was small and global economic conditions were changing rapidly and unpredictably due to new technology. But now that China is a middle-income country, to continue the analogy, the water is getting so deep that it becomes difficult to even find a stone. In order to get people across the river to a new safe haven, vision and leadership are now needed more than ever to provide a clear direction and to coordinate future development. Beyond its previous economic focus, the next phase of development will require deeper reforms, fresh ideas, and significant innovation in social and political concepts and practices. It will require better domestic management as well as adaptation to the rapidly changing global environment.

Some Westerners have been surprised to see the rapid pace of Chinese industrialization and economic achievement since Deng Xiaoping's reform and opening in 1978. No country in history has achieved so much in such a short period—only 40 years. They assume that either China has faked their data, or they have stolen secrets from the West. However, if we can step back and look at it from a historical perspective, China is actually just recovering from its misfortune of the past 200 years, a historical aberration; they are trying to return to their trajectory of over 2000 years as a thriving and vibrant society, leading and sharing with the world. China still has a way to go to recover its former status and ability, and despite some Western fears, things will never really be restored completely, nor should it be. Instead, we hope that the Western world can open its mind more to see that a flourishing China alongside an already powerful West will bring balance and peace to all of humanity—we should root for China's success, as we will all be better for it. As an integral part of the global supply chain and a significant part of the world population, China more than ever needs the support, understanding, and non-judgmental wisdom of the rest of the world.

SEVEN: ETHICAL CIVILIZATION AND GOVERNANCE

China is not a nation-state in the conventional sense, such as is the case with Germany, France, or the United States. It is much larger and more diverse than people can imagine, yet as a civilization it has survived and thrived for thousands of years while others, such as the mighty Roman empire, fell apart in a fraction of the time.

At the heart of the Chinese way was Confucianism, which has a strong focus on morals and ethics, effectively providing a guide on how to behave and live as a human. Expanding that to governance for an entire country, China's former success was built around governance by only those intellectually worthy and of high moral standard (there were exceptions, of course, but they typically didn't last long), as well as a mandate to serve the people.

Now, as China industrializes and attempts to become a better global citizen of the world, it is trying to adopt many Western institutions and ways while trying to reconcile them with its own culture, which has a much stronger emphasis on morality, ethics, and responsibility over rights. And it is attempting to do this on a scale non-existent in the Western world, ever. With a diverse population of over 1.4 billion people over a continental-sized territory, and an implied responsibility to keep every citizen fed, happy, and safe, the complexity behind every government decision is immense, and often unimaginable. Only a few observers in this world can truthfully explain the how, what, and why behind China's actions, which creates frequent misinterpretation for those who know little about the country's history and culture.

In this chapter and the next, we will attempt to gain some insight into the traditional Chinese way of governance and some core concepts that are unique to China, as well as exploring its more recent political structure and the changes and reforms underway as part of globalization and China's re-entry onto the world stage.

MODERNIZATION NOT WESTERNIZATION

The word "civilization" has generally been associated with Western civilization in the modern era, and many East Asian efforts to reform refer to catching up with the "advanced" Western civilization to become enlightened and solve their problems. In 2013, contemporary Chinese historian Jilin Xu wrote an important essay[37] called "What kind of civilization? China at a crossroads." He surmises that "modern civilization" is made up of at least two dimensions: the pursuit of wealth and power (via military might, capitalism, etc.), and the defense of values. He argues that civilization is universal and culture is local; civilization is about what is good and culture is about what is ours. The defense of values may not be universal but must be defended openly and convincingly in a universal setting. At the same time, by calling "the pursuit of wealth and power" a dimension in modern civilization, he implies that it is universal. What China has so spectacularly mastered since the beginning of the reform era is what Xu calls the "wealth and power" dimension of modernity. Xu argues that having beaten the West at its own game, China, therefore, must look inward to find the culture-appropriate values necessary to fill the current moral vacuum in Chinese society. He further hopes that a communitarian ethos will emerge from that search, which will enable China to contribute and even become a leader in establishing universal values for our world. Instead of arguing

---

37 Jilin Xu, "What Kind of Civilization? China at a Crossroads," *Rethinking China's Rise* (Cambridge University Press, 2018) https://readingthechinadream.com/xu-jilin-what-kind-of-civilization.html

that "China would be better if China were democratic like Western countries are," Xu instead asserts that "as part of modern civilization, China must join the world, defend its values, and make its contributions."

In Chinese civilization, particularly in Confucianism, secular ethics is central and core, which is unique in the world. Confucians consciously and purposefully resist wealth and power, treating it as corruption. Modern China's economic successes are not dependent only on "wealth and power," such as in Western imperialism and colonialism, or capitalism. Instead, it is the many tenets and ethos of traditional Chinese civilization and heritage, including strong and collaborative leadership, proper work ethic, flexibility, education, inclusiveness, social ethics, and harmony that is helping China to advance and modernize. Every country in the developing world would like to pursue wealth and power. China must redefine what that means to them and find their own way to succeed as a modern civilization while staying true to their culture. Many aspects of Chinese culture and heritage have become constructive again in our interrelated world, and such values should be defended as universal. Social Darwinism produced wealth and power that supported Western dominance over the past several centuries. But some Western cultural values have mistakenly been considered universal, only as a result of its dominance. Modernization is not Westernization, something which confuses many people, both Chinese and non-Chinese, including modern historians and intellectuals. It's time to change that assumption and re-evaluate what values truly should be universal in our increasingly multicultural and interconnected modern world.

You may recall from Part One that traditional Chinese thinking preferences are practical, holistic, integrative, broadmindedly inclusive, and readily adaptable to change. Humanity is an integral part of Nature, and all humans should be assumed to be born with innate goodness and virtue even though some may lose their way, overly influenced by human greed, desire, and indulgence. Though that may happen, goodness and virtue can be restored through introspection and education. Chinese civilization has developed a uniquely holistic yin-and-yang thinking paradigm to explain the world, seeking balance and harmony within human relationships, thereby simultaneously attaining peace within one's self and as part of Nature. Chinese people comfortably practice Confucianism, which is yang, and Daoism or Zen Buddhism, which is yin, depending on the circumstances. Similarly, the Chinese ruling bureaucracy governs by balancing between Legalism and Confucianism, depending on the situation or problems encountered.

Morality and ethicality are emphasized and taught in every life pursuit, playing an important role in social harmony. Some would call this a secular religion, different than preordained principles or religious supernatural beliefs. Chinese people are very practical and results-oriented. Moral judgments are made implicitly—whether in cultural, social, or political contexts—and are always based more upon what actions have been taken, rather than what was said in words. The Chinese believe justice is always in the heart-mind of each and every one of us. Over thousands of years, the moral lessons of history have become engraved into the language itself as poetic idioms and sayings that everyone learns in their childhood. These idioms carry cultural and moral guidance, renewable and expandable generation after generation, eventually becoming the cultural norms and heritage for the entire populace. It is a cultural narrative difficult to understand by those in other cultures because so many of the concepts and terms are complex and not easily translatable—they often have multiple meanings and interpretations with no direct equivalents in Western languages.

Since the Chinese believe people are all unique, with varying endowments in terms of ability and moral cultivation, the ideal Chinese society is organized into a hierarchy designed to encourage each person to perform to the best of his or her ability. Leaders who are ethical, capable, and intellectual with the altruistic intention to serve people will rise to the top, and the rest of the populace is content to play their part, being both served by the leaders as well as psychologically fulfilled and supported by a culture and community of caring and empathetic familial relationships. Such a hierarchy has unfortunately become almost taboo in the modern world. Daniel Bell and Wang Pei[38] used the term "Just Hierarchy" to contrast between a morally justified hierarchy and the many unjust ones, such as those based on race, sex, or caste. They argue: "Different hierarchical principles ought to govern different kinds of social relations: what justifies

---

38 Daniel A. Bell and Wang Pei, *Just Hierarchy: Why Social Hierarchies Matter in China and the Rest of the World* (Princeton University Press, March 2020).

hierarchy among intimates is different from what justifies hierarchy among citizens, countries... Morally justified hierarchies can and should govern different spheres of our social lives, though these will be very different from the unjust hierarchies that have governed us in the past." Using the family dining table as an example, the authors remind readers that children do not sit as equal to their parents at the table. From this point of view, a true Chinese hierarchy should be considered as one that is justified.

As many more countries, including China, enter into the modern world, it is valuable for them to look at the multiple examples available in the long history of the world, and not presume that Western civilization is the one they must follow. As an ancient civilization that flourished very early in world history and for thousands of years, China's success was built on a strong moral and ethical foundation, espousing humanitarian concepts such as civility, balance, and tolerance, while practicing harmony in diversity in order to unite and govern a large, diverse, and complex population. No other civilization has succeeded in building a peaceful and collaborative society at this scale, and sustained for thousands of years. The mighty Roman empire was a military conquest and relatively short-lived. The federated United States of America was reasonably successful during good times, but now is showing weakness when challenged, such as during the financial crisis of 2008, a growing anti-competitiveness, mismanaged globalization, a dysfunctional financial sector, and divisiveness during the 2020 election and pandemic. The European Union had an honorable goal, but ended up mainly uniting in currency; it still has a long way to go in becoming a political entity, and this may never happen. Our world should treasure and learn from China's unique achievement and historical experience, instead of simplistically labeling it as authoritarian, or even worse, totalitarian.

POLITICAL LEGITIMACY: THE HUMANE WAY

Chinese cultural and political thinking and philosophy has always favored strong, ethical, and capable leadership which can provide a clear vision and unified direction for everybody to follow and act upon for the collective benefit. How can an empire so large keep everyone working together effectively without coercion?

Throughout China's long tradition of political philosophy, the sole test of a good ruler has been whether they succeed in promoting the welfare of the common people. This is the most basic principle in Confucianism and has been tested throughout the ages, yielding both successes and failures. In order to serve the interests of the masses, the bureaucracy must first gain the trust of the masses. If the bureaucracy becomes corrupt or loses its moral foundation, the result is disastrous for social order. Therefore, a critical function of the bureaucracy is to dispense justice in a way that people can easily relate to morally and ethically, thereby building trust. Upholding justice for people is one of the most popular themes in Chinese opera and theatre.

The accountability of leaders and the government is ultimately measured by people's satisfaction in their daily life, not only materialistically, but also spiritually. Leaders should always lead ethically, so that most people need not concern themselves with which specific political principles, processes, procedures, or institutions they may have used to achieve these commonly accepted goals, or how leaders' visions and objectives are to be realized. Some leaders or officials are more strategic than others, but they should always have a clear objective in mind: working for the welfare of the people, both immediately and for the long term. In Chinese philosophy, since the only constant in the world is change, how to realize or achieve a vision or dream is best left to the judgment of the practitioner at various levels of execution. People implicitly know how good or bad their leaders are, and which government has collectively done the most for them and for future generations. Words can seldom properly articulate such feelings.

The politics of a proper mandate from the people is expressed as *Wangdao*, or popularly translated into English as "the Way of the Humane Authority." This is a representation of the Way of *Tian*, or Nature's Way reflecting history, culture, and the people's will. According to contemporary Confucian Jiang Qing,[39] legitimacy is the most important issue in politics, and this is manifested in the ruler's authority and the people's loyalty. If the ruler's actions lack legitimacy, he will need to constantly

---

39 Jiang Qing, *A Confucian Constitutional Order: How China's Ancient Past Can Shape Its Political Future* (Princeton University Press, 2013).

bargain with the people and he will never be able to win full loyalty from them. Political order will constantly be on the brink of chaos. Hence, the Way of the Humane Authority of Confucianism seeks to fully and wholly resolve the question of political power, and to establish a political order that is stable, harmonious, and sustainable. Rulers should always legitimize their actions using the Way, and not just act impetuously. Such political thinking is in stark contrast with liberalism and democracy in the West. But then again, we've already established that the basic assumptions, challenges, traditions, and histories are very different in the two cultures.

Jiang described three forms of political legitimacy that follow the Way: First, within the mandate, the ruler should set up sacred institutions and rituals between *Tian* and Earth. Second is cultural legitimacy—the ruler must examine his institutions and compare them with those of the "founders of the three dynasties," then judge them by their adherence to ethical values, which can be found in the ancient classics. Third is the ruler's own character and conduct, which ultimately is judged by the people. The "founders of the three dynasties" were legendary exemplary idols that Confucius used to perfect his ethical ideal, and they have become an important resource for many later generations. The Way of the Humane Authority seeks not only to judge the three forms of legitimacy, but also to ensure that they are in balance when applied.

Comparing this with the Western system, Jiang states: "Western democracy is built on the separation of powers, but from the view of the Way of Humane Authority, the separation of powers is a matter of implementation. Western democracies' legitimacy is based on the sovereignty of the people. This is said to be unique, supreme, absolute, exclusive, and inalienable. From a political point of view, there is nothing that can keep it in check. The Way of the Humane Authority is different. It holds that equilibrium is an issue not only in implementation but also in legitimization. It is not only to be used in determining the basic meaning and legal structure of political legitimacy itself. In the Way of the Humane Authority, no one form of legitimacy should be allowed to become sovereign over the others, for this will lead to political bias and failings." That is, according to Confucianism, the political ideal, and its institutions should be balanced among its sacred mandate to rule, its culture and history, and the will of the people, all of which must adapt to changes in the environment. The fluidity of this Confucian interpretation is consistent with Chinese acceptance of change as a constant in the world.

Jiang's work on political legitimacy references many ancient writings about the Chinese precept of *Wangdao* or "the Way of the Humane Authority." This ancient concept has been very influential throughout Chinese political history. *Wangdao* literally means "the King's way," in contrast with *Badao* or hegemony. Confucians consistently denounced hegemony in favor of *Wangdao*. Xunzi, the founder of the naturalist and rationalist school of Confucianism, even held that the difference between *Wangdao* and *Badao* does not lie in power, but in morality. He distinguished between the two by pointing out the former's ability to achieve the voluntary subordination of others through moral actions, and the latter's capacity to build alliances through the establishment of strategic credibility. Mencius similarly maintained that *Wangdao* practices *ren* (benevolence, humanity, compassion, empathy, caring, tolerance) whereas hegemony pretends it has *ren* while relying on might. *Ren* is central to Confucianism and describes the relational character and interdependence of human beings. A person of *ren* realizes himself and helps others to fulfill their lives, which is very different than individualism, which by nature tends to be more self-serving.

Confucius endorsed simple moral and political teachings: Love others. Honor thy parents. Through the process of self-cultivation, each individual self becomes part of a fiduciary community in order to realize the deepest meaning of humanity. Confucians have faith in humanity since they believe everyone is born with a good human nature. It is through the conceptualization and teaching of *ren* that the ancient Chinese were able build an ethical society, regardless of how powerful greed and desire can be. Without *ren*, there needs to be stronger reliance on law and order or religion, such as we currently see in Western philosophy. Interestingly, contrary to Confucian belief in human beings' inherent goodness, the Legalist school of Chinese philosophy assumed that humans were evil by nature and would commit crimes if the state authority did not discipline them, and since human beings are selfish and greedy, the only way a state can function is by issuing laws and severely punishing those who violate them. In times of social unrest, Legalism assumes its role, similar to what we see in the Western world. Traditional Chinese governance has always emphasized finding a proper dynamic balance between Confucianism and Legalism, consistent with our premise that our world will also benefit if we can find a dynamic balance between Western and Chinese ways.

DIFFERENCES IN POLITICAL THINKING AND SYSTEMS

Ethics answers the question: "How should we live?"

Politics answers the question: "How should we live together?"

There is little argument that Westerners and Chinese have developed very different perspectives on ethics, political ideals, and governance due to very different circumstances in their environments and history. Most Europeans were descendants of nomadic Indo-European migrants from the steppes and Ural mountain region of eastern Europe or Western Asia. River basins around the Mediterranean were relatively small, and the materials needed for buildings and larger scale farming were not readily available. Hence, they relied on trade by sailing across the Mediterranean to obtain many of the essentials for living. From their nomadic and seafaring traditions, they often had to battle with Nature, which was considered hostile and cruel. They became proud of their ability to face challenges from Nature and to conquer Nature. But they also feared the almighty Nature, and the supernatural.

The early gods represented in Greek mythology often showcased characters with great powers, some of whom were benevolent and others who were cruel. Western ethics comes from a belief that there is an almighty, all knowing, and perfect God. Humans are born into original sin and must live their lives with the ultimate goal of one day joining their God in His Kingdom. When Christianity dominated the Western world during the Dark Ages, the church was synonymous with morality. But ever since the separation between church and state, morality has become increasingly distant from the political arena. While Protestant values are ingrained in the American constitution, religious ethics are no longer taught in American schools because of political correctness. It is during these changes that American society started to lose its only traditional moral compass. It enabled extreme liberalism, nihilism, relativism, postmodernism, and recently populism, to gain ground and even at times dominate in American society.

Western political thinking can be traced all the way back to the governance of small ancient Greek city-states. Aristotle said that all knowledge can be classified into three categories: theoretical, productive, and practical. Theoretical knowledge involves the study of truth for its own sake; it is knowledge about things that are unchanging and eternal, and includes things like the principles of logic, physics, and mathematics. Pursuit of this type of knowledge brings us closest to the divine. Productive knowledge addresses our daily needs as human beings, and roughly means "know-how." Practical knowledge is the key to living a good life. Ethics and politics, which are the practical sciences, deal with human beings as moral agents. Ethics is primarily about the actions of human beings as individuals, and politics is about the actions of human beings in communities, although ethics and politics are closely linked together. Aristotle believed that mere abstract knowledge of ethics and politics was worthless. Practical knowledge is only useful if we act appropriately on it, but it will not tell us what virtue is. For the Greeks, the highest good is the happiness of individuals.

It is easy to see Aristotle's influence in modern Western political thinking, and how it is so different from Chinese thinking. For the Greeks, individual humans act as moral agents for God. Governance of a small city-state, such as Athens, easily supports democracy when all its citizens can simply cast votes in a town square. Plato dreamed of a "philosopher king" in his *Republic*, but thought it might be difficult to find a philosopher willing to serve. The Chinese could not afford such a luxury in thinking because the scale of their problem was enormous. They attracted a large population from early on, so they had to adapt to meet the challenges that came their way. They found it was more efficient and effective when people worked together collaboratively under strong and ethical leaders who could act decisively for everyone's benefit. This is one of the reasons why the Chinese are always so practical. We must take these contextual and historical differences into account when we criticize China for being less than liberal and democratic.

Western political science has always focused on form: elected leaders, democratic principles, laws and constitutions, procedures and institutions. Much of it can be traced back to Aristotle. For him, since he felt that a "philosopher king" would be too hard to achieve and even harder to sustain, the best form was therefore a mixed government, or "Polity," which was basically an aristocracy with a bit of democracy thrown in, supported by a strong middle class, slaves and women not included. He identified six types of constitutions—three that he designated as being fair (monarchy/ aristocracy/democracy), and three that were considered unfair (tyranny/ oligarchy/anarchy). A constitution is a monarchy if power is exercised by one person in conjunction with laws that protect the public good. But if the monarch uses the power for their own interests, then it becomes a tyranny. An aristocracy is when power is controlled by an elite group for the good of all but degenerates into an oligarchy if the leaders are bad. Democracy is the regime of the people but may turn into anarchy when demagogues take power. These simple political dichotomies work well in small city-states, but are totally inadequate to describe large complex political entities such as China.

Both the Western and Chinese systems have had their successes and failures over the years, and neither can be said to be perfect. The Chinese system puts extreme emphasis on having strong leadership in order to bring peace and harmony to all its citizens, and has evolved into a governing bureaucracy. Historically, it has encountered both success and failure, but by comparison, Chinese people have enjoyed more prosperity over a longer period of time. Governance of much smaller-scale Greek city-states had no need to complicate things, so they preferred simple forms, procedures, rules, and constitutions from which the democratic system of the West was created. The Western system has also had successes and failures over the years. Smaller states like the Scandinavian countries appear to have fared the best. But the workability for diverse larger states remains to be proven, as could be seen in the 2020 American election which showcased how divided the people were feeling, in turn preventing the country as a whole from effectively and speedily reforming and enacting the changes it needed.

There are some obvious pros and cons if we are to compare the two political philosophies and systems. In a culture of shame, Chinese philosophy demands self-cultivation and self- introspection from everyone, particularly its leaders, so ethicality and virtuosity become major social and political considerations which can be vague, ever-changing, and difficult to judge. In Confucian thinking, the rule of law is only necessary when a society becomes morally bankrupt and social persuasion is no longer effective. This is one reason why Westerners, who value the objectivity and impartiality of the Western political and judiciary systems, find the Chinese political and judiciary systems to be totally opaque and baffling. Similarly, Chinese people are often bewildered by many of the irresponsible, immoral, or even unethical things that the Western systems allow, as well as the inflexibility of their laws. Because the Western world embraces dualistic thinking, they tend to oversimplify things as black and white, good and bad, left and right, democracy and authoritarian, or capitalistic and socialistic. If you are my enemy, then you cannot be my friend, and vice versa. But the real world is increasingly full of shades of grey, along with many more colors people may not have noticed before. It makes it even more challenging for Westerners to interpret and understand China, its people, and its political system, as it cannot even be classified based on traditional European experience. Just as China has been studying the Western way for the past two centuries, maybe it's time the Western world returns the compliment and opens its mind to the vast ways of the rest of the world.

GOVERNANCE UNDER TIANXIA

The ancient Chinese philosopher Xunzi once wrote, "Men are weaker than cows, run slower than horses, why are they superior? The answer lies in that men are social beings, animals are not." Chinese thinkers further contended that, even if primitive humans were social beings, they were no better than animals because they fought one another until such time as virtues and morals were cultivated. Further, each person is distinctly unique according to their ability and their achievements in areas such as moral cultivation and education. In the Chinese view, it was not until the arrival of a strong leader, the so-called sage king, that humans attained civilization, established proper social order in a hierarchy of virtuosity and ability, and distinguished themselves from animals by taking responsibility for family and extended families, and eventually the rest of humanity and *Tianxia*. But individual human rights and the development of self-esteem or individuality were not really among their considerations until very recently. Instead, tenets such as benevolence, wisdom, humility, honesty, and willingness to serve others were essential qualities of good leaders.

Thus, the Chinese have one of the very few cultures in the world that are centered around human ethics and morality, and in which there is no dependence on any supernatural or religious belief.

In Chinese history, sage kings were wise rulers who were in tune with Nature and possessed superior virtue, political wisdom, personal integrity, family loyalty, and filial piety while having the humility and dedication to devote their life to working for the welfare of the people. While naturally not all succeeded, nonetheless this was traditionally the goal and still is today. Chinese philosophy starts with an assumption of unity and sees order as a process of integrating divisions and differences into an organic whole, ultimately into a world of greater harmony. Recognizing the distinctiveness of individuals is consistent with Chinese ethico-political thinking in that people have different contributions to make to society depending on their individual morality, self-cultivation, inclination, ability, and aspiration to serve. To the ancient Chinese thinkers and educators such as Xunzi, if we could all accept our differences and learn from others, past and present, social order and harmony can be attained, and even the weakest would be protected. The key lies within each of us, inside our own heart-mind.

Contrasted with Thomas Hobbes, who believed that humans are all equal as individuals and need a social contract with their government in order to have law and order to protect freedom and properties, Xunzi believed that good moral education through *li* and *yi* would produce a better social order, protection for the people, and a more harmonious society. *Li* (representing rites, social norms, proper behavior, and moral formats) is a traditional Chinese value that is applicable everywhere from ordinary daily life to diplomatic and political affairs. Confucius said: "if you do not learn *li*, your character cannot be established." Confucian education starts with introspection, authenticating one's heart-mind before cultivating relationships. *Li* is a vehicle to learn appropriateness in relationships, which is rooted and embedded in the culture. Wrongdoers are taught to feel ashamed of their improper actions through education and moral persuasion, very different from the modern precept of self-esteem.

Freedom without the constraint of *li* can easily give rise to violent social or political conflicts. No law is needed if we can all treat each other with proper respect. Ancient Chinese society was known for its harmonious aesthetic order, which was a product of combining *li* with music. Both *li* and *yi* (representing righteousness, justice, uprightness, appropriateness, and reasonableness) are defining moral qualities that anybody can uphold in practice, regardless of social status or wealth, as long as they can overcome their greed and selfishness. Historically, poor people consistently demonstrated these qualities better than rich people did. The precept of *yi* is one of the original Chinese moral codes shared by multiple schools of thought, including Confucianism, Daoism, and Mo'ism. Both *li* and *yi* presupposed achievement of self-cultivated *ren*. All these values have been accepted as social norms among the Chinese throughout history. More interestingly, such moral precepts have no equivalence in the West because they are secular in nature.

China views itself as being related to all others under the precept of universalism, or *Tianxia,* which also has no equivalent in Western culture. It is sometimes referred to as the Middle Kingdom dating back to the Zhou around 841 BC. *Tianxia* describes everything under *Tian* (Nature/ Heaven with no religious connotation). The Zhou justified its conquest of the Shang by citing superior moral grounds, first regarding the will of *Tian*, and subsequently via the new ideology of the "mandate of *Tian*" being reflected in the will of humanity. *Tian* and humanity are mutually influencing, sharing a future destiny. In fact, *Tian* and humanity cannot be separated, as humans would suffer if there was damage done to Nature. The Zhou aristocracy claimed *Tian* was a universal being, concerned with the welfare of all the world's people and operating on a stage beyond the limits of any nation. The Zhou kings reigned because they had received the mandate of *Tian*, and they could equally lose the throne if their performance did not satisfy *Tian*. Zhou kingship was thus founded on a conception of legitimacy, which depended on accountability to a universal *Tian* that listened to the people and guided the world of human beings on a moral course.

Nationalism was a Western creation after the French Revolution. The 19th century has been called the age of nationalism in Europe. Nationalism, translated into world politics, implies the association of a state or nation with its people according to ethnographic principles. National boundaries are drawn with consideration to race, culture, religion, language, and/or creed. But nationalism and national governments are social organizations that were relatively foreign to Chinese tradition until very recently. After the Opium War, China had no choice but to join the family of nation-states. Up until then their traditional political thinking had always been in terms of all humankind, with world peace as their ultimate goal. Family and nation were only considered transitional steps towards the perfecting of *Tianxia*, the world of humanity. It is this kind of benevolent pacifism and universalism which makes Chinese political philosophy distinctive, but when misunderstood, it strikes fear into Westerners, who misinterpret it as China's desire to take over the world. Even though modern China has to be a nation-state, the precept of *Tianxia* still persists in the hearts of the Chinese people. The ancient saying "we are all families under *Tianxia*" still resonates with the Chinese people and showcases the Chinese aspiration for world peace and togetherness. This is a key part of the cultural context behind China's recent rise on the global stage, often misunderstood by Western politicians and leaders, time and again causing suspicion and mistrust between China and the West. While Americans worry about being transcended by China, the Chinese are mostly focused on how to transcend themselves.

THE IMPORTANT ROLE OF THE *SHI*

Throughout the imperial history of China, emperors and their royal families relied on the mandate of *Tian* and high moral supremacy for their legitimacy as rulers. This was contrasted with the powerful, exclusive, and inherited lineage of European aristocracy. The traditional Chinese imperial system governed China through an emperor who, often despite his own failings, was to provide superior moral leadership, with a bureaucracy including a prime minister and supplemented by a cabinet of Confucian officers providing administrative assistance to the emperor. A relatively capable and virtuous bureaucracy is the reason why the empire was administratively stable despite many incapable emperors. The use of Confucian scholars, called *shi*, provided moral order and guidance, not only to the administration but also for the generally peaceful and hard-working agrarian populace. The system was broad-mindedly inclusive since *shi* could come from all walks of life and Confucianism was socially non-discriminative. Many authors translate the term *shi* into "elite." We much prefer to use *shi* directly because "elite" does not even begin to communicate the selfless, altruistic, and even missionary sense that the spirit of *shi* truly entails, and there is no equivalent word in English.

In Imperial China, especially after the year 622, when a formal examination system was institutionalized to select talent for government service, the *shi* (morally cultivated scholars) occupied a central position in state power and became an integral part of the ruling apparatus. The spirit of *shi,* which can be traced back to Confucius and his disciples' teachings or even earlier, is unique to Chinese culture for its altruistic intention and moral commitment. It is best captured by Fan Zhongyan of the Song Dynasty as being one who is "truly concerned with *Tianxia* and the universe before anybody else, and will be the last person under *Tianxia* to obtain enjoyment and happiness." It is an inwardly self-imposed duty of *shi* to take care of *Tianxia*. With such a high but humanly ideal, only very few individuals in the government could realistically attain it. But it has been very inspirational for generations of scholars throughout Chinese history. The rank of *shi* is broadly open to any scholars who embrace the spirit through self-cultivation regardless of their wealth, social background, or status. There is no declaration needed to join the ranks. But with such a large Chinese population, even if only a very small fraction of people attempt to practice it, there will still be enough *shi* ready to serve and make a difference. There have always been these few but special individuals throughout Chinese history. Some selfless *shi* would serve in the government under ideal conditions, otherwise they would often retire to the mountains, woods, or a farm to enjoy Nature and become a poet or teacher, even sometimes serving as a critic of the government on the people's behalf.

The problem of articulating a term or concept that has no equivalence in another culture can represent a major hurdle for cross-cultural communication. Linguistic, cultural, religious, and other traditions are present throughout our lives, contextualizing the present and serving as a source of ideas and possible solutions to problems that we face. As long as we are aware of the cross-cultural differences, we believe there are always ways in which we can recognize the value and integrity of each other's traditions, and bridge and extend those traditions. Frank recognition of the differences is an important first step. We mentioned earlier that the term *shi* is often misinterpreted in translation. A great example of how the cultural background of an individual can affect how they interpret situations is in the following two publications evaluating the political situation and the role of "Chinese elites" in contemporary China.

The first publication is in *China Tomorrow, Democracy or Dictatorship?*, authored by Jean-Pierre Cabestan[40] who studied the role of "Chinese elites" in shaping the political evolution of modern China. The "Chinese elites" studied included party-political elites, economic elites, intellectual elites, liberal elites, and counter-elites. The author, a political scientist, asked and concluded: "Which segment of Chinese elites can get things moving? Certainly not the party's political elites or a majority of elites, at least in the short term. There is a potential for politicization among private entrepreneurs to take risks to advance any cause other than their own economic interests, in the current Xi-imposed 'new normal.' As for counter-elites, they need to await better days just to raise their head... largest segments of the intellectual elite have good prospects of remaining invincible in the decade or two ahead." The author categorized elites broadly from a Western perspective, completely missing the possible existence of those who exemplify the true spirit of *shi*. The author was looking for a typical Western political evolution, expecting it to move towards liberty and democracy, and was obviously disappointed.

The second publication is by Xiaowei Zang and Chien-wen Kou,[41] *Elites and Governance in China*. It attempted to bring together elite studies and governance studies for an analysis of the relationship between elites and governance in China. The volume noted "the active and effective participation in governance by a wide range of the elites, including leading intellectuals, functionaries and grassroots or community elites. They have introduced new concepts such as social justice and good governance into PRC, guided and taken part in discourse on how best China will be governed, and turned central policies into realities. The findings also show the importance of community elites in maintaining social stability at the grassroots levels. Clearly, although the Chinese Communist Party has maintained a firm grip on power in PRC, governance in China has

---

40 Jean-Pierre Cabestan, *China Tomorrow: Democracy or Dictatorship?* (Rowman & Littlefield, 2019).

41 Xiaowei Zang and Chien-wen Kou, *Elites and Governance in China* (Routledge, 2016).

evolved into a complex political enterprise in which multiple key social actors have actively influenced, negotiated and participated in the process of governing, including decision-making and policy-implementation. The PRC is no longer the country in which the CCP led everything from 1949 to 1978." The term "Chinese elites" used here clearly has a sense of *shi* and makes sense when taking Chinese history into account.

Obviously, the two publications cited have drawn totally different conclusions from their study of "Chinese elites" and their significance to Chinese politics. It is interesting to note that both Jean-Pierre Cabestan and Xiaowei Zang share remarkably similar credentials: both trained as social scientists from top Western universities and are currently teaching in a university in Hong Kong, and both are renowned in their respective fields of expertise. But their backgrounds are very different. Cabestan is a renowned French expert in Political Science who also studied Chinese Language and Civilization at Jussieu University in France. Zang is an ethnic Chinese with a strong background in Chinese culture. How could these two people, both born, bred, and trained in the Western world, have such different interpretations and draw such starkly different conclusions about what the term "Chinese elites" means? If this can happen to academic experts trained in both political science and the history of Chinese civilization, just imagine how easily and how often this happens to regular people, and to our leaders and politicians who are democratically elected and come from all sorts of backgrounds?

A more recent article published in *The Chinese Journal of International Politics*, entitled *Historical-Geopolitical Contexts and the Transformation of Chinese Foreign Policy*[42] and authored by Colin Flint and Zhang Xiaotong is more encouraging. Colin Flint is an accomplished political scientist and Zhang Xiaotong teaches political science at Wuhan University in China. Their collaboration created some excellent historical-geopolitical context needed for understanding Chinese foreign policy from the perspective of world system analysis, and showcases the success of international cooperative efforts.

---

42 Colin Flint and Zhang Xiaotong, "Historical-Geopolitical Contexts and the Transformation of Chinese Foreign Policy," *The Chinese Journal of International Politics*, Volume 12, Issue 3, Autumn 2019, Pages 295-331.

One cannot over-emphasize the importance of *shi* in Chinese politics even though it has been mostly ignored in Western analysis. With Chinese pragmatism influencing the political selection of *shi*, the Chinese political system has evolved into a meritocratic governing bureaucracy where political officials are selected first and foremost through civil examination, followed by evaluation of their performance at different and increasing levels of government. Moral integrity is always judged ahead of ability or capability and is measured by actions, not just words. No one can rise to the top without proven extensive and outstanding performance at every level of government. President Xi Jinping, for example, has served as a lead executive, successfully running the equivalent of at least three different provinces or states before he became president, and each province or state was larger than most European countries. Meritocracy is the hallmark of the Chinese political system to this day, and is still evolving. The Chinese model for rigorous exam-based civil service was even adopted by England and France in the 19th century. But since Westerners believe more in the equality of every individual because we are all children of God, democratic election of leaders was a more ideologically fair and suitable method for the West. In the future development of democracy, however, it will be interesting to see if they can incorporate some Chinese experience by giving more consideration to ethics and on-the-job experience, rather than popularity or political platforms, during election campaigns.

One more recent example of the powerful spirit of *shi* is the now renowned historic conference at Mount Mogang north of Hangzhou in 1984. This was seven years after schools reopened in 1977 (after the Cultural Revolution), and at the beginning of Deng's Reform and Opening era that began in 1978. After the establishment of the first Special Economic Zone at Shekou, everybody in China knew that the Chinese economy needed to transform from a planned to a market economy, but nobody knew how to do it. A group of young economists from across the country volunteered to come together for a seven-day think-tank session on top of Mount Mogang. Disregarding age, status, or experience, 124 participants out of over 1300 applicants were selected to attend by an ad-hoc committee. Selection was based on a one article submission from each applicant on a current challenge facing the Chinese economy. Seven subgroups were formed at the session covering various topics ranging from price setting, market and financial reform, institution and tax reform, and all the way to the macroscopic future of the farming sector. After many enthusiastic and heated debates, they summarized their key conclusions and submitted them to the government for action. Some were actually approved at the Twelfth Plenum of the CCP and implemented as new economic policies. Many participants in the think-tank went on to become key contributors to the success of multiple Chinese political and economic reforms. In 2012, they created a new Mount Mogang economic think-tank that meets annually to discuss new challenges facing the country.

The tradition of meritocratic bureaucracy continues to evolve in China even today. Constitutional, legal, national, local, educational, and party reforms are all modern expressions of it. There is always a small group of contemporary *shi* in every walk of life in China; these are morally cultivated intellectuals ready to serve the country and its people, ready to self-sacrifice if needed. However, President Xi warns that future governance will need to rely more on the rule of law. Deep political and institutional reforms always involve redistribution of power, proportional responsibility, and revenue sharing between central, provincial, and local governments and institutions, all of which are ongoing under the current leadership, and this is ruffling a lot of feathers. True conviction and a collective willingness to make compromises are crucial to the success of such endeavors as they involve much give and take from everyone involved. Strong leadership that can keep participants focused on the vision of a shared common future is necessary, as is the Chinese spirit of *shi*. The Chinese political system is often considered a mysterious black box to many outsiders. To Western political scientists, it is full of contradictions, mostly because of cultural and thinking differences. It is easy to just brand the system as authoritarian. But it is much more complex than that and it is continuously evolving. Analyzing it using Western political science has proven to yield many misinterpretations and misunderstandings. Throughout Chinese history, *shi* have always been a key contributing group in imperial governance, and we believe they will continue to play a role in China's future. Our hope is that more people will recognize and revive the spirit of *shi* and that more academics will make efforts to understand governance in China from the perspective of their behavior and influence.

EIGHT: POLITICS IN CHINA

China became a republic in 1912. Even though there is no longer any emperor, political parties still follow the Chinese tradition by legitimizing their rule on high moral ground and vowing to serve the people. In fact, "Serving the People" was one of Mao's most popular slogans during the Chinese civil war, and it lives on as part of the pledge by all subsequent administrations, including the current one. How well these governments can deliver on that promise has varied over time. But it is under this historical context that we can understand why the recent anti-corruption campaign in China is so important to the government and its people. According to President Xi, the legitimacy and survival of both the CCP and People's Republic are at stake.

In building a system or institutions that can prevent corruption, there is much China can learn from the Western experience. The long term strategy is to transform the country from rule of people to rule of law, with the CCP playing a strong leadership role in the process of inventing a new judiciary system that gives importance to social virtue, both for party officials and people in business. The institution is slowly evolving, but will certainly look different than the Western judiciary we're familiar with.

In contrast with American democracy, which is known to be government "of the people, by the people, and for the people," Chinese political philosophy is to have ethical, competent, and stable government "of the people, by a meritocratic bureaucracy of *shi*, and for the welfare and security of the people." In American democracy, the will of the people is the sole source of legitimacy and there is no consideration given to the morality or the quality of its mandate. An unfortunate consequence is that individual popularity and election campaign financing can become major determinants of the success of a candidate. In the Chinese system, on the other hand, leadership, responsibility, and accountability are the major priorities, consistent with its cultural heritage. The Chinese government is judged by its ability to maintain personal and social security, as well as how well it meets the people's expectations, rather than on its observance of human rights or universal values. This has miffed many Westerners and even Western-educated Chinese, who feel there are not enough rules to govern the leaders and keep them in line. Some fear the government will abuse its power, and point to the many situations where it has been perceived to oppress certain individual freedoms. If these individuals could learn a bit more about the Chinese political system and where it's headed, perhaps they will begin to understand the sacrifices that must be made when you are responsible for the security of the largest population in the world, at over 1.4 billion people, recognize the reforms and massive changes being made to find a better dynamic balance with human rights and universal values, and acknowledge that with strong moral leadership always being a core objective, they deserve the benefit of the doubt and our efforts to try and understand them better.

From a political standpoint, that begins with understanding the Chinese Communist Party. It is easy to obsess over the label of "Communist," but labels are really just that. The CCP is drastically different than any other communist institution in history and understanding it requires putting aside preset biases to look at both the good and bad of its political structure today, as well as how it is continuing to evolve.

TRADITIONAL GOVERNANCE IN PRACTICE

Traditionally, the governing political philosophy incorporates Confucianism as the way to govern for the welfare of the people and a bureaucracy to design and deliver policy, supplemented with Legalism for situations requiring penal law. Very early on and throughout history, scholars with high morality and ability were selected into the govern-ing bureaucracy through local recommendation and examination. They formed a class of *shi* through an open selection system providing upward mobility and social stability for the country. Other social classes in the meantime, were taught to feel happy and emotionally content. Fulfillment and social support came from a network of well-defined relationships. Balance, sustainability, and stability were key to understanding the Chinese sociopolitical experience.

The accountability of the government was measured by the people's approval. There was no limit to a government's responsibility for people under such a system. Being very practical, people's judgment was usually results-oriented. The government would set its own goals and objectives and the people could just sit back and enjoy the benefits of being governed, a political concept totally different than American democracy. Under abnormal circumstances, like during a national emergency, this enabled the government to take extraordinary measures quickly and without restriction, such as shutting down the large eleven-million person city of Wuhan during the 2020 pandemic, calling for voluntary medical help from other provinces, and requesting personal sacrifice from everyone to stay home. People are willing to cooperate when there is enough trust in the leadership and people know the nation is heading in the right direction. No coercion is needed, and there is no questioning of intent. Having such a foundation of trust is crucial to a non-democratic country like China, so it becomes imperative for its leaders and officers to constantly communicate its intent and actions, building trust with the general populace. Sometimes the government has been accused of withholding information or restrict-ing expression and it is no doubt guilty of sometimes trying to tailor the messaging to maintain trust with its people and limit distractions. If you consider that the government may lose its mandate altogether if it fails to meet public expectations, they certainly have a lot on the line. Because the trust and judgment of the people is so critical to their continued gover-nance, it is almost hard to blame them when every other government also carefully tailors their messaging in different ways, but has a lot less to lose if they get it wrong. To ensure they are consistently meeting the needs of their public, the Chinese government constantly runs polls and surveys to monitor public opinion. If certain policies or actions fail to work, they must move quickly to reform and try other ideas.

To thoroughly trace the trajectory of Chinese political reform and evolution, we must start with the Opium Wars back in the 1800s. The Opium Wars marked a very low point for Chinese civilization. Even before it started, Chinese intellectuals had been looking for ways to renew their ancient country while it was on its decline. Intent on reforming the Qing Empire's political regime towards a constitutional monarchy, Emperor Guangxu and a group of Chinese intellectuals advanced the Hundred Days' Reform, which failed in obscurity. The Boxer Movement then brought the invasion of the Eight-Nation Western Alliance in 1900, an event which still leaves a bad taste in the mouths of many Chinese as the Western nations looted China, deeply hurt Chinese pride, and threatened many livelihoods. It sped up the demise of the Qing Dynasty, after which the imperial era ended with the Nationalist Revolution of 1911 and the establishment of the Republic of China in 1912. Over the next thirty-seven years, various forms of capitalist government were attempted with help from Western nations like America. Dr. Sun Yat-Sen's "Three Principles of the People: Nationalism, Democracy, and People's Livelihood" also played a part in those attempts, having already inspired Chinese political thinkers for many generations, and even many leaders of the communist movement. Even so, China failed to organize as a modern nation-state, and the Chinese economy and politics became more chaotic than ever.

At the end of World War I in 1919, China was further humiliated by losing Germany's concessions on its Shandong province to Japan at the Paris Conference, even though hundreds of thousands of Chinese non-combatant laborers had supported and sacrificed alongside the Allied Powers during the war. China never signed the Treaty of Versailles, and it sparked nationwide protests while strengthening the people's resolve to safeguard China's sovereignty, triggering the May Fourth Movement. This movement contributed much to further awakening Chinese intellectuals, as they tried to save their country by denouncing everything traditionally Chinese and advocating the learning of science and democracy from the West. Some even advocated total Westernization.

The May Fourth Movement became an inspiration for many anti-traditionalists, nationalists, reformists, and revolutionaries looking for ways to renew China. The nationalist regime from 1919-1949 was corrupt and chaotic, both economically and politically, subjugating China to further influence by major global powers. But despite all these setbacks and conflicts, the spirit of *shi* continued to thrive as it has for generations, influencing and inspiring many Chinese intellectuals around the turn of the twentieth century to educate themselves in order to build a stronger Chinese nation and civilization. Many went abroad to be educated at leading world universities, and participated in diverse political movements. They studied different political ideas and revolutionary ideologies from the West, including the French and American revolutions. Many lambasted traditional Chinese values and translated works by Western, Japanese, and Russian thinkers, constantly searching for new ways and ideas. A group of them became attracted to the liberalism of John Dewey and various forms of anarchism and socialism, Bolshevism and the October Revolution, and ultimately the ideal of communism. This small group of compatriots with names such as Chen Duxiu, Li Dazhao, and Mao Zedong became founders of the Chinese Communist Party in 1921. Zhou Enlai and Deng Xiaoping joined the party at a later date. They were attracted by certain tenets of classical Marxism, including a classless society, sharing with the underprivileged, and globalism, all of which resonated with traditional Chinese thinking and values.

From the time of the Japanese occupation of China in the 1930s, those communist compatriots fought two wars in succession: the Japanese Invasion followed by the Chinese Civil War. It was through fighting in these wars that the CCP grew stronger, more popular, and became a dominant national force. In classical Marxism, exploitation of the proletariat by the bourgeoisie was the basic injustice. Mao understood the Chinese peasantry well and was able to sinicize the classical Marxist doctrine to reflect local Chinese rural conditions. His party communicated well with peasants and was able to mobilize them to fight, and eventually win, the war against the Japanese and also the Chinese Civil War. During wartime, the party performed a role akin to the past imperial bureaucracy, as an intermediary between the emperor and the people. They used cultural tools such as slogans, songs, plays, and writings to propagate revolutionary and patriotic sayings and thoughts, and to communicate social and political ideas and policies among leaders, party members, soldiers, and civilians.

Many patriots and idealists joined their ranks from all over China during wartime. Bridging both traditional and modern methods, they succeeded in mobilizing everyone under a central communist banner, all prepared to sacrifice for the Party if needed. This type of popular and broad-based guerilla warfare proved especially effective in fighting a much stronger enemy.

The Chinese Communist Party decisively won the civil war in 1949, enabling them to form a government and build a new political system based on the ideals of communism, which until then was foreign to the Chinese nation and its tradition. When Chairman Mao proclaimed the establishment of the People's Republic in 1949, China was run, in reality, by prominent generals of the Chinese People's Liberation Army, all Mao's comrades in arms during the war. Though party membership was open to any progressive individual with a commitment to serve others, the new Chinese leadership basically consisted of revolutionaries, strategists, fighters, and some intellectuals, mostly armed with winning wartime experience, but no exposure to nationhood building, management, or state governance. Military leaders became politicians but continued to govern as if it was wartime, with Mao in central command. If Mao gave an order, the whole country would immediately mobilize to follow. The central politburo controlled every personnel appointment across all political institutions, the military, state-owned corporations, and public institutions such as the media, schools, and universities. The Party created whatever institutions they needed for governance of the country according to their socialist ideals and values. Everything was structured as it was in the military, and while it made it easy for them to run social experiments as they learned on the job, it was disastrous for the Chinese people due to their idealism and inexperience. Much injustice was committed in those few early years of the Republic under Mao, such as in the Land Reform Movement, Anti-Rightist Movement, Great Leap Forward, People's Communes, and many ad-hoc sociopolitical campaigns. This was the era when China was still struggling to feed its own people. Over 80% of the population were peasants, and the literacy rate in China was very low (much less than 20%). Most of the people suffered in various levels of poverty until Deng's Reform and Opening decades later, which finally pushed China back towards its traditional evolutionary trajectory of conservative moderation, social harmony, and stability.

Deng Xiaoping, a pragmatist general, came to power after Mao's death in 1976, and brought China back from the brink of revolutionary socio-economic chaos. Deng's Reform and Opening strategy, while maintaining the same basic organization used during Mao's time, transformed the CCP to become a governing bureaucracy, while bringing back more traditional methods for political management, control, and state-governance. Deng and his successors, Jiang and Hu, transformed China from a planned to a market economy by learning from both Western capitalist nations and from Asian economic models like in Singapore, Hong Kong, South Korea, and Japan. China joined the World Trade Organization (WTO) in 2001, coinciding with American led globalization that required cheap manufacturing overseas. Since then, China rapidly became a leading global manufacturer and exporter. Its export-oriented economy made some people rich, but the majority remained poor, working in the lower to middle levels of the global supply chain. Even at that low level, China has managed to lift hundreds of millions of people out of extreme poverty within a few decades, giving it a little boost to proceed more confidently.

From 1978 to 2008, the Chinese government has been following Deng's pragmatic approach to "cross a river by feeling the stones." This turned out to be the best strategy since it encouraged everyone to focus on the main commitment to economic growth, and effectively removed distractions such as ideology, particularly critical at a time when globalization and technological advancement made it so that no predetermined strategy could possibly react fast enough to keep up with the pace of change. During such times of rapid change and when a country has much to fix, a centralized government with a learning mindset adapts and responds most quickly and effectively. And so, over a period of just thirty years since Deng's reform, China became the world's second largest economy in 2010. It is now about two-thirds the size of the US economy and set to overtake it this decade. Despite that, the per capita income is still among the lowest in the world, ranked sixty-eighth in 2019, which is even lower than Costa Rica, according to the World Bank. Even with a newly found middle class of 400 million people, which is larger than the entire population of the United States, China still has one billion people living in relative poverty, which is why it is also the largest developing nation in the world.

Today, the basic structure of the Chinese political system has not changed for seventy years, except for a drastic increase in complexity, sophistication, diversity, economic scale, and depth of operations. Mao's dictatorial leadership, however, has now been replaced by "decision by committees," albeit headed by its core leader who provides vision and direction, and encourages collaborative management. Many other crucial adjustments to governance have also been made in order to modernize, while becoming more responsive to people's needs, with increasing emphasis on quality instead of just quantity, as it was in the past era. This allows them to adapt to the fast-changing global environment, which has recently turned hostile towards them, and become much more challenging. The Trump administration deployed every bullying and demonizing tactic in their arsenal, even using lies to try and start a new Cold War before leaving office, but they still failed. During the 2020 pandemic, American social scientist Francis Fukuyama[43] named three political ingredients for passing that brutal stress test called COVID-19: capable states, social trust, and effective leadership. China was able to pass all three with flying colors, while the United States had some of the lowest ratings in the world. Other traditional Confucian East Asian countries such as South Korea, Vietnam, and Japan all also managed that stress test well, indicating that the cultural fabric of society may also be factor, more so than ideology as those are all democratic countries.

Social trust continues to be a core requirement of Chinese governance, and the Chinese people continue to value social security as their top need. Even though China is still one of the developing countries, it is building a new social security system that includes health and old age security, for both urban and rural citizens, and unemployment protections. Because most of its large population is still relatively poor, many trade-offs have been needed to find a way to balance civil rights versus responsibilities, stability versus freedom, economic growth versus social welfare, etc., and the bureaucracy is rapidly responding, adjusting, balancing, and evolving. So far, other than the initial pains during the first thirty years of the Republic, the people's satisfaction has

---

43 Francis Fukuyama, "The Pandemic and Political Order," *Foreign Affairs* (July/August 2020).

been consistently very high, according to a Harvard report.[44] Chances are that the CCP party-state will survive its mandate until those surveys show otherwise. No foreign entities can change this reality no matter how much they try to demonize it with things like trade wars, banning companies like Huawei, or blaming a pandemic on it.

In contrast, Western political heritage and tradition has such a strong emphasis on human rights and political form that sometimes it struggles to put limits on the demands for human rights. For example, the US continues to protect the freedom to own a gun even though an average of 100 people die every day from gun violence. If the form of government is good, such as in a liberal democracy, and if the government, by law, does what it is supposed to do, the people will accept whatever outcomes or consequences it leads to, including the death of hundreds of thousands during the 2020 pandemic. Dissatisfaction is normally expressed in the next election, or in street demonstrations.

While it is no doubt important to strike a balance lest there be too little emphasis on rights and freedom (something China does struggle with at times), it is still interesting to note that when surveyed, the Chinese people consistently place much greater value on their security over their freedom. For them, having food, shelter, and medical services, as well as a society free of criminals and predators, means they are more than willing to share their personal information for security purposes, for example. While this gives China an interesting edge in our Information Age, they must handle the privilege carefully and learn to also protect individual privacy whenever possible. Both systems work well in ideal situations. But there are always different types of corruption which can cause unexpected failure in any ideal system.

Chinese intellectual circles are continuously searching for a suitable future path. There are constant debates among Chinese political scientists on Maoist equalitarianism (the Left), American neo-liberalism (the Liberal), and Confucianism (the New Confucian). Many Left intellectuals are looking for Asian solutions, as well as socialist solutions that engage

---

44 Dan Harsha, "Taking China's pulse," Harvard Gazette, July 9, 2020, https://news.harvard.edu/gazette/story/2020/07/long-term-survey-reveals-chinese-government-satisfaction/

but are not limited to either Chinese or Western/universal norms. Liberals are looking for ways China can develop universal or global norms while drawing from Western liberal thinkers. New Confucians are looking for Chinese solutions from political traditions and the classics, while re-interpreting ancient writings. These debates will be key to shaping and realizing the stated governmental ideal of "building a socialist market economy with Chinese characteristics." From the roots of Chinese heritage, we believe that tenets such as holistic and long-term strategic thinking, broadminded inclusiveness, balance, justice and fairness, sustainability, and social harmony will remain key to their future success.

STRUCTURE OF THE CHINESE POLITICAL SYSTEM

The ability for the bureaucracy to govern is an integral part of Chinese heritage. Since 1949, the bureaucracy has been organized into a one-party political system with two different branches: the Chinese Communist Party (CCP) and the State, replicated across the five levels of government—central, provincial, city, county, and township or village. These crisscrossing lines of authority produce a governmental matrix that is both collaborative and functional. Formally, the party and state are separate organizations, with a Party Secretary and Premier, respectively, at the top of each branch. In practice, the two are intertwined—each functioning differently, but in close collaboration, and both leaders are members of the seven-member Politburo Standing Committee, which is the party's top ruling body. The Party Secretary usually provides vision, direction, and policy and the State carries out the implementation. The spirit of collaboration, not competition, is emphasized through the entire organization. Such cultural inclination is often misinterpreted by Western observers. It appears opaque to uninitiated outsiders because it is balanced between people-based and law-based, and most of the time, decisions are contingent upon the input of new data and facts, and often can only be understood under its own cultural context; it is more flexible and negotiable than outsiders give the Chinese credit for. The Chinese system has gone through many iterations leading up to the present stage, and many of its experiences continue to be reviewed and institutionalized.

Membership of the CCP was greater than ninety-one million in 2020, more populous than the countries of Germany and Croatia combined, yet still a fraction of the overall population, which totals over 1.4 billion. In addition to the national Politburo, both the party and state are governed by several functional committees. Together they provide long-term goals, direction, leadership, regulatory enforcement, and accountability for the central government and lower governing levels. Each important central government function (including economics, culture, environment, rural and agricultural development, urban planning, foreign affairs, etc.) has a corresponding committee to report to. President Xi, as the Party Secretary and President of the state, is the core leader and ultimate arbitrator who heads every important national committee. Sometimes when decisions are difficult, pilot projects are initiated to test the parameters or the viability of the proposed policy or evaluate the consequences of a policy. Projects are fact-based and results-oriented, each one aimed at solving a well-defined problem. Once a project is agreed upon, each committee member is held accountable for his or her segment and is responsible for passing the committee decision down to subsequent levels of government, all the way to the appropriate level for the decision to be implemented. Well-defined objectives, results orientation, communication, collaboration, and accountability are all key to how projects are completed at such a fast pace in China—the now renowned "Chinese speed."

In the State Government branch, there are three political institutions: the State Council headed by the Premier, the People's Congress headed by the third highest ranking member, and the People's Political Consultative Conference (CPPCC) headed by the fourth ranking member. All are in different stages of active evolution due to institutional reform initiated by the party. These three institutions exist in tandem at all five levels of the political hierarchy—the capital, the provinces, the municipalities, the counties (including county-level cities or city districts), and the townships (or street administrations in urban areas). Joint appointments can be made across the entire bureaucracy and are controlled by the Organization Department in the State Council. More details can be found in Lance Gore's book[45] on how the mechanisms and integration operate between the party, state

---

45 Lance L. P. Gore, *Chinese Politics Illustrated: The Cultural, Social, and Historical Context* (World Scientific 2014).

council, NPC, and CPPC. Information is widely available with full details, so we will not elaborate further here. The main points we want to highlight are that top-down hierarchy, meritocratic bureaucracy, and pragmatic collaborative attitudes are core to operating effectively in every part of such a political establishment.

The only institution that is conceptually uniquely Chinese is the people's political consultative conference (CPPCC). According to Gore, the CPPCC is an "advisory body" to assist the rule and broaden the base of support for the CCP. It was the first legislature of the PRC established in 1949, as a result of the united front the CCP built with eight other political parties in a common struggle against the Nationalist Government. In 1953, after the founding of the PRC, the National Party Congress (NPC) was created and the CPPCC was relegated to the status of an advisory body. Under Mao, both the NPC and CPPCC were dismissed by outsiders as rubber-stamped window-dressing bodies for the CCP. But they have both evolved since, with NPC becoming a national legislative institution for the country, similar to the US Congress, but with no party association for its members, and the CPPCC becoming an institutionalized official think-tank.

With the market economy, globalization, and information revolution, Chinese society has become increasingly pluralistic. Influential social elites such as public intellectuals, entrepreneurs, scientists, etc. (including some *shi*), have emerged outside the political establishments. These elites excel in different professional fields or segments of business and society, but many of them do not want to join the CCP. In response, the CCP has invited them to join the CPPCC in order to serve collaboratively with the government as advisors, supplying professional information crucial for legislation and policy making using their expertise. In this way they have effectively become official outspoken *shi* collaborating with the party, but also holding the establishment accountable for its actions. Many of their recommendations and proposals get forwarded to the People's Congress to be legislated into law or implemented for action by the government. In this way, we see the same Chinese traditions being applied: ultimately legitimacy for the government lies in the people's satisfaction, so a good government must embrace those that speak out to the benefit of the people, lifting them up to give them a voice.

In fact, many governmental objectives and power are slowly transitioning from purely dictatorial to becoming more service and regulatory functions. A party secretary is accountable for many things within their jurisdiction, but because of ongoing environmental concerns they might designate a captain (often the highest ranking member including the party secretary) to be accountable for any mishaps in the ecosystem of a lake or even a section of a river. It becomes that captain's responsibility to identify risks and coordinate to make sure everybody knows and implements what is needed to safeguard the ecosystem, including coordination with authorities outside their jurisdiction. As a brief aside, since we are talking about environmental issues and protecting ecosystems, it is interesting and encouraging to note that we should see many changes in this area in the next few years since one of China's newest goals is to become an ecological civilization that demonstrates harmony between humans and nature.[46]

Another important reform is in the divisional power between the central government and the provinces, which also determines the corresponding fiscal budget policy. The central government no longer sets growth rate targets for the provinces, encouraging them instead to develop economic strategies for themselves. The Chinese believe that people are all distinctively different, and hence contribute in diverse ways to family, community, and nation, according to their ability and virtue. Likewise, Chinese provinces all have personalities that contribute differently to the nation, according to factors such as their size, capability, resources, accumulated wealth, and local culture. The average population of a European country is about fourteen million. With a population of over 1.4 billion, China is like a conglomerate of 100 average-sized European countries. The average province is about the size of Spain. The largest province Guangdong has a population of about 113 million—approximately the same as Germany combined with Uganda. The scale is immense in comparison. China has thirty-one such large, diverse, and independently-governed provinces, and

---

46 "Xi Focus: Xi stresses strategic resolve on building eco-civilization," *Xinhua,*
May 1, 2020, http://www.xinhuanet.com/english/2021-05/01/c_139919713.htm,
accessed July 1, 2021.

more than 2,000 counties, all now fiercely competing with each other on nationwide goals such as green economic growth.

Competition for performance at various levels of government has become quite intense, providing incentives for leaders to perform and distinguish themselves under a socialist political system normally known for disincentive and inefficiency. Promotion is very competitive and supposed to be based purely on merit. Merit is based on a measurable set of parameters to measure local performance. Unfortunately, there are always bad sheep in any crowd, so even though promotion should be based solely on capability and past performance, China has been continuously battling corruption in many areas; there is a department in the State Council that is responsible for planning, training, and positioning potential leaders on a career path within the organization that is also tasked with implementing proper checks and balances to monitor and discipline party members. Hence, party leaders are professionally trained to be politicians, something that doesn't exist in the current Western system.

Politically, China is formally centralized, but according to Kroeber,[47] it is also highly decentralized in practice, which is another Chinese contradiction to outsiders. By the simplest quantitative measure, the proportion of fiscal revenue and expenditure handled by the local governments—revenue 40%, expenditure 73%--in China is by a wide margin the most decentralized country on earth. Local governments' share of revenue and expenditure are more than twice of what's typical in developed OECD countries (revenue 19%, expenditure 32%), and still more decentralized than developing nations (revenue 9%, expenditure 14%). This statistic is difficult for Westerners to explain, even for some renowned social sciences experts. It is the large scale and diversity of the Chinese provinces that makes China competitive and allows the central government to trust professionally trained provincial leaders to experiment with different political and economic policies before nationwide implementation, a luxury not found in any other country. It is unique—it took China five millennia to come to this particular juncture in history.

---

47 Arthur R. Kroeber, *China's Economy: What Everyone Needs to Know* (Oxford University Press, 2016).

In some ways, the current political organization is similar to the traditional imperial court of the past eras. The emperor and its cabinet can be likened to the seven-person Central Politburo and its committees. The entire bureaucracy works towards a common objective, that is, a better life for its citizens as in the imperial Chinese mandate. For the first time in history, the Politburo is now comprised of social scientists, historians, and economists, not engineers as in the previous two administrations. Both President Xi and Premier Li are established professionals with doctoral degrees in economics and law, for instance. They are very different from Mao's military generals. With such strong and diverse professional qualifications and experience in the leadership team, and with the support of its industrious and enterprising people, and the holistic and long-term strategic thinking of the Chinese tradition, the Chinese nation has been hitting many of its goals. Fortunately, with a stated overarching goal of world peace and social harmony, and a personal goal of seeing the rejuvenation of the Chinese nation by the middle of the 21st century, the world should root them on instead of throwing obstacles along their path. China has come a long way recently, but as Premier Li keeps reminding us, China is still very much a developing country, with annual income less than one fifth of that seen in the US in 2020, so there is still a long way to go.

MODERNIZING CHINA WITH CHINESE CHARACTERISTICS

As the leader of every main committee, President Xi wasted no time after the 18th party congress in 2012 to start working towards his goal of "modernizing China with Chinese characteristics." During his first tenure between 2012 and 2017, he focused internally on what was called "the deep reform" of advancing China through science, education, intensely coordinated regional development, rural revitalization, and environmental improvements, to name just a few. As one example, China needed a quality workforce for its development of innovation-driven scientific and industrial communities, so Chinese universities are now graduating millions of engineers every year. In 2013, China graduated seven million students of higher education, 40% of which completed their studies in a STEM (science, technology, engineering, and math) subject—more than twice the share of US graduates.[48] Since then, growth in the number of engineering students has been particularly explosive. Many Fortune 500 companies are doing research in China because of the abundance of talent available.

To advance urbanization and industrialization, they built 35,000 kilometers of high-speed railway by 2019, which now connects most of the key centers and cities, bringing new industries and businesses to some of the smaller cities and towns along the way. Major supercities grew even bigger through aggregation to become super-metropolises because of fast transportation to nearby cities. Technologies such as the Internet, big data, social media, the Internet of Things, and artificial intelligence are all helping development in this regard. Then there are the areas around Beijing, Tianjin, and Hebei that had potential based on their proximity to each other and the complementarity of their development, but needed coordination. In these situations, strong leadership is extremely beneficial to unite them with a well-defined objective and direction as well as mediate effectively between all the different local interests. Under Xi's personal supervision, these three regions are becoming a model of development for the rest of the country in showcasing a uniquely coordinated blend of culture, education, science, government, research, ecology, and industrial development with well-defined individual functions for each city or area. The project will be continuing through to the middle of this century and beyond. Another development of national priority is the highly coordinated development of cities along the mid-Yangtze river which crosses multiple provinces. Again, centralized leadership benefitted the project tremendously. Cities such as Chungking, Chengdu, Xian, and Wuhan are now the fastest growing industrial cities in China. If this project succeeds it will further join with the lower-Yangtze river cities between Nanking, Hangzhou, and Shanghai, forming one of the most prosperous waterways in the world.

In 1978, only 18% of the Chinese population lived in cities. Thirty-five years later, the urban population had swelled to 54% of the total, at a rate twice as fast as the comparative period in the US from 1830 to 1930. Growing at a rate of sixteen million people per year, China would have had

---

48 National Bureau of Statistics of China and the US Department of Education

to build a new city every year for thirty-five years, each city comparable in size to greater New York City and greater Boston combined. To reach an urbanization level of 82% like the US will still take many more years. To achieve that requires further industrialization, urbanization, more green and clean housing, education, jobs, food supplies, environmental and social services, plus mechanization of large-scale farming.

Aggregation is a new trend for global urbanization, based on learnings from the development of overly populated cities in the US such as New York, Chicago, Los Angeles, or Detroit. With modern infrastructure, China is in the process of building more super-metropolises in both the Yangtze and Pearl river deltas, and around Beijing and Tianjin. With modern fast transportation such as high-speed trains, many cities can be joined together to form a supply chain within one to two hours of travel. This type of aggregation is an efficient way to avoid the big-city problems and degradation often found in many global metropolises. Increasingly, ecological balance and cyber-management will also be crucial for design and planning. The Chinese government has previously been criticized for building ghost cities, but given enough time every one of those cities has become filled. As part of the overall plan to lift the country out of extreme poverty, people were expected to gravitate towards urban centers, and hence the ghost cities demonstrated the government's foresight and long-term strategic approach to social and industrial planning rather than their backwardness, as critics had assumed.

Another example to illustrate Chinese political creativity is the way in which the government accomplished President Xi's pledge in 2015 to totally eradicate extreme poverty by 2020. According to the World Bank,[49] China lifted 730 million people out of extreme poverty from 1990 to 2015 due to high economic growth and policies that favored improvements in the livelihoods of the poorest and most disadvantaged. Consequently, there were only fifty-five million people still living in poverty in 2015. In 2016, the World Bank further noted that China's state-sponsored programs, such

---

49 Ho Wah Foon, "China set to eradicate poverty by 2020," The Star, Jun 16, 2019, https://www.thestar.com.my/news/nation/2019/06/16/china-set-to-eradicate-poverty-by-2020#m3mAi1j52LzyX2H3.99

as for early childhood development, provision of quality education and healthcare, cash transfers to poor families, construction of rural infrastructure, and giving of subsidies to rebuild homes were all effective in alleviating poverty. But it was even more inspiring to see how the government mobilized the rich provinces to help the poorer ones, and incentivized rich and profitable enterprises, both public and private, to help train and teach people in remote rural regions to make a better living—for example, some now sell their wares or expertise online and others turned their remote locations into resorts for urban workers to escape to. The cooperation between these enterprises and the general populace ensured that China met its goal by the end of 2020, despite a pandemic, and nobody anywhere was left behind.

Our world is changing rapidly with increasing complexity, causing knowledge to be easily outdated. Following its heritage and tradition, the Chinese government is proud to be recognized as committees of learners. As a fast-developing nation, China is facing more domestic and global challenges than any other nation of our time. In order to obtain an in-depth understanding on issues of current significance or on a subject in advanced science and technology, the central Politburo invites top experts in every field to lecture them on a wide range of topics on a nearly monthly basis. In addition to sharing knowledge, group participation encourages meaningful in-depth discussion on current challenges and places each member on equal footing for more collaborative decision-making. Decision-making at the scale of Chinese national or provincial levels will never be simple, but learning and studying together enables groups to arrive at consensus easier.

The sheer size and complexity of the Chinese governing bureaucracy tells us that any simple label of "dictatorship," "totalitarian," or "authoritarian" is inadequate to describe such a massive organization. Even though there is no interparty democracy in their political system, there is intraparty democracy, and in-committee decision-making within the government. One can view the Chinese system as akin to the running of a multinational corporation, which is also nondemocratic. The Head Office is in the capital city of Beijing and the provinces report to the Head Office as subsidiaries or independent holding companies. A CEO and Board of Directors (the Central Politburo) must be strategic and decisive in decision-making, keeping in mind the best interests of their employees, clients, and shareholders (the welfare of the people) every moment in operation. The Corporate Head Office, all subsidiaries and their management and employees (the governing bureaucracy) must implement the Board's decisions and realize company objectives before the corporation (the country) can be profitable and successful (as measured by the people's satisfaction).

Of course, the Chinese experience and system is definitely not for everybody. As President Xi repeatedly emphasizes: "only your foot knows whether or not your shoe fits," meaning that only people living in a country know whether or not the political system works for them. Culture, history, thinking, and the attitudes of the people play a major role in determining the best system for any nation. To succeed, the Chinese system requires long term strategic thinking and vision, strong and capable leadership, and commitment from its people, who are all culturally interdependent and committed to win-win relationships. Chinese people are traditionally more willing to sacrifice personal freedom for the common good, which is in stark contrast to the individualism of the West, where democracy thrives. During the pandemic of 2020, people in America fought for their right to wear a face mask or not, turning it into a highly publicized battle and political issue for months. It was incomprehensible to many Chinese that some Americans would prefer to die rather than subjugate themselves to the state, even though it was for their own good.

It is worth reminding our readers again that China is still a developing country and many of its citizens are quite poor. It will be some time before it is developed to a level comparable to our home country of Canada. On its way, it will face many challenges. As a diverse, complex, and large country with a long history, the challenges it will face are enormous and multifaceted. The future of China will depend on how well its leaders and its people can effectively synthesize and further internalize different values from the diversity of traditions and ideologies in their past experiences. From the revolutionary tradition of Mao's era, egalitarianism and social justice were the important concerns—classical Marxism, such as the concept of a classless society and dialectic materialism are still rooted in the minds of many Chinese intellectuals. From the forty years of Deng's reform and opening period, Western resources from the Age of Enlightenment, such as democratic values and liberalism are still considered important in segments of Chinese society. But most importantly, China is increasingly returning to its traditional roots to find ideas in its heritage that can help create an improved Chinese modernity. Many traditional tenets such as broadminded inclusiveness, harmonious relationships, moderation, balance, peace for all, self-transcendence, and many other ancient Chinese teachings are increasingly applicable in our even larger, more diverse, complex, and interrelated world. More than ever, innovation in science and technology needs moral guidance and leadership, an area where ancient Chinese wisdom can be quite complementary and useful. China will never be democratic as some still wish for, but that doesn't mean it is wrong. It is still actively developing this "modern China with Chinese characteristics," and there is a long way to go. What will emerge ultimately is likely a new ideology and tradition that nobody has seen before. With its uniquely large scale, diversity, and history, it will certainly be one to watch and have far-reaching effects on not just the Chinese, but also on everyone in the world, and on our collective future.

NINE: THE CHINESE ECONOMY

An economy is a complicated organism. It is the totality of ideas and actions, and the livelihood of every member of a society or nation. Adam Smith summed it up when he wrote that economic progress depends upon a trinity of individual prerogatives: pursuit of self-interest, division of labor, and freedom of trade. Since then, pursuit of self-interest has become the heart of modern Western capitalism, with the other two prerogatives complementing it. Adam Smith helped produce a world of individuality, autonomy, and personal fulfillment.

In a more recent popular book *Capital in the Twenty-First Century*,[50] French economist Thomas Piketty focused on wealth and income inequality in Europe and the United States since the 18th century. He found that when the rate of return on capital is greater than the rate of economic growth over the long term, the result is concentration of wealth, and this unequal distribution of wealth causes social and economic instability. To Piketty, the inequality we are witnessing today is not an accident, but rather a feature of capitalism, which can only be reversed through state intervention. His book thus argues that unless capitalism is reformed, the

---

50 Thomas Piketty, *Capital in the Twenty-First Century*, English translation by Arthur Goldhammer (Harvard University Press, 2014).

democratic order will be threatened. This is another way of saying that capitalism and socialism should learn from each other to attain a dynamic balance. The Scandinavian countries did just that and created their own brand of socio-capitalism. China is in the process of creating another brand: the socialist market economy.

EVOLUTION OF THE CHINESE ECONOMY

The Western experience was defined by three socio-economic events that were profoundly significant in the formation of the modern economy: capitalism, the free market economy, and globalization. Capitalism is an effective way to accumulate capital and wealth; the free market economy is an efficient way to allocate resources; and economic globalization is a way to facilitate specialization and stratification, or division of labor. The modern West excels on all three counts. In addition, innovation and advancement in science and technology is increasingly playing a crucial role in our modern global economy, and Western countries are leading the way.

It is interesting to note that, historically, China has never been able to truly develop capitalism because of its distinctive cultural and historical context. Contemporary China chose to stay with socialism instead of capitalism as its state ideology, because that is more compatible with the traditional Chinese precept of sharing, hence the economic model that has worked for them is a slightly different flavor than what has worked for the rest of the Western world. Out of the four traditional social classes: *shi* (morally cultivated scholar), farmer, carpenter, and merchant, the class of merchants ranked last in the Confucian social hierarchy. Chasing after personal financial gains was not encouraged in Confucianism or Daoism, even though both agreed that there was nothing wrong with money if ethically earned.

In modern China, the Reform and Opening economic strategy of Deng and his successors transformed the country from a state-planned to a free market economy as an effective way to allocate resources. This enabled China to meet all three requirements for a modern Western economy and drove its recent economic success. In 2018, the Chinese economy was reported to be US$13.37 trillion, second only to the US at $20.58 trillion.

Average annual growth of the Chinese economy was 9.4% between 1979 to 2018, unprecedentedly high in world history. Even though its growth has slowed to around 6% over the past couple of years, it is still considerable compared with other countries.

Also in 2018, the Australian National University published a book[51] that brings together the work of many of the world's leading scholars on the Chinese economy and is the most authoritative and comprehensive compilation found anywhere. As stated in the introduction: "In 31 separate contributions, they reflect and present views on policy reform, economic growth and structural change over four fateful decades (1978-2018). These were the years in which China moved from being a poor, backward country to achieving living standards above the world average and now approaching those of the high-income countries. Over these four decades, China moved from near economic isolation to be the world's largest trading economy." For those interested in diving deeper to learn how China's economy changed so dramatically, the full book has five parts and is a gigantic, yet thorough, study of the different factors contributing to the transition, and multiple interpretations from the world's leading scholars on the topic.

The modern Chinese economy is extremely complex because of its continental scale, diversity in population and geography, distinct cultural, social, and political history and ideology, and the distribution of its natural resources and commercial activities. The diversity and scale of the Chinese economy make it unique, allowing regions to compete and grow at their own pace, depending on resources and skills available. With direction from the central government, regions can help as well as compete with each other just like siblings within the same family, a very Chinese concept.

The Chinese economy historically has done well in wealth accumulation, economic stratification and division of labor, trade and commerce, as well as urbanization and technology, all of which peaked during the Song Dynasty (960-1279) when circulation of commerce, trade, urbanization, and technology became widespread and China became a leader

---

51 Ross Garnaut, Ligang Song, and Cai Fang, *China's 40 Years of Reform and Development: 1978-2018*, (Australian National University Press, 2018).

in foreign trade. With improvements in maritime technology, including the use of the compass, an adjustable centerboard keel, and cotton sails in place of bamboo slats, China came to dominate trade in the South China Sea and beyond. The end result was that the seaports, rather than the old land routes, became China's principal contact with the outside world. With many expeditions during the Song, and later in the early Ming with Admiral Cheng He's journeys to the east coast of Africa, China led the world for the first phase of globalization and economic development. The recent modern Silk Road initiatives proposed by China are just another attempt to reconnect the Eurasian continent through both land and sea, a win-win proposition for everyone on its path.

Arabs and other people along the various silk roads have always played a crucial role in China's global development. In fact, for most of human history, China and India persistently contributed over half of the global economy because of their relatively large populations. The West became dominant only in the last two centuries, after the Industrial Revolution. Some Westerners seem surprised and even feel threatened by the current economic success of modern China. But the fact is China was historically the most developed country in the world and nobody in Asia felt threatened by its power because China always promoted peace. Now China is just trying to get back on its previous trajectory and recover from the woes of the past two hundred years. In his book, Charles Hucker[52] wrote:

> In the eleventh and twelfth centuries, China was not only the most populous and urbanized country in the world; it was also the most advanced and sophisticated country in the world in agriculture, industry, marketing, and trade. In retrospect, Song China seems to have been on the verge of developing a genuine "modern" economy –commercialized, industrialized, monetized, and to some extent even mechanized. In most respects, eleventh-century China was at a level of economic development not achieved by any European state until the

---

52 Charles O. Hucker, *China's Imperial Past: An Introduction to Chinese History and Culture* (Stanford University Press, 1975).

eighteenth century at the earliest. These set the stage for the later empire's explosive population growth. But the pace of economic development then slowed. The complexities of the economic system seem eventually to have outgrown China's managerial competence.

Hucker's perceptive words foreshadowed what was to follow in modern-day China. If economic success is not coupled with appropriate political reform and better business management and state governance, all gains are eventually headed for failure. Modern China is painfully aware of its past failings, so its current strategy includes deep reform tackling political, social, and judicial concerns at the same time. Modernizing state governance and governing capacity is on the agenda to be accomplished by the middle of the 21st century. Hence, to truly understand how China is evolving economically, we need to take a deeper look at both its economic and political reform.

The original plan of the Four Modernizations of Deng Xiaoping during the period 1979-82 was focused on a commitment to modernize Chinese industry, agriculture, science and technology, and national defense. It was designed to match world levels by the year 2000 and make China a great economic power by the early 21st century. As described by Arthur Kroeber,[53] the goal of China's industrial policy has been to create a set of industries, with Chinese companies progressively producing goods of greater technological sophistication and higher value, and gradually becoming more globally competitive. By 2020, those aims have largely been achieved. China has moved from being a producer of low-end textiles and cheap consumer goods in the 1980s to a country with successful and large-scale automotive, shipbuilding, machinery, electronics, chemicals, and precision instrument industries. The technological sophistication has risen as well. The global competitiveness of Chinese production has steadily risen, as shown by its growing share of global manufactured exports. For most of the 2000s, foreign enterprises accounted for more than half of the exports

53 Arthur R. Kroeber, *China's Economy: What Everyone Needs to Know* (Oxford University Press, 2016).

and as much as two-thirds of the trade surplus. By 2014, the foreign share of both was under half, with domestic firms significantly increasing their share. The aggregate trade surplus of China's non-state enterprises is now twice as big as the foreign-enterprise surplus.

But China has not been equally successful in all industries, according to Kroeber. The FDI model means that certain industries, such as automobile and electronics, have been built mainly by foreign firms, and it has sometimes proven hard for Chinese companies to break in. This shows that the Smithian capitalist path of industrial development has a big advantage when accumulation of technological know-how and capital is the prerequisite for further development. The highest-value components of the technology value chain—design and marketing of final products, design of integrated circuits, and original software development—remain firmly in the hands of global giants such as GM, GE, Toyota, Volkswagen, Apple, Samsung, Intel, IBM, and Microsoft. This is why international trade is still a win-win proposition worth protecting by all countries. China may be the largest consumer market in the world, but it is also the biggest beneficiary and strongest defender of global free trade.

Today, China faces a new challenge on a global scale arguably greater than any it has had to overcome in the past. This challenge is to shift from a growth model based mainly on the mobilization of resources to one based mainly on the efficiency of resources used. With a middle class of more than 400 million, China is in the process of moving up the global supply chain in manufacturing, improving the business environment for investment by reducing taxes, fees, and red-tape, and encouraging innovation and entrepreneurism. Simultaneously, it will focus future technological development around 5G, the 5th generation of mobile networking. Its emphasis now is on improving the quality of its products to satisfy the domestic needs of the people and its service industry. This task is complex, requiring an intricate series of reforms in its financial, enterprise, governance, and legal systems, as well as an ability to respond flexibly to unexpected situations such as a trade war or global pandemic.

CREATING AN ETHICAL AND SOCIALIST MARKET ECONOMY

Harvard philosopher and author of the bestselling book, *Justice*, Michael J. Sandel, explores a central question of our time in his most recent book:[54] *The Tyranny of Merit: What's Become of the Common Good?* Sandel argues that to overcome the crises that are upending our world, we must rethink the attitudes toward success and failure that have accompanied globalization and rising inequality. The book showcases the hubris that a competitive meritocracy generates among its winners and the harsh judgment it imposes on those left behind, tracing the dire consequences across a wide swath of American life. He offers an alternative way of thinking about success that is more attentive to the role of luck in human affairs, more conducive to an ethic of humility and solidarity, and more affirming of the dignity of work—solutions that sound more Confucian than we would expect from a Harvard scholar.

Very few people, even in the Western world, know of Adam Smith's other great work, *The Theory of Moral Sentiments,* published in 1759, and revised by Smith in 1761. Both volumes share the same fundamental passion about the moral foundations of social life. At the heart of each of these books is an explicit recognition of the fundamental contradictions within the market economy. Smith demonstrated that the free market is an immensely powerful force for impelling economic progress, but also has deep internal contradictions from an ethical standpoint; that is, the division of labor and the pursuit of profit. Smith believed that class stratification was a necessary condition of economic progress because it facilitated the accumulation of capital and division of labor. However, he acknowledged that the arrangement would amplify the possibility of not only class conflict, but also the corruption of morals through the construction of social values that justified neglect of the poor. The current fractured social conditions in America amply demonstrate this point. But Smith offered no solution to this contradiction.

Adam Smith's penetrating analysis is of the deepest significance in China's search for a moral touchstone to help the country find its way

---

54 Michael J. Sandel, *The Tyranny of Merit: What's Become of the Common Good?* (Farrar, Straus and Giroux, 2020).

forward in the years ahead. Regional and wealth disparities are of incalculable concern to the Chinese government, but both are the outcome of specialization and the stratification effects of globalization and a market economy. Yet, it is misleading to suggest that Smith provided unqualified support for the free market. He did not, and his reservations were clearly of relevance to China's situation today. The central preoccupation of Chinese political practice for thousands of years has been the attempt to find a function for the state and nurture a social ethic that enables the economy and society to operate in a way that serves the wider social interest. Chinese philosophy has always centered on human needs and the improvement of government, individual and social morals, and the value of human life. The traditional Chinese economy was far more dynamic and market-oriented than many people have realized. Thus, it has become a complex challenge for the Chinese government to address the problem of income disparity and wealth distribution, adhering to the principle of social justice and equality, without intervening in the free market economy.

The common theme of both Confucius and Adam Smith, according to Peter Nolan,[55] is that the market is not an intrinsically moral entity that should be allowed to dominate society. This point was thoroughly demonstrated during the financial tsunami of 2008, when nobody on Wall Street or in the US government was ever truly prosecuted. Restraint of selfishness, or more simply the promotion of benevolence, is a human moral foundation, unlike the pursuit of individual self-interest endorsed by the free market fundamentalism in the United States. Both Confucius and Smith emphasized reciprocal social obligations and duties as the foundation of a good society. Both regarded the pursuit of wealth and position as damaging to individual fulfillment. Both regarded education as the foundation of self-fulfillment and morality that forms the cement for social cohesion. Both understood individual happiness to be the primary goal of a successful society. And they both believed that this was not to be achieved through the pursuit of ever-greater material consumption. Nolan navigates his way through a broad spectrum of perspectives from economic, business, industry, and through to history, philosophy, art, and society at large.

---

55 Peter Nolan, *China at the Crossroads* (Polity Press, 2004).

Nolan was invited to meet with Deng Xiaoping in June 1979 to discuss how to apply these thoughts in combating corruption in China. One of the biggest challenges that the Chinese people face is to establish a market economy and corresponding social institutions that account for all these ideals and ethical considerations. They refer to this endeavor as the building of a "socialist market economy with Chinese characteristics." This should be understood as a Chinese effort to modernize China by combining Western socialism and the free market economy with traditional Confucian ethics and morality, hopefully incorporating concepts like the traditional spirit of *shi*. One of their biggest projects is the Chinese "One Belt One Road" (OBOR) Initiative, promoting economic growth through improved connectivity to the underprivileged developing areas of Asia and Africa.

Giovanni Arrighi et al.[56] published an analysis that found there are actually two possible paths for industrialization—"Braudelian capitalist" and "Smithian capitalist." The West followed a Smithian dynamic during the Industrial Revolution by concentrating on new technology and accumulation of capital. East Asia, China in particular, followed a Braudelian capitalist dynamic which they called an "industrious revolution," focused on reorganizing where and how people worked. Such people-orientation versus machine-orientation is consistent with the differences between Chinese and Western thinking and worldviews, resulting in subsequent differences in their political, socio-economic, and industrial structures and hence institutional development.

In the Western model, a company typically grows larger by building bigger and better machines and/or increasing their accumulation and usage of capital, then begins to dominate their segment, sector, and gradually becomes a "too big to fail" multinational with global capital and technology diffusion growth, eventually dominating the free markets of the regional and world economy. This was the path taken by the West during and after the Industrial Revolution, in all subsequent phases of globalization, and even in our present Information Age. Growth is from the top

56 Giovanni Arrighi, Takeshi Hamashita, and Mark Selden, *The Resurgence of East Asia: 500, 150, and 50 Year Perspectives* (Routledge, 2003).

down, and then gets spread all over the world. But in his most recent book *People, Power, and Profits*,[57] Nobel prize winner Joseph E. Stiglitz claims the situation is now dire, and challenges us to throw off the free market fundamentalists and the monopoly of powerful high-tech multinational corporations, and reclaim our economy so that a middle class life can once again be attainable by everyone.

In China and some East Asian countries, however, the industrious revolution went from the bottom up. Because of China's previous planned socialist economy, all companies were state-owned and everybody worked for the government. There was no private ownership of property after the 1950s, before Deng's reform. During Mao's era, members of a family would all work for the same state-owned company, which provided food and shelter for everyone. In fact, State Owned Enterprises (SOEs) served social as well as economic functions for the entire populace. Literally hundreds of thousands of workers worked in a single SOE, such as in an oil field. But state-owned enterprises were not known for their efficiency. So as part of Deng's reform and opening in 1978, transforming from a planned to market economy, efficiency began to matter, and consequently some more industrious people were encouraged to venture out and start privately owned businesses such as a little local cafe or a home-grown machine shop. Soon, private businesses flourished everywhere alongside State Owned Enterprises. People were also able to own private properties and housing again.

During those early days of Chinese industrialization, there was no shortage of labor, but capital was limited. Instead of buying expensive machines to produce a large quantity of products, Chinese entrepreneurs distributed production to many privately-owned small companies, each employing only a few workers. Such a distributive system of production required very little startup capital and had the advantage of being flexible and adaptive to any change in consumer demand and/or market conditions. This model was socio-economically significant since it could create the massive employment needed for a developing country without a

---

57 Joseph E. Stiglitz, *People, Power, and Profits: Progressive Capitalism for an Age of Discontent* (W.W. Norton Company, 2019).

massive capital injection. Later, it also enabled China to stably transform its economy from export to domestic-oriented. Chinese development often started from the bottom, with people spreading out everywhere to find opportunities or pockets for growth. Even in traditional China, entrepreneurship was a means for people to accumulate wealth. When advanced technology is added as a part of its evolution, such a bottom up approach can be quite scalable, as evidenced by the fast Chinese development of their own Internet and the millions of applications for individuals and businesses.

In the 1980s, the genius of Steve Jobs created smart phones and Apple, the company, a pretty typical Western success story full of heroics. Chinese phone manufacturer Xiaomi, on the other hand, did not exist until 2011. Xiaomi prides itself on making little changes that have impact, building one little improvement at a time from the bottom up. By working closely with their customers, they were able to keep a close eye on what was important to consumers and adapt quickly while keeping their costs relatively low. Contrast this with Apple working from the top down to bring their founder's vision to life, Xiaomi became a US$16 billion company with 15,000 employees in the short space of seven years, using exactly the opposite model—building from the bottom up. This model also works well in other developing countries such as India and Africa where investment capital is the strong limiting factor.

Another interesting business comparison is between Amazon and Alibaba, both companies specializing in e-commerce marketing. People can buy anything online *from* Amazon. It is Amazon who sells you the product regardless of where the product comes from. Contrast this with Alibaba, which provides a platform where companies can register to sell their products. Consumers buy directly from the registered companies and Alibaba facilitates the transactions and delivery. Again, the Alibaba business model is distributive, involving many small entrepreneurs with minimal initial capital outlay, consistent with the general model of distributive online businesses. By mid-2020, there were over 900 million Internet users in China empowered to be e-commerce consumers, traders, business owners, and producers through the Alibaba platform. This group is gaining momentum, and due to its initial domestic success, Alibaba is expanding to facilitate cross border e-commerce so that Chinese people can buy and sell to the world.

A lot of the recent rhetoric from the United States claims that China has been stealing technology and Intellectual Property (IP) from the US in order to rapidly create its own competitive businesses. In some ways, it is inescapable that late comers in technology need to learn from the pioneers as they industrialize—in this case the West. Not too long ago, it was the West that learned most of their early technologies from China in order to industrialize, and the Chinese were more than willing to share their innovations. Whether there is industrial espionage now and how much is fair is not for us to judge, but using politics and the economic embargoes to try and hinder Chinese entrepreneurs and development only serves to distract and ultimately harm growth on both sides. Instead of continuing to point fingers, it may be time to establish some international rules for fair intellectual property protection and enforcement, or accept that a certain amount of learning from each other is normal and even beneficial for the overall good of humankind because it can trigger the type of competition that will help us all advance even more quickly.

Any opportunity to learn from the Western experience is indispensable, but China sees an opportunity to improve the Western model even further by incorporating an additional ethical dimension into its institutions, a dimension that is lacking in the present Western system. Adam Smith's analysis of the market mechanism tried to lay down fundamental laws governing economic development, assuming that the free market, guided by the invisible hand, was a reasonable arrangement for organizing economic life. But in traditional Chinese ideology, it is reasonable for the visible hand, or the government, to get involved as long as it works for the welfare of its people, preferably with a spirit of *shi*, as described previously.

On December 30, 2020, China and the European Union announced the conclusion in principle of a Comprehensive Agreement on Investment (CAI), concluding discussions that began in 2013. The EU presented the agreement as "the most ambitious agreement that China has ever concluded with a third country." The agreement binds China's liberalization of investments and prevents backsliding on conditions of market access for EU companies. In addition, it provides for the elimination of quantitative restrictions, equity caps, or joint venture requirements in several sectors, including automotive and health. The CAI will also facilitate EU market access in other sectors including Research and Development (R&D), telecommunication/cloud services, and air and maritime transport. It is a win-win agreement of great profundity to both China and EU, showcasing that collaboration and diplomacy can work better than confrontation in international relations.

China is still very much in the process of developing its own modern market economy, sociopolitical institutions, commercial laws, laws for economic management practices, and rules for corporate governance that are best suited for a socialist economy. Innovation is the key to success since this is a totally new concept. There is still much work to do on reviving traditional Chinese ethics and morality and figuring out how to fairly incorporate it into the institutional fabric with the right checks and balances. But China is still following Deng's strategy to be fast and adaptive to changing conditions, and that has been serving it well. Similar to achieving the lofty goal of eliminating extreme poverty by 2020, they are well on their way towards meeting another goal—that of modernizing China by 2049, the centenary year of the People's Republic.

CASE STUDY: THE SHEKOU/SHENZHEN MODEL

To better understand Chinese economic accomplishments over the past forty years, it is instructive to follow how Deng's vision of "open and reform" was implemented in practice. The irony is that there was never any grand design. Deng's main instruction was for the people to "cross a river by feeling the stones." What this unleashed though was the confidence for people to follow their instincts, being both practical and resourceful in adapting to new surroundings and situations. One of the first examples of success in applying this was the development of a little place called Shekou.

In 1979, Shekou was a small insular village at the southern tip of the larger city of Shenzhen, in Guangdong province. It faced Hong Kong across Shenzhen Bay, so was a prime location for China to open up to more market-led economics and trade. Hong Kong, of course, is one of the most beautiful cosmopolitan port cities in the world, ceded to Great Britain in 1842 after the Opium War. After the Korean War, Hong Kong became the only window to the world for China because of the economic blockade imposed by the UN and is still one of the few free ports open to the world. The majority of people in Hong Kong are of Chinese descent, many of whom escaped from China after suffering during either the Japanese invasion, the civil war, or political persecution that was part of the Chinese revolution. They are very proud and pragmatic people with tremendous energy and ambition. Combined with the administrative efficiency, professionalism, and the effectiveness of British legal and financial services, Hong Kong quickly became one of the world's best for port facilities, commerce, finance, and trade. Unfortunately it is also one of the most limited in resources such as labor and land, and has significant environmental concerns.

Because of its proximity to Hong Kong, Shekou was a natural choice to become the Shekou Industrial Zone, the precursor to the Special Economic Zones initiated by Deng Xiaoping in 1980. The opening of Shekou was good news to entrepreneurs in Hong Kong. Many of them could now move their manufacturing facilities to Shekou where both labor and land are cheap, and since Chinese commercial and environmental laws were not in place yet, there were even more opportunities to make money. The local government was purposely flexible and business friendly, formulating a series of preferential policies to attract foreign investment and allow businesses to thrive. Within a relatively short period of time, multiple industrial parks cropped up and the local community started to grow. After adding schools and shopping centers, it started to resemble a modern metropolitan hub. As it continued to expand into the larger city of Shenzhen and beyond, many other cities along the Pearl River delta started becoming suppliers, and the whole area quickly became one of the most competitive manufacturing regions, exporting goods out to the world through the port of Hong Kong. In order to connect with suppliers more efficiently, the next step was to build better transportation, such as high-speed rail and freeways. This process of taking "a seaport," then building "an industrial park," then "a city," and finally "a region" is now known as the "Shenzhen/Shekou model," and this plan has since been replicated many times across China, and even in some other developing countries.

In 2017, the city of Shenzhen recorded nominal output of 2.2 trillion yuan (US$338 billion), which at the time was comparable economically to Singapore and Hong Kong. It boasted an urban population of over 10 million and was known as "the world's factory" because so much of what the world uses was made there. In fact, Briony Harris reported[58] that 90% of the world's electronics came from Shenzhen, including toys, televisions, air conditioning units, mobile phones, and drones. It should be noted that even though the simple Shenzhen/Shekou model worked well for China, those achievements would not have been possible without the simultaneous development of advanced technology. In China, Beijing is the main incubator for innovation and technology because many of their top universities, academia, and national laboratories are situated there, providing deep bench strength for generating innovative ideas. But it is Shenzhen where those ideas are implemented and tested, and many graduates from Beijing go to work in Shenzhen where most of the major high-tech firms are now located. It is also a business-friendly city and has become the home base for many large enterprises such as Huawei, a privately owned corporation with a strong focus on long term research and development. Huawei made a name for itself as a global corporation with its advanced 5G development, which also unfortunately drew the competitive ire of the US, wanting to stop them from dominating with their first mover advantage. Run very differently than most Western businesses, it dedicates between 10-20% of its annual total sales to research, and its founder controls only 1.4% of the total shares in the company with employees owning the rest.

Another important observation about the Shenzhen model is that it takes time—the whole evolution from seaport to thriving business region took thirty to forty years. With learnings from that experience, other zones have grown more quickly, but it still takes twenty to thirty years to fully develop a zone. It is typical that large infrastructure projects such as these require heavy initial investment for many years before you start to see the returns. Western governments often have a four-year election cycle to consider that prevents them from undertaking and completing truly large-scale projects. Similar to businesses, they also need to justify and demonstrate a return on investment (ROI) within a reasonable timeframe. Hence,

---

58 Briony Harris, "The astonishing rise of Shenzhen, China's gadget capital," World Economic Forum, November 9, 2017, https://www.weforum.org/agenda/2017/11/inside-shenzhen-china-s-gadget-capital/

they typically shy away from such long-term investments or experiments where the risks and rewards may be difficult to determine.

In contrast, because of Chinese cultural and political traditions, long term strategic planning is much more routine for the Chinese government and businesses. We mentioned ghost cities earlier, which are a perfect example of this. Starting as early as 2006, Westerners started reporting the existence of under-occupied developments in many Chinese cities—even Shenzhen was included in its early days. But once people started relocating from the countryside towards these hubs seeking the opportunities that the infrastructure developments enabled, those ghost cities quickly filled with people, demonstrating that it was, in fact, all part of a longer-term plan. Whether or not a country can successfully execute longer-term plans depends very much on the cultural attitude of its people as well as the political system and structure of the country. Democracy has enabled individualism to thrive, which means that if people's goals are not aligned on a project it can easily seem like herding cats. For smaller scale projects there are many ways to overcome this, but when large-scale and longer-term projects require strong collaboration and a large upfront investment with minimal initial ROI, then cultures and countries with a more collectivistic attitude typically are more willing and able to invest and see it through.

After eight years of construction, the longest bridge in the world (fifty-five kilometers) now joins Hong Kong, Macau, and the city of Zhuhai at the western mouth of the Pearl River delta. There is a national plan in China to combine the economies of both Hong Kong and Macau with nine other cities in the delta to become the latest "Bay Area," possibly by 2035. All eleven cities in the area are within a few hours by car or one hour by high-speed rail. By combining the entrepreneurism, technological expertise, and innovative industrial potential of Shenzhen, the international network and global financial services experience of Hong Kong, and the resource power of workers and suppliers within a population of over 70 million in Guangzhou and neighboring cities, this area is set to become a powerhouse for manufacturing, global trade, and commerce. According to the national plan, the combined economy will create USD $1.4 trillion of business opportunities for the area, the success of which could affect all of southern China, and may eventually rival comparable metropolises such as New York, Tokyo, and San Francisco.

The Shenzhen/Shekou model has proven successful in creating many similar thriving regions across China and continues to expand. Each of those initial investments took years, even decades, of patience, hard work, and faith in order to see results. But once the base infrastructure was in place it fueled exponential growth for the businesses and communities surrounding it, enabling the "China speed" that has astonished watchers in the West, something that truly could only have been achieved because it was China and the Chinese people. We can already see China extending this model beyond its borders, hoping to invest in similar success internationally, partnering with other countries along the modern Silk Road to Europe and beyond. The pace and potential of these developments will be immense, and we hope those in the West can start to look more at the future possibilities that it is trying to enable rather than criticizing immediate efforts which typically get interpreted as either futile or domineering. Better yet, if the West can acknowledge the power of Chinese resources and commitment to a long-term vision and start to contribute their own expertise, we can all start to see the results and reap the benefits even more quickly, helping to lift so many more countries and people out of poverty to truly become part of our modern globally interconnected world.

UNIQUE CHALLENGES AND OPPORTUNITIES AT SCALE

China is distinctive when compared with others because of its large scale—in population, territorial area, ethnic and cultural diversity, and its thousands of years of history as a continuous and unified political entity, initially developed almost in isolation to the rest of the world. The land spread of modern China is about the same size as the US including Alaska, but with a population four times that of the US. This large scale presents China with an unusual set of constraints and possibilities. Every challenge it faces is always larger than our imagination, but the resources available to alleviate any problems are also impressive. Structurally, the Chinese government is in a commanding position to solve any economic problem under its jurisdiction and make long term plans for its future. Such Chinese scale is unique and unprecedented in our world, and only understandable within the Chinese context.

Historically, China has always been self-sufficient from a resources perspective. Chinese culture discourages excessive consumption, so most people live well within their means. During the heights of Chinese civilization such as during the Han, Tang, and Song Dynasties, a creative symbiotic inter-relationship between state and market existed that was well managed as an integral part of good government. For much of Chinese history, the Chinese state strongly encouraged the development of a traditional Chinese market economy, which peaked during the Song Dynasty. But it couldn't have succeeded without an equally stable Chinese hierarchical bureaucracy that emphasized the importance of ethics and education, promoting an inclusive civil examination system for selecting leaders, and managing a meritocratic evaluation system to provide upward mobility for officials. This system is well-preserved and continuously evolving throughout Chinese history, even today.

It was also dependent on the people, an important human resource when organized constructively. Tenets such as Confucian social ethics, the ideal of a harmonious society, and a collective preference to integrate rather than divide and confront contributed much to order and stability. Confucianism supplied values and behaviors that enabled each individual personality to manage his or her existential tensions, giving meaning and coherence to the central social values that defined the structure of society. The overriding values were those of the primacy of order and stability, of co-operative human harmony, of accepting one's place in the social hierarchy, and of social integration. All of these encouraged and enabled the Chinese people to willingly work together for the shared common good. Such Chinese organization and political thinking are distinctly different from Western liberalism and individualism.

Conceptual disparities have made many Westerners misinterpret China, even Karl Marx. In Marx's view, according to Peter Nolan, Asiatic despotisms (including, but not limited to China) were characterized by the absence of private ownership of land; large scale, state-run irrigation systems in agriculture; autonomous village communities; passively rentier or bureaucratic cities; and a despotic state machine which obtained the bulk of the economic surplus. Unlike the European political economy, which Marx viewed as progressing from slavery to serfdom, feudalism, capitalism, socialism, and ultimately communism, the Asiatic mode was merely cycles following the rise and fall of dynasties, but not an evolutionary history.

European experience, of course, was very different from the Chinese one, yielding contrasting contexts and interpretations. Many modern economists also believe that it was the traditional Chinese state that stifled the creativity of the Chinese nation and crushed the development of the ancient Chinese market economy. Nolan maintains that one answer to the "Needham question" of why China failed to achieve an "Industrial Revolution" despite a high level of technical development is precisely because markets were so highly developed that any local bottlenecks could be met through the market mechanism. The state stepped in whenever markets failed not only in respect to immediate growth issues, but also in relation to the wider issues of social stability and cohesion. It actively nurtured and stimulated commerce, but refused to allow commerce, financial interests, and speculation to dominate society, or produce excesses that would threaten stability. Stability is a prerequisite for social harmony in a large-scale community. A key responsibility of the CCP is to provide stability for the contemporary Chinese economy to advance and grow.

The rejuvenation of the Chinese nation is one of the stated objectives of the current Chinese administration. One interpretation of this is that it intends to use some of the ancient ways and past experiences to solve current problems. The government is becoming renowned for its long-term strategic thinking, which is often easily misunderstood if viewed on a short-term basis or with Eurocentric thinking biases. China's large economy combined with an industrious populace and traditional benevolent governance can be advantageous. With such a large pool of resources, both natural and human, the country has been able to industrialize and urbanize within only a few decades and is still going strong. Advances in infrastructure and construction have led to tens of thousands of kilometers of high-speed railway connecting the country along with mega airport terminals, providing a level of connectivity never seen anywhere before in the world or history. Much of it has been enabled by effective and efficient central governance that gives clear direction for the country and facilitates collaboration and healthy competition among diverse cities, provinces, and regions. As a result, China has grown a middle class of 400-millon over the past two decades and is projected to double that number by 2035.

Still, unexpected events beyond anyone's control can always happen. The global financial crisis of 2008, or the US's attempts to unchain and deglobalize, for example, have presented huge challenges to the export-driven Chinese economy. They are dealing with it, but with profound consequences. One must remember that China is still a developing country with a very low per-capita income. It is not until very recently that China finally solved the problem of feeding its own people. Chinese culture works like water flowing down a stream—when you put a boulder in its way, it often just finds a way to go around it. In many of these cases, the irony is that Western strategies to punish and deter have only served to make China and its people more self-sufficient, forcing them to become stronger faster.

Rapid economic ascendance in China has brought on many challenges, including increased inequality within the large urban centers, between urban and rural areas, and between the industrial east and remote under-developed west. The country is trying to adapt in many ways. The building of more and even better infrastructure is in the plan. They've promised a new progressive tax system that will be fairer for everybody. Plans for future socio-political development have a stronger emphasis on the central and western provinces rather than the major metropolitans of the east. Already, the economic growth rate in western cities such as Guiyang, Xian, Chungking, and Chengdu are surpassing Shanghai. Increasing rail traffic between Chengdu and Europe through central Asia is further helping the industrialization of western China. The future of China will depend on how well they develop the underdeveloped rural regions, which will help to increase Chinese per capita income to the global average.

China also faces demographic pressure related to an aging population. Relaxing the one child policy has helped, as well as better and more innovative care for the elderly. But attempts to increase the birthrate have not been entirely satisfactory because of the high cost of bringing up a child with good education. Thankfully, there are already many innovative ideas springing up to help solve the problems of childcare and elder care. There is much we as humans can share, not just resources like housing and helpers, but also our time, company, and care. It is becoming increasingly critical to revive the traditional values of filial piety and respect for the elderly and the teachers. Also, China is welcoming foreign investments and competition to advance its service industries, including health and elder care.

China is still in the process of deep and comprehensive economic reforms. These reforms will transform the economy from export to domestic consumption-oriented, and from industrial to service and supply-side focused. It will include new government and legal institutions, policies between central and provincial authorities on power and revenue sharing, state-owned corporations for better efficiency and allocation of resources, and a new social benefit system. The stated objective of the government is to provide a good business environment that eliminates obstacles to industrial and business development through institutional and policy reform, provides better service and easier financing to smaller businesses, and encourages innovative entrepreneurism. At the same time, they plan to implement better rules and regulations for monitoring and security of all businesses to prevent corruption. In parallel, China will open more to the world for finance, trade, investment, and service industries. In particular, they are seeking bilateral and regional free trade agreements wherever possible, such as the multiple comprehensive regional trade and investment agreements they signed with both Asian and European countries at the end of 2020.

After their initial success in building domestic supply chains, and especially after kicking off the Silk Road initiatives, China began to participate in matching supply and demand on a global scale, which is known as global supply chains. It has thrived in this arena and continues to be the most attractive region for production sourcing and in the building of better global connectivity. Some mistakenly assume that the low cost of Chinese goods was the sole driving force behind China's success, but that is not the case. Successful global supply chain management requires implementing the appropriate framework of concentration, complying with international regulations set by governments and non-governmental organizations, and recognizing and handling appropriately the risks involved, while maximizing profit and minimizing waste. It is a very complex undertaking in strategic, logistical, and operational management, which is ideally suited to Chinese cultural aptitudes and experiences. In addition, market access, supply chain performance, quality, infrastructure, and its win-win diplomacy have emerged as the dominant drivers for continuously increasing production volume in China.

Due to its large scale, China is the top nation in terms of manufacturing output, consistently contributing a quarter to a third of global economic growth over the past two decades. In 2018, China shipped US$70 billion of smartphones to the US, along with US$45 billion worth of computers. At one point, Apple CEO Tim Cook commented on why Apple makes iPhones in China: "China has moved into very advanced manufacturing, so you find in China the intersection of craftsman kind of skill, and sophisticated robotics and the computer science world. That intersection, which is very rare to find anywhere, that kind of skill, is very important to our business because of the precision and quality level that we like... But for us, the number one attraction is the quality of the people. China has extraordinary skills. And the part that's the most unknown is there's almost two million application developers in China that write apps for the iOS App Store. These are some of the most innovative mobile apps in the world, and the entrepreneurs that run them are some of the most inspiring and entrepreneurial in the world. [...] The truth is, the process engineering and process development associated with our products require innovation in and of itself. Not only the product but the way that it's made, because we want to make things in the scale of hundreds of millions, and we want the quality level of zero defects."[59] China has indeed come a long way from when it was considered the low-labor-cost country where the world produced its goods. You can still get the worst of the worst "made in China," but they now possess the ability to produce the best of the best as well. Just as Japan was once known for being the great copycat of the world, causing it to become so motivated to change that it is now known for how uniquely elegant and beautifully designed their products are, there is no doubt that "made in China" will no longer be scoffed at by the world for low cost production quality, and that day may be sooner than you think. With its large consumer market, the world has already begun to "make for China" as well.

---

59 David P. Goldman, "US-China decoupling: a reality check," *Asia Times Financial*, April 14, 2020, https://asiatimes.com/2020/04/us-china-decoupling-a-reality-check/

It is difficult to quantify how well countries are doing in the global supply chain beyond standard statistics. In 2011, Ricardo Hausmann et al.[60] published *The Atlas of Economic Complexity*, which attempted to measure the amount of productive knowledge that each country holds, by visualizing the differences between national economies making use of "complexity statistics" in 128 countries. The book concludes with hints at "how difficult and complex it may be for government planners to kick-start a new industry—while showing that there are new industries that will struggle to get started without help." In our current Era of Knowledge, strong leadership and a large well-trained labor force further explain why Chinese high-tech companies are now gaining ground in the global supply chains. There is no doubt this global trend will persist into the future, fueled and furthered by increasing partnerships similar to the Regional Comprehensive Economic Partnership (RCEP) in Asia and the Comprehensive Agreement on Investment (CAI) in Europe.

---

60 Ricardo Hausmann, et al., *The Atlas of Economic Complexity* (Puritan Press, 2011).

Part III:
Building a Harmonious Future

Who doesn't want world peace? But when we look at the news these days, it sometimes feels so far out of reach. Our politicized communities and cities are highly fragmented and polarized. There seems to be no end to the conflicts, the differing opinions, and the societal problems that now seem insurmountable—over the decades, they have become really big and complex. Often, to keep our sanity, all we can do is to focus back on the things we can change in our day to day lives. Every choice we make, however small, has an impact, whether good or bad. What is most difficult but most meaningful, though, is to make a conscious and educated choice rather than to just follow along with what everyone else is doing. When the news is not always reliable and trustworthy, when our social feeds tend to confirm our biases, it's easy to just blindly follow along and feel confident we are on the side of right. But increasingly there is no right or wrong in our world. Just a massive spectrum of grey. And we need to become more aware, even more comfortable, living in that grey area.

We believe it is indisputable that China is well on its way returning to the glorious country it once was, hopefully even better, and if we want our increasingly interconnected world to be peaceful, then the Chinese and Western worlds must embrace each other for the benefit of all humanity. Because we've established now that they are indeed very different, we believe that if these two can find ways to resolve their differences, be willing to work with and learn from each other, that will be the strongest and broadest foundation on which a peaceful world can be built. This requires an effort from everyone: to empathize more with other ways of thinking and behaving, to seek to better understand the historical context and lessons of our own and other civilizations, and to dream bigger about advancing our collective humanity—not just the country, religion, or culture we were born into. Regardless of which world we associate more with, learning will broaden our minds to different ways of thinking, which will gradually influence the choices we make and how we act. It also helps us better understand ourselves. If many people can start to do this, then we will have a movement, and as civilization has shown time and again, a movement has the potential to change the world.

TEN: PLAY THE INFINITE GAME

The COVID-19 pandemic of 2020 was a wake-up call in many ways. It showcased huge differences in how governments and people responded, based on their cultural preferences. Regardless of the outcome, it will profoundly change the world's economic and political order and international relations. But more importantly, it creates opportunities for cultural changes of the sort required to challenge a world cultural order that has long been dominated by a powerful liberalism, especially since that liberalism has proven impotent, sometimes even counter-productive, to efforts or actions preventing the spread and progress of the pandemic.

Cross-cultural scholars Roger Ames and Peter Hershock, in *Confucianisms for a Changing World Cultural Order*,[61] asked: "When we look for the cultural resources necessary to respond to global predicaments, primary among them are resources suited to replacing the familiar competitive pattern of players strengthening possibilities for coordination across national, ethnic, and religious boundaries. As is now widely appreciated, Confucian cultures celebrate the relational values of deference and interdependence. That is, relationally constituted persons are to be

---

61 Roger T. Ames and Peter D. Hershock, *Confucianisms for a Changing World Cultural Order* (University of Hawai'i Press, 2018).

understood as embedded in and nurtured by unique, transactional patterns of relations—a conception of person that contrasts rather starkly
with the more familiar model of discrete, self-determining individuals that is an artifact of the eighteenth and nineteenth-century Western
European approaches to modernization and nation-state building that has
become closely associated with liberal democracy. Might a contemporary
Confucian ethic that locates moral conduct within a thick and richly tex-
tured pattern of family, community, and natural relations be a force for
challenging and changing the international cultural order?"

INFINITE GAMES

Ames and Hershock offer James P. Carse's game theory[62] as useful in beginning to think through how Confucian values could make a difference in a
newly emerging cultural order. Carse distinguished between finite games,
which are played to win by single actors according to a finite set of rules
over a finite period of time, and infinite games, which have no limit.

A finite game is a zero-sum game of sorting out winners and losers.
The pervasiveness of what has become an ideology of individualism and
rational-choice theory makes finite games a familiar model for the way in
which we are inclined to think about our daily transactions as particular
persons, corporations, and as sovereign states, across a range of activities that entail competition—including sports, business, education, and
foreign affairs.

Infinite games are different. They are not played to win, but rather to
enhance the quality of play. Infinite games have no discernible beginnings
or endings, but most importantly, rather than focusing on competition
among single actors, they focus attention on strengthening relationships
with the ultimate goal of sharing in advancing human flourishing, not
sorting out winners from losers. The relationship among family members
might be a good example of the infinite games we play, where parents are
resolutely committed to strengthening the relationship they have with
their children so that together they can respond productively to whatever
increasingly complex problems their lives together might present. In the

---

62　　　James P. Carse, *Finite and Infinite Games* (Ballantine Books, 1987).

case of infinite games, the interdependence of relationships means that the success and prosperity of parents and children are coterminous and mutually entailing—they either succeed or fail together. Infinite games are always win-win or lose-lose.

Eurocentric thinking and social Darwinism were responsible for driving Western nation-states to imperialism and colonialism, dominating the world as they became very powerful after industrialization. They always won and everybody else lost. The most powerful imperialists became hegemons, leading and shaping the Atlantic world, and later on the Indian Ocean, the South China Sea, and the Pacific. Over the past centuries, we have seen hegemony transferred among European imperialists from Portugal (1450) and Spain (1530), to Holland (1620), France (1740), and Britain (1815), and finally after two devastating world wars, to the United States, which is still the only superpower in the world, dominating the world in every possible human endeavor. In Europe, it took two decades for Europeans to finally come to some peace with its neighbors after the establishment of the European Union in 1993. But finite thinking still prevails in the Western world and in dealing with others.

INFINITE HUMANITY

> Confucius replied, "To be humane is to spread five practices in the world."
> Zizhang asked, "And those are?"
> Confucius said, "Respect, tolerance, trustworthiness, diligence, and generosity. If you're respectful, you won't be insulted. If you're tolerant, you'll win the hearts of the people. If you're trustworthy, people will have confidence in you. If you're diligent, you'll get things done. If you're generous, people will do things for you."
> - The Analects of Confucius 17:6

The Chinese Way always starts with the heart-mind of the internal self. How we self-cultivate virtue is by introspection and controlling negative desires. Nature is always moral and just. As an integral part of Nature, humans should also be moral and just. If humans do not do what is good, they must have lost some of their original power, which can only be restored through self-reflection, self-cultivation, and education. There has been an explosion of interest by Westerners over the last few decades in practices such as meditation, quieting the mind, practicing self-reflection regularly, even reflective daily journaling; all are techniques one may find helpful to restore the virtuous good that Confucians believe is within each of us, and find our way back to be in harmony with Nature and The Way.

Ancient Chinese have a deep-rooted sense of morality and a willingness to sacrifice self-interest for the common good, both ideas well preserved in the Chinese language as sayings and proverbs. Those sayings, in addition to the many Confucian and Daoist traditions of China, have empowered Chinese people to weather many hardships through multiple generations over the past two millennia. As a result, Chinese people know how to save and conserve during the good times, and how to persevere during the storms. They embrace that change is a constant, a dynamic fluctuation between yin and yang where one cannot exist without the other, and together are part of a greater whole. Following the Chinese Way is also analogous to flowing water, which the Chinese admire for being soft yet strong enough to cut through rock, and so adaptable such that should it come across a boulder in its path, it will just go around it.

The ideal Confucian *shi,* in particular, have roots cultivated wide and deep into Chinese sayings and traditions that enable humans to enjoy life, and thrive as one part of the great whole of Nature, even when there is very little materialistic support. Many folk stories throughout Chinese history continue to inspire people, often praising their endurance and resilience. Such spirit of *shi* empowers people to minimize their negative desires and serve others altruistically by espousing Confucian *ren* and *yi,* sacrifice aspects of their own life if that is what it takes, and yet derive happiness from within themselves by doing so. We do find similar stories and actions in other civilizations where this spirit of generosity is also displayed, but the Chinese emphasis has been both deeper and wider, having been reinforced through Confucian teachings for the last two millennia.

All Chinese relationships are familial, which can be understood as an infinite game of win-win in which every member is working to improve the whole family, including extended family. Through an early and constant emphasis on self-introspection and self-discipline, Chinese people are taught to take responsibility for things themselves instead of relying on external laws or constraints to guide their actions. Dignity is earned through moral actions. Western society stresses individual rights, freedom, dignity, and independence, but seldom insists on self-discipline. Chinese cultural tradition, Confucian in particular, emphasizes communal values and the propensity to self-sacrifice. An "individual" is at the center of all relationships, but has both rights *and* duties. One of the most important duties is to do whatever is necessary to harmonize with the other centers (individuals), with their community, nation, and Nature. Admittedly, very few humans can actually live up to the full Confucian ideal, but it is an inspiring Chinese utopia that we should at least understand, as it differs greatly from a Western utopia.

Chinese people admire the spirit of Confucianism in every profession. For example, a Confucian businessman embodies the Confucian ideal of a fiduciary society by emphasizing traditional values while honoring his commitment in business, maintaining his credibility, and committing himself to doing what is right instead of what is profitable. One can find Confucianism and the spirit of *shi* in every profession in modern China, but especially among educators, scientific workers, social entrepreneurs, and those in the medical professions. A recent example of self-sacrifice was in 2020 when over forty thousand medical workers and health care volunteers from all over China relocated to the epicenter in Wuhan to help in the fight against the coronavirus (COVID-19) pandemic. That kind of sacrifice is both common and respected, even revered, throughout the country. The Chinese government also performed its duty, acting like the head of a family, taking care of and protecting its people against the self-desire of a few, resulting in getting the pandemic under control two months after the Wuhan shut-down, a feat that the West refuses to recognize since it is a concept in stark contrast with Western liberal rights and individualism. Confucianism reached its lowest point during Mao's cultural revolution because it contradicted Mao's revolutionary ideals. But current Chinese leaders endorse it as an essential element of being Chinese. Confucianism is again breathing and thriving with new life across the country and at the same time modernizing itself in a renewed Chinese Way, both in China and in East Asia.

In 2014, there was an inaugural conference for a World Consortium on Research in Confucian Cultures held at the University of Hawaii, and attended by scholars of traditional Confucian culture from China, Korea,

Japan, and Vietnam. In a special issue commemorating the establishment of this consortium,[63] Ames and Hershock asked the central question: How has Confucianism functioned historically, generation after generation, within the specific conditions of an evolving Chinese culture to try to make the most of its circumstances? In response, they shared the following observations:

> However we might choose to characterize "Confucianism," it is more than any particular set of precepts or ported ideology identified post hoc within different phases or epochs of China's culture narrative. Confucianism is not so much an isolatable doctrine or commitment to a certain belief structure as it is the continuing narrative of a community of people—the center of an ongoing "way" or "dao" of thinking and living. Approaching the story of Confucianism as a continuing culture narrative presents us with a rolling, continuous, and always contingent tradition out of which emerges its own values and its own logic. A narrative understanding of Confucianism is made available to us by drawing relevant correlations among specific historical figures and events. Confucianism is importantly biographical and genealogical—the stories of formative models. And in reflecting on the lives of Chinese philosophers—a survey of often passionate, sometimes courageous intellectuals who as heirs to the tradition of the "scholar-official" (shi) advance their own programs of human values and social order—we become immediately aware that any account of the existential, practical, and resolutely historical nature of this tradition makes it more (and certainly less) than what would be defined as "philosophers" doing "philosophy" within the contemporary Western context.

63　　　Roger T. Ames and Peter D. Hershock, "Introduction to special issue commemorating the establishment of The World Consortium for Research in Confucian Cultures," *International Communication of Chinese Culture*, Vol 3, 543-547, (2016).

Ames and Hershock's characterization of Confucianism as a narrative certainly explains why it has survived through generations in China, as well as spread to other countries in East Asia. It is a living narrative contingent upon the histories and conditions of its hosts. The conference discussed the evolution of Confucian culture in Korea, Japan, and Vietnam, where its influence is rapidly spreading and growing. In some ways, because many of those countries did not experience Mao's suppression of Confucianism and education, they adhere more closely to the traditional Confucian culture than even China itself does—there is much even the Chinese must re-learn about their Confucian roots.

There are many in Asia today who believe that Confucianism and the Chinese Way can provide a great framework to build upon in constructing a new world cultural order. While the world was dominated by the West over the past two centuries, everybody learned the Western way—its culture, worldviews, religion, values, and institutions. We all have benefited from its enrichment of our lives. But as the world becomes increasingly pluralistic and better connected, and as the West becomes less dominant overall, there are many valuable traditions, narratives, values, and perspectives that the non-Western world has to offer. In many ways, the Chinese Way is a natural guide for living humanely and in harmony with Nature, strengthening our souls through introspection, and building a growth mindset in how we adapt to change. If we can cultivate this in our day to day lives, and even more importantly try to teach it to our children from the very beginning, humanity will be stronger for it.

INFINITE TIANXIA

The field of International Relations (IR) became an academic discipline relatively recently, when *The Twenty Years' Crisis* by E. H. Carr was published in 1939. Based mainly on European experiences, early IR studies focused on the need to find a system of collective security for Europe to replace the power system after WWI. Carr was called a "realist" for his analysis, as a leading critic of the more traditional "idealists." Since the late 1980s and early 1990s, constructivism has become one of the major schools of thought within IR. Constructivist theorists believe that the fundamental structures of international politics are social rather than material, and significant aspects of IR are historically and socially constructed, rather than inevitable consequences of human nature or other essential characteristics of world politics. Obviously, the field of IR needs to continue to mature as more data and case histories from the non-Western world become available for study.

Chinese civilization, on the other hand, has been developing along a totally different paradigm because of its relative continental isolation and conditions. With insurmountable Himalayan mountains in the south and southwest, the Gobi and other deserts in the west, northwest, and north, and the equally insurmountable four seas in the east, Chinese civilization was developed virtually in isolation from the rest of the world since ancient times. Chinese called their world *Tianxia,* all-under-Heaven, representing all of humanity and Nature, with humanity as an integral part of Nature. It is important to note that the word "Heaven" used here is sacred, with great respect, but without any religious connotation. In some ways, it is synonymous with all the lands and people that live under the sky above us. According to one of the Confucian classics, *The Book of Rites,* "When the great Way prevails, *Tianxia* is for everyone." Thus, the Chinese Way includes values like *ren, yi, li,* harmony, balance, humility, and broadminded inclusiveness, which extends to all humanity without exception, regardless of religion, race, or creed. These key concepts form the basis of how Chinese civilization has ended up playing an infinite game, embracing all of humanity in East Asia as an extended family living and thriving together under *Tianxia.*

Chinese differentiate people mainly by their level of civilization, judging based on how well they treat each other. "Things you don't want, don't give to others." In Confucianism, this can be achieved through self-cultivation and education, being honest with yourself and others, and acting responsibly in life. This embodiment of the spirit of *shi* provides a narrative for what a true Confucian would do in practice, thereby enriching the Confucian tradition. A similar differentiation among nations produced a hierarchy of social entities with the Middle Kingdom practicing the Chinese Way in the center and a periphery of lesser civilizations or states with different degrees of ethicality and morality around it in every direction. Based on China's history, culture, and traditions, it has always built the strongest relationships with its closest neighbors, then with others, depending on the distance or difference in positions between the countries. China's worldview was not initially one of interaction between equals, but instead a traditional self-centered land under the *Tianxia* view.

Although China's worldview now has a stronger sense of equality, the influence of Confucianism is still apparent. Countries in east and southeast Asia, as culturally the closest to China, are still their best trading partners. For example, on November 15, 2020, a group of fifteen Asia-Pacific nations signed the Regional Comprehensive Economic Partnership (RCEP) which brings together 2.2 billion people, about 30% of humanity, into a new economic cooperative agreement that is arguably the largest in world history. The ten members of the Association of Southeast Asian Nations (ASEAN), which initiated and led negotiations for the partnership agreement, include the poorest and least-advanced nations in Asia, as well as the most well off, and everything in-between. Sacrifices were needed by countries like China, Japan, and Korea, who were relatively more advanced, in order to properly support the poorer nations, which desperately need help in their development. It took eight years, but all parties were able to put aside political and cultural differences, and leverage their Confucian roots as well as infinite thinking to create an arrangement that maximizes the long term interests of every member of the group, not just the most powerful ones. It is very Asian, and also a great example of harmony in diversity.

Traditionally and culturally the most ethical and moral, the Middle Kingdom embraced *Wangdao* (the Humane Authority) in dealing with others, not hegemony. In Mencius' teaching, powerful larger states should always exemplify the spirit of *shi* and be altruistic in their dealing with lesser states. China has been a dominant power in central Asia, east Asia, the South China Sea, and the Indian Ocean during its long history. But China's interests were always related to culture and trade, never hegemonic. Because Chinese people suffered so much from natural calamities, they learned early on how to live collaboratively with each other under a shared *Tianxia*. This precept of *Tianxia* was uniquely Chinese, truly worlds apart from the former dominating zeal of European nation-states.

Tianxia has no permanent boundaries. Like many Chinese concepts, the term is mainly cultural and cannot be exactly defined, but the Chinese have never had a problem communicating about it among themselves. The geographic location of the so-called center has shifted many times during Chinese history. The center can become the periphery and the periphery can become the center as cultural conditions change with time. This flu-idity has enabled China to survive as a political and cultural entity even when the nomadic Mongols and Manchu occupied the country. Over time, both the Mongols and Manchus became peacefully assimilated into the big Chinese family of races. China has fifty-five minority races, and to this day, many Chinese people treasure their national integrity and unity more than many other people in the world do because of their feeling of kinship under *Tianxia*. For the class of *shi* who treat *Tianxia* as their life mission, humanity is their extended family.

When in isolation, China traditionally took centuries to assimilate various minority races into its multiracial family. For example, Muslims have been living peacefully in China since the Tang Dynasty. But recent events, such as the case of the Uyghurs in Xinjiang, have caused the Chinese government to feel the heat. It started with violence and deaths in some Chinese cities caused by a group of extremists trained by the same "East Turkistan Movement" that trained terrorists in the Middle-East for the Islamic State. In response to the terrorist acts, the Chinese government detained many extremists and put them through "re-education camps." This has caused a massive outcry around the world, suspecting China of various forms of abuse and attempting to indoctrinate people into the Communist ways through internment camps and forced labor. Though the United States and other countries ask for worldwide support of their military-based antiterrorism efforts, they seem to show little to no sympa-thy for Chinese efforts towards antiterrorism. This double standard has left the government with no choice but to quicken the process of assimilation through language education and job training. People can argue over which method is more effective, and unfortunately, China's politics sometimes prevents the world from getting a truly clear and factual picture of things, but it is important at least to recognize there are different ways to address the same problem, and there is often more than meets the eye. Hopefully, over time the world will come to learn the truth behind this situation.

Complementary to Confucianism, Daoism also talks about *Tianxia*, frequently under the context of relationships between humanity and Nature. Laozi, the founder of Daoism, said in *Daodejing*:

Cultivate Virtue in yourself, and Virtue will be real.
Cultivate it in the family, and Virtue will abound.
Cultivate it in the village, and Virtue will grow.
Cultivate it in the nation, and Virtue will be abundant.
Cultivate it in Tianxia, and Virtue will be everywhere.

Here, the broader the range in which one cultivates virtue, the greater one's virtue will be. Daoist philosophy further extends humanity to be unified with Nature. The precept of *Tianxia* provides a resource that allows us to see our world and our international relationships organically and holistically. *Tianxia* offers a different and workable cultural alternative to nationalism. In other words, while nation-states use the traditional logic of a finite zero-sum game and political borders for its players, *Tianxia* offers a new infinite paradigm where it's win-win or lose-lose for everyone since we live together on this planet, and so ideally all humans should share a future destiny, caring for and loving each other like a family despite any differences we may have.

In an essay entitled *The Clash of Civilizations*,[64] Samuel P. Huntington, a political scientist, claimed that international political conflicts and the future of human development can both be explained in terms of a clash of civilizations. In 1996, he further maintained that in the future, a divergence between Western and non-Western civilizations, rather than political and economic differences, will define the battleground where international conflicts arise. He asserted that the clash between traditional Confucianism on the one hand, and both Islam and the non-Islamic West on the other, will be the focal point of international conflicts. These conflicts will determine the future structure and orientation of international politics. Huntington's point of view is readily interpretable, even predictable, according to our characterization of traditionally confrontational Western thinking preferences and worldviews.

In contrast, Tu Wei-Ming, Huntington's historian colleague at Harvard and a renowned Chinese Confucian, strongly disagreed.[65] Tu asserted that

---

64 Samuel P. Huntington, "The Clash of Civilizations?," *Foreign Affairs* (Summer 1993).
65 Tu Wei-Ming, Bingyi Yu, and Zhaolu Lu, "Confucianism and Modernity—Insights from an Interview with Tu Wei-Ming," *China Review International*, Vol. 7, No.2, pp 377-87

it is a *dialogue* of civilizations, not a clash, that appropriately characterizes the current mainstream of our world. Moreover, conflict exists not just between civilizations; it arises internally, within each civilization system as well. Tu pointed out that countries and regions around the world are confronted with the conflict between improving material life and maintaining moral and spiritual values, between fostering economic growth and preserving the environment, between protecting individual rights and safeguarding the community, between change and stability, and so on. Problems that are common to different civilization systems indicate that a wide-ranging dialogue between different civilizational and cultural streams is both possible and necessary. Through such a dialogue of civilizations, Western and Eastern cultures will come to understand and complement each other better for the sake of coexistence and co-development.

Of course, which interpretation to choose depends very much on the background of the interpreter. But they do seem to confirm our observations that Chinese look for similarities and accommodation between people while Westerners tend to look at the differences. The precept of *Tianxia* helps us understand Tu's point of view on cross-cultural dialogue. Tu is a respected Chinese historian well-rooted in Chinese culture and tradition, likely infused with the spirit of *shi*, and looking for ways to make his contribution to humanity and *Tianxia*. Many of his writings reflect his altruistic commitment and scholarship. Interpreters with only Western backgrounds, however, may consider him naive. Having taught at Harvard for decades, he has started many initiatives to engage Western scholars in meaningful dialogue between the East and West, and he is definitely aware of how our future destiny is already linked, regardless of which identity or nationality we belong to. Like Tu, we believe it is only through continuous cross-cultural dialogue that our future generations will be able to better understand and accommodate each other in sharing this beautiful planet.

INFINITE POLITICS

Chinese studies of international relations can be traced all the way back to the Warring States era (475-221 BC) over two thousand years ago. Similar

(University of Hawai'i Press, Fall 2000).

to the European birth of IR inquiries, it was the era where the warring states in China were seeking lasting peace under *Tianxia*. As Chinese scholar Xuetong Yan wrote in his book, *Ancient Chinese Thought, Modern Chinese Power*:[66]

> ...on the grounds of protecting their own security, [the pre-Qin state] sought to develop and resolve the relationships among themselves and the central royal house and thus they accumulated a rich and prolific experience in politics and diplomacy. This complicated and complex political configuration created the space for scholarship to look at the international system, state relations, and interstate political philosophy. The pre-Qin masters wrote books and advanced theories, trying to sell to the rulers their ideas on how to run a state and conduct diplomacy and military strategy while they played major roles in advocating strategies of becoming either a humane authority or a hegemon...

So it was the topic of war and peace that has inspired thought for both Chinese and Western IR scholars. But due to contrasting thinking preferences, worldviews, and collective experience, their approaches to war and peace were very different, leading to different paths of subsequent development. What we can learn from Chinese experiences during the Warring States era may have relevance to our current global multistate system, as Yan suggested in his writing, especially considering that our current nation states are very interdependent, which is an outcome of globalization and technological advancement over the past few decades somewhat analogous to the situation during the Chinese Warring States era. Emperor Zheng of Qin finally unified the country in 221 BC, marking the end of the Warring States era. He ruled through powerful organization, centralization, and standardization, weaving the country closer together by constructing more roads and canals. Future global systems will also need better integration, not differentiation, and more connectivity and less

---

66 Xuetong Yan, *Ancient Chinese Thought, Modern Chinese Power* (Princeton University Press, 2011).

walls, with inclusive organization and an infinite *Tianxia* mentality. Just as China needed to be united during the Warring States period, our world and its people need to be reconciled for peace in order to move forward. This trend was well illustrated during the 2020 COVID-19 pandemic—the best results were attained where and when people banded together to fight it instead of fighting for their individual rights. We need to be more global and less tribal.

During the Classical Age of China, different schools of military strategists competed with their ideas on how kingdoms should conduct themselves domestically and in their dealings with each other. They were basically all extended families of the Zhou Dynasty, and exemplified the precept of *Tianxia*. Debates usually centered around topics of morality, righteousness and profit, war and peace, just wars, moral wars, leadership, good versus bad governance, and universal order. Most favored justice, benevolence, and morals over power of any kind. Daoists emphasized powerful examples in Nature such as water, which is soft and never resistant, yet also very strong, capable of cutting through canyons. The Mo'ists denounced all aggression, favoring more humanly love. Humans should be as inclusive as the ocean, infinitely tolerant, receptive to all, and never spilled or filled. Then there was the Legalist school, which insisted that people were evil by nature and would commit crimes if the state authority did not discipline them.

For the more mainstream Confucian, a true king rules his kingdom by exemplifying the highest morality and caring for his subjects. By extension, his kingdom deals with others, especially weaker ones, through benevolent intentions and actions, and by providing morally-informed leadership. In contrast, a hegemon relies on tyranny and fear to have its way with others. Confucians believed *Tianxia* would be peaceful if it were ruled by a true king with altruistic intentions, and there would be wars if it were ruled by a hegemon. This is the historical context behind why modern Chinese leaders have all pledged on numerous occasions that China will never seek hegemony. At the same time, it will stand firmly for peace if it feels bullied, no matter how powerful the other parties are.

China's economy has come a long way over the past forty years, now second only to that of the US. Recent Western literature has promoted the argument that geo-economics is a new form of power relations that has gained importance since the end of the Cold War. This argument is an extension of a long-standing approach to the so-called "economic state-craft," in which a state uses its economic strategy to pursue foreign policy goals. In this case, it is used in a negative sense because China is labeled as a non-democratic, non-liberal, authoritarian communist country. With a Cold War mentality, or if applying finite game logic, China's intentions are obviously suspicious. In Flint and Zhang's 2019 article, they recommended the alternative term "economic diplomacy"—a long-term strategy that uses economic means for both diplomatic and economic purposes. We believe this is a better term because it fuses, or entwines, economic and political processes, rather than creating a false binary.

But the term still fails to convey our understanding of Chinese foreign policy, which we consider to be relational, holistic, and having a longer-term strategic view in comparison to its Western counterparts. Couple this with an additional ethical component which is seldom considered by Western politicians but is important to the Chinese. But most importantly, we view Chinese foreign policy as a logical extension of its domestic philosophy promoting the Chinese Way of human relationships under *Tianxia*. According to Shao Binhong,[67] the rise of China's concept of world order can generally be divided into three phases: The first phase was during China's feudal period more than 3,000 years ago, spanning from the Western Zhou Dynasty to the Spring and Autumn period. At the time, China viewed the world as an outward projection of its influence. The relationship China had with other territories depended on the proximity of those countries to the son of heaven; in other words China is at the center, followed by the inner ring, the outer ring, tribute countries and peripheral countries, the all-encompassing *Tianxia*, just like an extended family. The second phase was the era of the tribute system. After having transitioned through the Warring States period and the unification of Qin/Han, the son of heaven became emperor of dynasties. The country would generally not engage in direct conquest of the neighboring countries beyond China even though China was the dominant power in the region, but rather, only

---

67 Shao Binhong, *Looking for a Road: China Debates Its and the World's Future* (Brill, 2017).

request that the neighboring territories provide tribute and pay respect to the emperor. Sometimes, the value of the return gifts from China would surpass the value of the tributes paid. But this relationship was by no means equal; rather, it was self-centered, illusionistically extending to infinity in all directions. China was ignorant of events beyond its own border. The third phase is contemporary China. The Opium Wars brought China back to reality.

Historically, until the Opium Wars, the Chinese Way followed the logic of an infinite game with China at its center, potentially with an infinite number of players, contingent rules, infinite time to play, but with a single purpose of enhancing the quality and experience of the player-community, not sorting out winners and losers. In the brave new world of nation-states, China has no choice but to play the finite game, both culturally and psychologically, but Chinese people still identify and consider the world to be their *Tianxia*. Under such a cultural context, it is natural for China to propose its modern Silk Road initiatives and the precept of a shared human destiny for the world. Chinese people are fully supportive of this, as it is effectively their default. But without such a contextual understanding, traditional Eurocentric politicians often misinterpret Chinese intentions and actions and regard them as a challenge to American hegemony that needs to be resisted. At this juncture of global development, especially in the post-pandemic era when the world needs to collaborate in bringing back growth to our global economy, China has much to contribute. When we look at how divided the world is, our work is cut out for us—whether at the individual level or at the level of international politics, we must all work hard to build trust and confidence in each other now, more than ever, thinking infinitely to enact the best win-win solutions for everyone.

ELEVEN: CONNECT EVERYTHING

All the continents on our Planet Earth were joined together as the super-continent Pangaea during the late Paleozoic and early Mesozoic eras, approximately 335 million years ago, until they began to drift apart about 175 million years ago. Our solar system lives in a seemingly nondescript neighborhood of the vast Milky Way Galaxy, which is only one of thousands of billions of galaxies in our universe. Space-time is close to infinite on a human scale. In relation to these, our human species is still in a very early stage of evolution, its infancy, if you will. Only two thousand years ago, very few humans, if any, knew how large their Eurasian continent truly was, not to mention the existence of other continents like the Americas or Antarctica. A few centuries ago, we were still debating whether the Earth was round or flat, and whether the Sun goes around the Earth or the other way around. We were able to connect with other continents only very recently through the burning of hydrocarbons. But the use of fossil fuel has already heavily upset the delicate ecological balance on Earth, and humanity is starting to pay the price.

Human ingenuity is quite amazing if we use it constructively, as seen in the many ways it is connecting people all around the world. But we are only just beginning to realize the impact we are having on each other and on our planet in this increasingly complex and interconnected world. The 2020 coronavirus pandemic was a great reminder of how helpless humanity can become when facing almighty Nature. Over one million humans died while tens of millions were infected. It is becoming apparent that to meet future challenges and survive on this planet, we will need to expand our scientific knowledge on Nature, and put aside our many differences, identities, and ideologies, and work together as a team to save the future of humanity as a whole.

ANCIENT CONNECTIVITY

Back in the Stone Ages, our ancestors were very ignorant of their living environment. Tribal wars over resources were a common occurrence due to scarcity. For a long time, fighting and adapting for basic survival was the main goal in life. As cultures and civilizations developed, initially mostly independent of each other, they began to acquire different characteristics reflective of each choice made in life, in living, or in how to see and interpret their own world. Some faced many hardships where certain basics—such as water or food for human survival—were not readily available, such as in high mountains or deserts. In such cases, the people may have developed ways of thinking or types of relationships that supported their own comfort and protection in the harsh environments surrounding them. For example, nomadic people developed a culture in which individual members must be independently strong, courageous, and resourceful, while also being somewhat desensitized to other people's feelings and sufferings. The instinct to fight and conquer was a key part of their cultural norms. On the other hand, other ancestors may have been more fortunate, living in an environment of abundance, but often challenged by natural disasters such as floods and drought. Under such conditions, people had to work genuinely and cooperatively as a team. Strong, capable, and moral leadership was necessary to manage the resources and maintain social harmony. The bigger the group, the greater the need for social ethics and government. In this way, we are all products of generations of cultural choices and environmental adaptation that influenced how we chose to connect, which in turn, determined what kind of society or political system we lived in.

Before 1500 AD, societies generally gained historical significance only when they connected with other people and created something greater than themselves. China became populous very early due to the abundance of natural resources, and an environment which was amenable to the early development of agriculture. With a large population over a continental-scale territory, developed in isolation to the rest of the world, collective security and human relationships were a major cultural concern. To survive natural calamities caused by their mighty rivers, Chinese people learned early on how to handle conflict and work collaboratively with each other to attain social harmony and security. Slowly, China evolved into a civilization well-known for people's hard work, fairness, inclusiveness, tolerance, deference, adaptability, and sustainability. As agrarians, peace and stability was always the goal, to allow people to have a happy and fulfilling life.

With many early inventions, China led the world[68] in many technical fields including agriculture, metallurgy, medicine, ship building, writing, and printing, so much so that long before 1800 AD China was the most sophisticated and technologically advanced nation on earth. Chinese people were already culturally, socially, economically, and politically fully connected in their own world when the first emperor of the Qin Dynasty unified the country in 221 BC. More significantly, China did not rely on aggression and conquest to sustain itself. Instead, it focused on internal migration, commerce, technological change, innovation, and cultural inclusiveness to generate the surpluses required to sustain a large bureaucracy for governance. This social and political achievement was unique in the world at that time. Large interconnected, inclusive, and technological advanced communities facilitated specialization and stratification, and the country was hierarchically organized according to the ability and moral capacity of each individual. Very early, China had invented silk for clothing, brass and iron for tools, bamboo and paper for writing, and many other comforts of life. They had also created a bureaucratic system to select leaders for their government who were deemed both virtuous and capable, and yet willing to work diligently and selflessly for the people's benefit.

---

68 Robert Temple, *The Genius of China: 3,000 Years of Science, Discovery, and Invention* (Inner Traditions, Revised ed. Edition, 2007).

The system may have failed multiple times in history, but was sustained, renewed, and rejuvenated every time.

Chinese civilization, with its large population and size, was one of the earliest and strongest communities, and the first to connect the Eurasian continent, which extended all the way to east Africa in the sixteenth century. By the start of the second millennium, China's presence in the market of West Asia was already keenly felt, a result of both land and sea Silk Roads. Silk and porcelain were the commodities most highly sought after by elites and royalties in the rest of the Eurasian continent, and this provided incentive for intra and intercontinental connections. Under the Song Dynasty, centuries before the Portuguese discovery of eastern Africa, maritime trade was already flourishing between China, and east and southeastern Asia, as well as nations around the Indian Ocean, extending to West Asia and East Africa. Trade created the linkage for this embryonic world economy, but China's technology made it possible. Eventually, many Chinese inventions found their way to Europe at various periods in time, facilitated by the Mongols, Arabs, Indians, Persians, and many other Asians. During the Ming Dynasty in the sixteenth and seventeenth centuries, China unfortunately turned inward to isolation as maritime activities were prohibited, and the Chinese people became disconnected from the rest of the world after Admiral Chenhe's seventh journey to west Asia, just when the rest of the world was beginning to flourish and Europeans started to explore the world.

WAVES OF GLOBALIZATION

During the sixteenth century, human society experienced a fundamental change in how humans were interconnected. With newly found technologies from east Asia, previously isolated European communities suddenly found themselves dangerously exposed to new global forces. The experience positively transformed many societies; others were enslaved. The discovery of silver and gold in the Americas provided Europe with the means to participate directly in the huge Asian economy, thus transforming intersecting regional trade networks into global relationships. The Atlantic Ocean was then globalized and connected all the way to the Pacific through the Indian Ocean and the South China Sea. Robbie Robertson[69] called this the first wave of globalization where Europe was "the epicenter of a revolution that transformed global relations." With the Scientific Revolution happening in Europe, human knowledge of our world and our ability to connect improved drastically.

For the first time, foods were exchanged globally with new supplies from the Americas, helping populations to expand rapidly and enabling Europe to utilize scarce land for nonagricultural purposes. As a result, the pace of urbanization in Europe accelerated. The spice trade also helped the South and Southeast Asian populations increase as these regions' economies were monetized and globally integrated. All of Asia's fiscal systems soon reacted to the huge influx of silver and gold. Chinese tea plantations expanded. Silk and porcelain were even more popular in Europe. Spice production increased, and textile workshops expanded in India. Unfortunately, European nations such as Great Britain became worried about the continuous depletion of their silver stock. This caused anxiety and greed, one of the consequences of which was the building of opium plantations by the British East India Company, followed by the opium trade flourishing in 1773, and eventually leading to the Opium War. Thus, Robertson's first wave of globalization ultimately had a destabilizing effect in both Asia and Africa. And Europe had only just begun sorting out their winners and losers.

Robertson's second wave of globalization, driven by technology instead of the trade and commerce that initiated the first wave, began in 1800. It was the age of imperialism and colonialism in the wake of a successful Industrial Revolution in Europe. Abundance of cheap human and natural resources acquired from colonies fueled industrialization, and urbanization, and further improved global connectivity, even though people in underdeveloped countries had to pay a hefty price for it. The global impact of the second wave was much deeper and more rapid because it inherited the preexisting networks of the first wave. Improved communications and transportation systems reduced distances and enabled the movement of

---

69 Robbie Robertson, *The Three Waves of Globalization: A History of a Developing Global Consciousness* (Zed Books, 2003).

goods and people on a scale never before possible. The Europeans benefited most from this mobility. Unlike the Chinese, who tend to be players of the infinite game because of Confucianism, Europeans were culturally more attracted to finite games. People in most other continents suffered heavily from the resulting colonialism and exploitation, but global immigration, commerce, and trade also flourished because of improved connectivity.

According to Robertson, more than sixty million people left Europe for the Americas, Australasia, and southern and east Africa between 1815 and 1914. One million went to north Africa alone. The continent of Africa was divided among European imperialist powers into colonies. As was said in Africa: when the white men first came, we had our land and they had their Bible; now they have our land and we have their Bible. But Europeans were not the only immigrants during this century. Nearly twenty million Chinese and Japanese also migrated, as did some two million Indian citizens, as they escaped from poor conditions at home. The second wave also inherited industrial systems of production that connected new sources of raw materials, again on a scale that seemed to constantly escalate. Production on this scale generated wealth that surged through industrial economies much more impressively than even the Spanish bullion. Indeed, there seemed no end to the production and reproduction. This era also saw the beginning of nationalism, with political borders drawn between nation-states, and in the colonies between the Western powers, a permanent political feature of the modern world.

Robertson's third wave of globalization began with a sense of globalism that earlier waves had lacked. Robertson claimed that democratization, in addition to the presence of technology, was a fundamental dynamic of globalization led by the United States. Indeed, as the US became the only superpower in the world after the Cold War, it was positioned to shape the rest of the world with its liberal ideology, capitalism, and global market economy. Under this phase of economic globalization, multinational corporations outsourced production to developing countries, thereby helping their industrial development, simultaneously reaping huge profits for America. Countries such as Japan, Singapore, Korea, China, India, and many other nations benefitted and are in different stages of industrialization.

This development in globalization was also accompanied by rapid technological advancement, otherwise known as the "Information Age" or Alvin Toffler's third wave civilization at the end of the twentieth century. We are in the midst of changes of immense proportion and with profound significance, drastically changing life as we know it. Our knowledge-based society is responsible for many of the changes that we see in today's world, including new family and social relationships, ways of working, loving, and living, and a new economy. Powerful new technologies reshape our world daily, including moving electronic platforms, supercomputers, instant communication, jet and space travel, applied medical and bio-technology, renewable energy sources, cloud computing, quantum computing, big data and artificial intelligence, virtual reality, autonomous vehicles, smart cities and management, and many more—the list goes on and on. These are creating a sudden explosion of human and machine connectivity around the world on a daily, and often real-time, basis.

But even though globalization and technological development have generally improved human conditions and connectivity, global society has become increasingly vulnerable, uncontrollable, and unpredictable, since national governments can no longer solve problems that are global in nature, and there are no effective global mechanisms or institutions capable of doing it. Problems such as global epidemics, regional and global financial crises, income disparity, wars, hegemonic bullying, environmental degradation, climate change, and extreme weather persist, increasingly dominating and destructive, threatening the security and life for people around the world. Better cooperation, management, and governance on a global scale are becoming imperative for future development, but these seem difficult to achieve when many global citizens are becoming more national, provincial, even tribal, especially in wealthy developed countries.

Better connectivity and increased globalization are supposed to improve efficiency, strengthen economic growth, and generate more wealth for the world. Indeed, according to Francois Bourguignon,[70] before the 1990s, global inequality greatly exceeded inequality within any

---

70 Francois Bourguignon, "Inequality and Globalization: How the Rich Get Richer as the Poor Catch Up," *Foreign Affairs* (January/February, 2016).

individual country. This observation should come as no surprise, since global inequality reflects the enormous differences in wealth between the world's richest and the world's poorest countries, not just the differences within them. Much more striking is the fact that, in a dramatic reversal of the trend that prevailed for most of the twentieth century, global inequality has declined markedly since 2000 (following a slower decline during the 1990s). This trend has been due in large part to the rising fortune of the developing world and is continuing, particularly in China and India. This trend unfortunately seems to be making wealthier nations turn inwards to become more isolationist, in an attempt to protect their fortunes.

But even as global inequality has declined because of improved connectivity, inequality within individual countries has crept upwards, gaining on average more than 2% in terms of the Gini coefficient (which measures the degree of inequality in distribution of income/wealth) between 1990 and 2010. The countries with the biggest economies are especially responsible for this trend—particularly the United States, where the Gini coefficient rose by 5% between 1990 and 2013, but also China and India and, to a lesser extent, most European countries. To counteract this trend, nations should pursue policies aimed at redistributing income. Unfortunately, not very many capitalist countries can or will follow such advice. Only when unexpected factors such as an uncontrollable epidemic threaten their economies are they forced to help the poor. This is where a socialist country like China, coming from a culture where the performance of the government is judged by the welfare of its people, has an advantage.

CONNECTING THE WORLD

Over the past forty years, China has made great efforts in advancing domestic and global connectivity, particularly in building infrastructure. One stellar example is the network of over 35,000 km of high-speed railways they built by the end of 2019, joining every province from the affluent east to the less developed and remote central and west regions. Cities in industrialized regions are now connected to each other within one to two hours of fast transportation, creating super-metropolises. Farm roads in rural regions are even well-connected to cities now through a network of high-speed motorways and trains, ferrying fresh agricultural produce to satisfy the palates of city dwellers. The trains that connect China and Europe through central Asia are just like the camels on the ancient Silk Road. And as a top global manufacturer and exporter, Chinese container cargo ships and airlines are already connected with every major seaport and airport on every continent, along with other global traders.

The ancient Chinese precept of *Tianxia* could be seen when President Xi Jinping announced his Silk Road initiatives, also known as One Belt One Road (OBOR), in 2013. He launched this groundbreaking initiative to connect the world with transport routes, infrastructure, industrial joint ventures, teaching and research institutions, cultural exchanges, and much more. His stated objective was to construct a large unified market that makes full use of both international and domestic markets, utilizing cultural exchange and integration to enhance the mutual understanding and trust of member nations, thereby creating a dynamic and innovative pattern of capital inflows, a large talent pool, electronic networks, and technology databases. The RCEP is a good example of this. To advance OBOR, China proposed five connectivity initiatives around policy coordination, facility connectivity, unimpeded trade, financial integration, and people-to-people bonds that are aimed at achieving connectivity and trade facilitation across Eurasia. OBOR is a multi-trillion investment project— clean, green, open, and sustainable, with investments already in more than 150 countries and international organizations and growing rapidly.

Embodied within OBOR is the precept of *Tianxia*, encouraging nations to benefit from their comparative advantages, creating win-win situations for all involved. The OBOR objectives were included in the Chinese constitution in 2017. It is the paradigm of the infinite game behind this initiative which has been constantly misinterpreted and misunderstood, and even demonized, by politicians using a finite paradigm of winner and losers. Many Western countries feel threatened by the Chinese initiative, viewing it as a challenge to the existing global order.

From the perspective of the developing countries, however, infrastructure is vital to their economic development and growth, so they welcome any help they can get. And after centuries of building across their massive land at world-renowned "China speed," the Chinese have developed some impressive expertise to share. In 2012, China constructed a new port in Djibouti, Africa, and then built a 756 km electrified railway and related infrastructure between the Ethiopian capital of Addis-Ababa to Djibouti in 2015. In 2018, Ethiopia built fifteen industrial parks along the rail lines to speedily transport products made in the industrial parks to the port of Djibouti for shipping abroad, creating much needed growth and employment for its economy.

China also built a diesel-powered Mombesa-Nairobi SGR (Standard Gauge Railway) called the Madaraka Express in Kenya, which carried its first fare-paying passengers on June 1, 2017. Elevated on huge concrete pillars, the SGR can withstand Kenya's fast rains and huge elephants, and is lined with wire fencing to ward off attacks and big game. Viaducts have been crafted so that families of large animals, such as giraffes, can pass under. The main selling point to the Kenyan public was that it would haul 22 million tons of freight a year, slashing cargo transport times from two days to eight hours. And the passenger line is even faster. The Chinese construction contractor hired 25,000 Kenyans to work on the railway, generating a huge boost in employment, and continues to operate it today. The Madaraka Express was initially envisaged as part of an East African Railway Master Plan that would connect Kenya to Ethiopia, Uganda, Rwanda, Tanzania, South Sudan, and eventually go all the way to the Democratic Republic of Congo—another beautiful win-win situation benefitting both sides, pumping blood through the veins of developing countries by connecting them to the world.

On the morning of July 30, 2019, the "Africa Pride" tourist train entered the Benguela Railway Lobito Railway Station. It departed from Dar es Salaam, the capital of Tanzania on the Indian Ocean, embarking on a 4,300 km journey, passing through Zambia and Congo, to arrive at the port city of Lobito on the Atlantic Ocean in Angola. For the first time ever, the Indian Ocean and Atlantic Ocean are connected by rail on land, marking another great milestone in China's efforts to connect Africa, and by extension, the rest of the world.

One may wonder why China is expending so much effort on Africa? For the Chinese, it's mostly normal course of business—going where there's a need and opportunity to apply their expertise while creating a win-win scenario. But for Europeans, Africa is very important to the global world order. If we consider how much European countries have suffered from the refugee crisis caused by wars in Iraq, Syria, and Libya, can we even imagine a refugee crisis caused by failed African states? The scale of such a calamity would dwarf our imagination. Instead of criticizing Chinese efforts in helping African development, the West should join in as soon as it can. China has been working hard at the grassroots levels, building much needed infrastructure to enable trade, agriculture, and light industrial development. But Europeans have even more knowledge and experience with these former colonies, so would be ideally suited to help connect and develop Africa. The potential win-win could be tremendous for all parties if the West, China, India, and Africa could effectively work together to expedite agricultural and industrial development and service industries. This is an infinite game all humanity can join in and benefit from. Taking it a step further, such collaboration would trigger global economic growth and employment that could even help pull other developing countries out of poverty.

Increasing connectivity is a persistent global trend, and our human need for better connectivity is stronger than ever. According to an Indian-American specialist in international relations, Parag Khanna,[71] connectivity has replaced division as the new paradigm of global organization. He believes that human society is undergoing a fundamental transformation, after which functional infrastructure will tell us more about how the world works than political borders do. Functional infrastructure includes mega-cities, highways, railways, pipelines, Internet cables, and other symbols of our emerging global network civilization.

As Khanna describes:

> If the world population has a common goal, it is the quest for modernization and connectivity—the latter a principal path to the former. Connectivity is unquestionably a greater force than all the political ideologies in the world combined. Deng Xiaoping, who managed to dismantle the Soviet-style communes of Mao's Great Leap Forward and even opposed the Cultural Revolution, subsequently launched the reforms

---

71 Parag Khanna, *Connectography: Mapping the Future of Global Civilization* (Random House, 2016).

of the 1970s that connected China to the world economy and catapulted it from backwaters to superpower. The same is true of religions. In most places, religion and the marketplace peacefully coexist. The religious revival among the newly minted middle-class Indians and Chinese has much to do with showing gratitude and praying for continued success in the global economy. Both societies know that without connectivity they would have much less to be grateful for.

He further observes:

Connectivity has become the foundation for global society. After all, individuals connect with the rest of the world not through politics but through markets and media. Supply chains literally embody how we (indirectly) feel each other: Low-wage Asian workers keep the price of mobile phones down for consumers worldwide, al-Qaeda militants attacking a Saudi oil refinery spike gas prices for urban commuters, and Indian and Filipino call center workers solve everyone's tech conundrums... Nothing connects rich and poor, East and West, North and South, like supply chains. Tenuous as these links may be, we are more likely to care about things we are connected to than those we are not. Pollution floating over the Pacific from China to California makes Americans think about climate change more than sinking Pacific Ocean islands... Connectivity enables the empathy that guides our ethical evolution.

In his view, a new supply chain global order is not a libertarian fantasy in which markets rule the world. Nor is it a universal socialist paradise. It is an evolutionary reality, and we should seek pragmatic strategies to create an ethical community versus a market society that neglects community bonds. Rather than waiting for governments to provide justice, dignity, and opportunity, people are forming new associations—professional, commercial, and virtual—not as a substitute for local social capital, but as an essential new kind of global social capital.

As part of his conclusion, Khanna further expounds:

The time has come for even bolder thinking about how to leverage near-total connectivity to advance large scale human development. Infrastructure, markets, technologies, and supply chains are not only logically uniting the world but also propelling us toward a more fair and sustainable future. But there is still a long way to go. Billions are still without roads and electricity; food is scarce; money is a luxury. Bad infrastructure and bad institutions stand in the way of bridging supply and demand. It is a moral imperative to overcome them.

This passage perfectly echoes our sentiment that there is no time like the present to band together as a human race and think infinitely. The theme of the 2008 Beijing Summer Olympics was "One World, One Dream." We are living in an age of greatness, where improved global connectivity as a result of globalization and advanced technology has brought humanity closer together than at any other time in history. Our world is already so interconnected that if you, too, long for the dream of a peaceful humanity on Earth that can handle whatever crises Nature may throw at us, it is imperative that we immediately start creating a new global conscience and effective governance for the world.

TWELVE: LEARN FROM HISTORY

Mark Twain once infamously said in his autobiography, "There is no such thing as a new idea. It is impossible. We simply take a lot of old ideas and put them into a sort of mental kaleidoscope. We give them a turn and they make new and curious combinations. We keep on turning and making new combinations indefinitely; but they are the same old pieces of colored glass that have been in use through all the ages."

Some days it feels like we are watching the same mistakes being made over and over again, sometimes even generation after generation. If you take individuals with a similar cultural background and worldview and present them with the same situational trajectory, people tend to come to the same conclusions on how to act; hence, history repeats itself in a myriad of ways. As we become a more global society, it is becoming imperative that we understand, not only our own history, culture, and circumstances, but that of other societies and cultures. If we could somehow read through the lessons that have been learned by all of humanity over time, learn how to empathize from a different perspective, or find new and different ways that others may have handled the same problems or situations, would we make different or even better choices?

PUBLIC ENEMY #1

Peace finally arrived in 1945 after the Allies decisively defeated Germany and Japan in World War II. This was the last war the United States fought in which the President asked Congress for a declaration of war. Since then, the US military has been involved in many foreign interventions around the world, against adversaries, in the name of democracy, liberty, human rights, and national security. The Cold War followed World War II and lasted forty years, as a response by President Harry Truman and successive presidents to try to contain Soviet aggression and communism, creating another ideological war to protect the "Free World." Truman gave a speech to Congress on March 12, 1947, establishing what became known as the Truman Doctrine, warning of the communist threat:

> At the present moment in world history nearly every nation must choose between alternative ways of life. The choice is too often not a free one. One way of life is based upon the will of the majority, and is distinguished by free institutions, representative government, free elections, guarantees of individual liberty, freedom of speech and religion, and freedom from political oppression. The second way of life is based upon the will of a minority forcibly imposed upon the majority. It relies upon terror and oppression, a controlled press and radio, fixed election, and the suppression of personal freedoms. I believe that it must be the policy of the United States to support free people who are resisting attempted subjugation by armed minorities or by outside pressures.

The personal freedom of individuals and the form of government are the major issue here. Three years later, in April 1950, Truman approved a secret policy paper known as NSC-68, which laid out his strategy for containing communism around the world.

The Soviet Union, unlike other hegemonic predecessors, was animated by a new faith in its own brand of communism, which was antithetical to the values of the Free World, and sought to impose its absolute authority over the rest of the world. Our world was at the brink of a nuclear holocaust during the Cuban Missile Crisis in October 1962, threatening the survival of humanity. But when the Berlin Wall finally came crumbling down in 1989, and with the dissolution of the USSR, along with the Warsaw Pact, the West had decisively won the Cold War.

In the summer of 2020, senior officials in the administration of US President Donald Trump started casting the United States and China as antagonists in a new Cold War, even though the global situation is totally different; decades of globalization have made the two economies intertwined. Speaking to the Arizona Commerce Authority in June 2020, US National Security Advisor Robert O'Brien compared Chinese President Xi Jinping directly to the Soviet dictator in power when the original Cold War began: "Let us be clear, the Chinese Communist Party is a Marxist-Leninist organization. The Party General Secretary Xi Jinping sees himself as Josef Stalin's successor." To dispute this misinformation, Michael McFaul, US Ambassador to Russia from 2012 to 2014, wrote an article published August 10, 2020 in *Foreign Affairs*, entitled: "Xi Jinping is Not Stalin: How a Lazy Historical Analogy Derailed Washington's China Strategy."[72] In that article he observed: "Stalin's regime was far more totalitarian in its control over every aspect of Soviet citizens' lives. Stalin also killed millions and imprisoned millions more, rivaled in brutality only by Hitler and Mao. Xi does not make the list." Yet, extreme right-wing politicians continue to make China their enemy number one.

On July 23, 2020, American Secretary of State Mike Pompeo, at Richard Nixon's Presidential Library in California, gave a speech about Xi that President Truman could have delivered about Stalin: "General Secretary Xi Jinping is a true believer in a bankrupt totalitarian ideology," adding that Xi's ideology "informs his decades-long desire for global hegemony of Chinese communism." Echoing Truman's speech to Congress on March 12, 1947, Pompeo framed the fight with Xi and the CCP as one in which only one side ultimately could win: "If the free world doesn't change... communist China will surely change us." Misunderstanding the Chinese cultural heritage, Secretary of State Pompeo also seems ignorant of the

---

72 Michael McFaul, "Xi Jinping Is Not Stalin: How a Lazy Historical Analogy Derailed Washington's China Strategy," Foreign Affairs, August 10, 2020, https://www.foreignaffairs.com/articles/united-states/2020-08-10/xi-jinping-not-stalin

fact that Mao's communist China is very different from Xi's communist China. He ignored the detail that one in fourteen Chinese in China is a CCP member in 2020, that they are from every walk of ordinary life, and this is not the case of a small minority forcing their views upon the majority. Chinese people are now free to travel the world, on a scale never seen before in history. Any outside attempts to change the regime in China will end in vain because the government is strongly supported by its people.[73]

It is depressing to see someone still fighting a war of a past era. Pompeo's choice of Nixon's Library to deliver the plea to the world was not an accident. The Trump administration wanted to signal an end to Nixon's journey of reconciliation and peace with China because China failed the US's expectation that it would become another democratic America. They forgot that it was Nixon's rapprochement with China that isolated the USSR and made its dissolution possible. As punishment for being too Chinese, the Trump administration started a trade war, closed down the Chinese consulate in Houston, applied a string of sanctions against CCP members and their families, expelled Chinese journalists and students, and banned multiple Chinese technology companies such as Huawei and TikTok, forcing a decoupling of American technology from the Chinese with the so-called "clean Internet," all aimed at a new cold war and deglobalization to protect the "America First" policy.

Continuing to treat China as an enemy is not going to benefit either side or the world. Arguably, it is also not accomplishing what America and the Western world wants from China. China has repeated many times its vow not to be hegemonic. If America wants to continue having a competition on who is the greatest, at this point, that is a race to the bottom with itself. China's focus is purely on how to do better and self-transcend. With globalization and China's rapid growth trajectory, America's usual strategies for keeping others in line are bound to backfire. They use trade embargoes, long-arm jurisdiction, lies, and hypocritical bullying tactics to show their power and capacity for trouble-making which only generates intense resentment from the Chinese people. Attempts to prevent or slow-down

---

73 Wenfang Tang, "The 'Surprise' of Authoritarian Resilience in China," *American Affairs*, Vol II, Number 1, Spring 2018.

Chinese advanced technological development have forced the Chinese to be more self-reliant even faster, often developing better solutions themselves, such as the case with 5G, GPS, supercomputing, quantum computing, space technology, and artificial intelligence.

Coming into the 2020 election year in the US, the Trump administration was known for its "alternative facts and truth." Mr. Pompeo's declaration of war on China could be dismissed by people as election rhetoric to divert attention from its own failures. However, there has been much misinformation from the American government and in the media over the previous years. The Trump administration fought to protect American hegemony at all costs and "make America great again." Unfortunately, with the significance and power that America holds, these actions have only served to fracture and poison the global community. It is sad to see beautiful friendships between Americans and Chinese people being brutally eroded, utilizing labels such as the "China virus" to create distrust and hostility.

There are some that say America wants a war, even needs one to help fuel its economy. Ever since the American Civil War, there has not been a single war fought on American soil. But because the US has one of the strongest military forces in the world, Americans have benefited politically and economically from almost every war they've participated in overseas, until very recently. In contrast, the Chinese people have suffered so much from wars and natural calamities in its long history that they treasure peace and harmony, striving their hardest to avoid provocation and conflict. Yet, if you recall, "under conditions of high threat, a defensive reaction in the form of nationalism fueled by a narrative of great civilization versus historical victimization is activated." Currently this is taking the form of retaliatory measures, an eye for an eye, and that war is being fought on economic and other battlefields instead of through real military confrontations. It is disturbing to watch, as continuing to escalate based on ideological differences will lead to no good for anyone, and the relationship is already suffering in multiple ways. Instead, a shift of mindset and elimination of rhetoric is badly needed to bring us to the same side before the war starts to take lives. Empathy and trust, seeking to understand before we act and assuming the best intent for each other, is becoming more critical than ever in today's world.

LESSON ONE: EMPHATHIZE WITH YOUR ADVERSARIES

More than three million people were killed in the Vietnam War, and millions of others remain deeply haunted by what happened during those years. As far as we know, this is the only case in history where both adversaries met after the war to document what happened and determine what could be learned from the tragedy. In six sets of unprecedented meetings held in Hanoi, Vietnam, between November 1955 and February 1998, and a seventh meeting held in Italy in July 1998, scholars, along with former civilian and military officials from both Vietnam and the United States, met to engage in a sincere dialogue about the war. They moved beyond blame, that is, beyond us and them. Instead, for the first time, they examined the complex interplay between two opposing sides and the unspeakable tragedy to which this interplay led.

Robert McNamara, secretary of defense in the Kennedy and Johnson administrations, documented these frank, revealing, and sometimes astonishing dialogues in which the two groups walked step-by-step through the war, analyzing each decision and action from both sides, and ultimately producing the document, *Argument Without End: In Search of Answers to the Vietnam Tragedy.*[74] In the document, McNamara and his colleagues described precisely where the Americans and North Vietnamese made crucial mistakes that first resulted in the war, and later led to a prolonging of the war. We also see irrefutably why the war could not have been won militarily by the United States unless it had either resorted to genocide or triggered a devastating war with China or the Soviet Union.

McNamara and his colleagues wrote an inspiring chapter, "Learning from Tragedy: Lessons of Vietnam for the Twenty-First Century," where they singled out the central failure of empathy and communication. Each side fundamentally misread the mind-set of its enemy and there was an absence of high-level contact between the two sides even when the war began escalating. One of the most striking features of these dialogues is the profundity of mutual ignorance and its dangerous consequences. McNamara recounted:

---

74 Robert S. McNamara et al., *Argument Without End: In Search of Answers to the Vietnam Tragedy* (Public Affairs, 1999).

As Chester Cooper commented on the first day of the June 1997 conference, American ignorance of Asia was such that "we did not know what we did not know. And that was one of our problems when we got involved here in Vietnam." Later in the same session, focusing on the mindsets of both sides during the early 1960s, Nicholas Katzenbach suggested that the ignorance was mutual and that "one of the reasons for the misconceptions in these various mindsets comes from the fact that... each country is focused on its own problem." There is a natural tendency for a party to a conflict to focus disproportionately on its own problems and, therefore, to mistakenly attribute the actions and motivations of others to factors affecting one's own situation but not the adversary's.

This is indeed a valuable lesson, one which McNamara, as American defense secretary, was well qualified to draw because of his direct personal involvement in the war. He contended:

In every way, American ignorance of the history, language, and culture of Vietnam was immense. Vietnamese ignorance of the United States and U.S. decision-making was at least as great. This profound mutual ignorance encouraged each side to project onto the other motivations and objectives that had little, if any, semblance to reality. Indeed, each projected onto the other motivations and intentions that ultimately proved to be tragically wrong... The American obsession with the global chessboard of the Cold War blinded leaders in Washington to the decisive importance of Vietnamese nationalism and the desire of the Vietnamese people for reunification.

Mutual ignorance of the situation, culture, and history of their adversaries resulted in tragedy for both the Americans and Vietnamese. We have repeatedly seen Western thinking focused on the simple dichotomies of extremes, like the free world versus communism, ignoring key factors in a conflict. In this case, it was Vietnamese patriotism, and the difference between European communism and nationalist communism that is common in Asia. Based on the Western experience in Europe, everything made sense—it was simply the Free World fighting against the communist insurgence. But in fact, before American involvement in the war, it was French colonialism that the Vietnamese were fighting against, and for even longer, Vietnam had been fighting the Chinese for their independence. Unlike the Soviet military occupation to install communist regimes in eastern Europe, Asian communism was led by indigenous nationalists and patriots to whom ideology was far less important than independence from colonialism—an irony that both the French and Americans failed to grasp. Just imagine how thrilled Ho and Vietnamese people would have been if, instead of taking over the war after the French defeat, the US actually offered them unification on terms acceptable to the Free World. That one action, creating an independent country of Vietnam, would have triggered eternal gratitude to America and made Americans welcome throughout Asia.

In 2007, after surveying the histories of both Western and Chinese cultures, we observed that historically ignorance, misinformation, misconceptions, misunderstandings, or miscalculations are often cause for wars between states or animosity between people, resulting in tremendous unnecessary human suffering and sacrifice. We wrote the first lesson from history then—in order to avoid a preventable war, understanding each parties' true intentions and justifications, and having empathy for our adversaries, are both mandatory:

> *Lesson One: Values and value judgments are often culturally dependent. Therefore, the use of force is never effective in achieving a permanent resolution of conflicts. Before going to war, we should reconsider our justifications by placing ourselves in our rival's situation, within their cultural and historical context. By doing so, we may find a way to achieve our objectives without unnecessary sacrifice and while avoiding compromising our own values and principles. We should empathize with our antagonist!*

Even at war, it is important to keep communication channels open, build off common ground, such as a mutual desire to stop bloodshed and save humanity, and take every view into consideration to avoid unnecessarily prolonging the war. These lessons always have relevance, even more so in our interrelated world today when politicians, public, and social media fill the news with misinformation, misconceptions, alternative truth and facts, populism, terrorism, polarized and fragmented societies and states, and international conflicts.

In the daily news, we constantly hear labels being thrown around by Westerners and politicians, habitually differentiating countries as "communist" versus "capitalist," "Christian" versus "non-Christian," "multi-party rule" versus "single party rule," "authoritarian" versus "democratic," and "capitalist economy" versus "socialist economy." They often make it sound like a country is either an "ally" or an "enemy"—you're either with us or you're against us, there is no in-between. We support our allies but always fight or even demonize our enemies. Likewise, simplistic labels are used to describe individuals or groups of individuals as black or white, liberal or conservative, left or right, pro-gun or anti-gun, pro-choice or anti-choice, etc. As a result, both Western societies and the world are increasingly fragmented and polarized along the fault-lines. Together with an insistence on political correctness and the advent of social media, other points of view are increasingly needed for deepening and broadening our understanding and to enable better compromises in a democratic society, and the world in general.

Unfortunately, China is a country that can easily be labeled as an enemy because of its differences from the West, which controls the global sociopolitical narratives. China is a communist, non-Christian, and undemocratic state with single party rule and a socialist economy. In fact, it is arguably the only country in the world which is currently qualified to be an enemy of the United States: opposite political ideology, non-Christian, and a size and population worthy of a competitor. In addition, the economic rise of China over the past forty years has made some Americans feel paranoid and fearful. The Chinese economy is now second in the world only to the United States, and if there can be only one leader in the world, then China is an obvious threat based on Western experience.

In a publication entitled, *Destined for War*, Graham Allison[75] asked, "Can America and China Escape Thucydides' Trap?" In that book, Allison

---

75 Graham Allison, *Destined for War: Can America and China Escape Thucydides's Trap?*, (Mariner Books, 2017).

presented twelve historical examples that resulted in war when the friction created by a rising power challenged an established power. Out of the twelve, there were only four cases where war was avoided. Allison focused on the examples he considered to be most instructive: the Peloponnesian War, World War I, and the Cold War. By his projections, the factors favoring war between the US and China are overwhelming: two powers with narratives of their own "exceptionalism," China's sense of past humiliation and present restoration, incompatible cultures and political systems, and a series of entangling flashpoints and alliances.

Unfortunately, what we see on the global stage these days seems to support Allison's projections. There seems to be no end to the rhetoric and provocations on both sides. Our only saving grace may be the highly interdependent trade relationship and stable nuclear deterrence on both sides, as he rightly points out. But like so many other Western dissertations based just on political form and not on historical content and context, he fails to see the differences in the two cultures and civilizations. It is true that American ignorance of other cultures and histories, as well as an emphasis on democracy versus authoritarianism makes China an easy target. But different from the USSR, China historically does not export ideology or aim to propagate a "Chinese model." Beijing has repeatedly assured the world that China has no hegemonic intention to replace the United States. In fact, China has been acting as an avid defender of the current global order built by Americans. It is the US that is backing off from its global leadership and commitments, focusing disproportionately on its **own** problems, mistakenly blaming China for problems they are encountering, and subsequently attempting to cut ties with China. But because the two economies are already extremely intertwined, and even complement each other in many ways, attempting to decouple will most certainly cause heavy damage to the global economy.

LESSON TWO: AVOID SELF-RIGHTEOUSNESS

It is sadly ironic that Adolf Hitler came to power in a democratic German election. Democracy is a means to an end, not an end in itself, but some politicians claim it as though it is absolute. People are vulnerable, and can easily be coerced or convinced into cooperation with demagogues. In

Racial Hygiene,[76] Robert Proctor documented how historians, scientists, anthropologists, and other academics were lured into advancing Nazi scientific research. It was chilling to learn how a passive scientific community failed to grasp the reality of what would happen to the Jews as medical scientists actively designed and administered key elements of the National socialist policy. Proctor also presented a comprehensive account of German medical involvement in the development of sterilization and castration laws, the laws banning marriage between Jews and non-Jews, and the massive program to destroy lives not worth living. His study traced attempts on the part of doctors to conceive of the Jewish problem as a medical problem and revealed how medical journals openly discussed the need to find a final solution to Germany's Jewish and Gypsy problems. Proctor was careful to make us aware that such thinking was not unique to Germany. We find its counterpart in Japanese militarism in Asia; it is just less well known to the Western world.

There are multiple lessons one can learn here. In the 1932 German presidential election, the Nazi party shared power in only one of the German states, Brunswick, which at the time was highly polarized politically. Hitler's quick ascent to power was fueled by economic and political nationalism, where conservative politicians were willing to share power with an extremist party, ignoring moral considerations, and eventually they were outmaneuvered. The lesson of Nazi Germany highlighted aspects of human behavior that can affect all societies, especially in the West. These include the susceptibility to scapegoating and the desire for simple answers to complex problems, the potential for extreme violence and the abuse of power. It also highlighted the roles that fear, peer pressure, indifference, greed, and resentment can play in social and political relations and demonstrated the fragility of all societies and of the institutions that were supposed to protect the security and rights of all. It showed how these institutions can so easily be turned against a segment of society. It also demonstrated the dangers of prejudice, discrimination, and dehumanization, be it the antisemitism that fueled the Holocaust, or some other

---

76 Robert N. Proctor, *Racial Hygiene: Medicine under the Nazis*
(Harvard University Press, 1988).

form of racism and intolerance. All these issues are highly relevant in our current world.

In particular, the United States has much to learn from twentieth century Germany. As an increasingly polarized America fights over the legacy of racism, Susan Neiman's book, *Learning from the Germans: Race and the Memory of Evil*,[77] asks what we can learn from Germans about confronting the evils of the past. She delivers an urgently needed perspective on how a country can come to terms with its historical wrongdoings. As a white woman who came of age in the civil rights-era South, and a Jewish woman who has spent much of her adult life in Berlin, she is immensely qualified to address the topic. She asks: How should a nation's history be told to new generations? Should monuments to Confederate leaders be removed? Should there be reparations for slavery and other historical injustices? Her book does an excellent job of acknowledging the victims of racism and slavery in the US, encourages reflection and empathy, and identifies constructive steps for addressing the past and present to create a different future. She reminds us that it is never too late to reflect and act.

Self-righteousness in the name of religious or ideological beliefs has been rampant through history and even today, showing that humankind often falls victim to a sort of disease of the mind that has the power to devastate cities and destroy civilizations, killing millions of people. Al Qaeda, or Islamic State, carried out its horrific actions against humanity in the name of Islam, which is a gross perversion. Religious wars are the cruelest because human beings are maimed and killed in the name of the divine. The Crusaders, the Conquest and the Reconquest, the Irish war between the Catholics and Protestants, and the religious war between India and Pakistan are all good examples of this horrible irony. Social and economic woes can be corrected, but religious faith is very resistant to change. Religious, ethnical, and ideological conflicts and extremism can turn genocidal when one disputant believes that right and good is completely on its side. For example, the savagery of the oppressive Stalinist era was committed in the name of communism, an ideology that, ironically,

---

77 Susan Neiman, *Learning from the Germans: Race and the Memory of Evil* (Farrar, Straus and Giroux, 2019).

embodies the socialist dream to liberate the poor and oppressed masses. Far too many times in human history, political and ideological propaganda has deceived masses of people.

This brings us to Lesson from History #2 from our previous book:

> *Lesson Two: The worst crimes and the greatest evils against humanity are often based in self-righteousness and committed in the name of the highest virtues. Fanaticism, especially of a political or religious nature, has been one of the major causes of mass human suffering. To avoid such suffering, we must first disallow our political and religious leaders the use of ideology as a cause for discrimination. Secondly, we must learn mutual tolerance and respect for other races, religions, customs, and traditions.*

This second lesson clearly echoes the atrocities committed by the Nazis and Japanese armies (i.e. at the Nanking Massacre) during World War II. The Nazis provided one of the most vivid examples of self-righteousness in their development of nationalist and racist myths promoting the superiority of the Aryan race, an ancient northern European people, and the inferiority of the Jewish people. The resulting millions of deaths remain a permanent scar on the twentieth century. We should be vigilant, as our world is highly polarized and fragmented, and extremism, racism, and populism are on the rise in many developed countries as an outcome of extreme wealth disparity, greed, over-consumption, and immorality.

When discussing political or religious fanaticism, we are reminded that traditional Chinese culture is very practical, seldom ideological, and always trying to seek a neutral middle ground away from the extremes. Distinct from the West, Chinese civilization has always been concerned with ethics and harmony. Early Confucianism was very practical in nature, and its virtues were allied with human spontaneity and education. But as Confucianism became more ideological and political during the Han Dynasty, its doctrines grew increasingly dogmatic, and proponents sank into hypocrisy. Then in the name of Neo-Confucianism, the Ming and Qing Dynasties became rigid and despotic. Society stagnated, and the people suffered. Modern China also suffered during Mao's extremist revolution ideology, and many died unnecessarily. It was not until Deng boldly put aside all ideologies that China was able to return to the path of economic reconstruction, initiating the growing national prosperity we are witnessing today. Because of their different thinking preferences, the Chinese encounter an entirely different set of problems in their culture, such as corruption, human rights abuses, and suppressing of individual freedoms.

The COVID-19 pandemic is one of the greatest global crises of this century. Its depth and scale are enormous, threatening each of the 7.8 billion people on Earth. It has also become a litmus test for world governments. Proving to their citizens that they can manage the COVID-19 crisis will buy leaders some political capital. But those who fail find it hard to resist blaming others for their failure. In the short term, the crisis will give fuel to all the various advocacies in the Western world. The hyper-nationalists, the China hawks, anti-globalists, and the neoliberal globalists will all see new evidence for the urgency of their views. Given the economic damage and social collapse that is unfolding, it is hard not to see a reinforcement of movement toward great-power rivalry, decoupling, and hyper-nationalism in the Western world. Even US President Trump utilized the situation to pursue his personal political agenda—justifying xenophobic tendencies, closing borders, further restricting the mobility of immigrants, and blaming China for any and every negative effect of the pandemic.

It is interesting to study how different countries respond to the pandemic, based on their culture. Western political culture emphasizes form, so many pundits immediately highlighted the contrast between democratic and authoritarian governments, demonizing any positive news from countries considered authoritarian. But politicization of the crisis is easily challenged—how can one rationalize the success of democratic South Korea or communist Vietnam in comparison to other democratic Western countries in Europe and North America? Why did Vietnam have so few causalities from COVID-19 compared with thousands of deaths in Russia? The data simply does not support any correlation between results and ideology—whether a country is democratic or not seems to have no bearing. Instead, it seems that East-Asian countries fare better than the Western countries. A key factor may actually be that East-Asian countries have a stronger collective Confucian foundation built into their culture for practicing self-control and feeling responsibility towards the common good that is stronger than their need for individual rights and freedoms. Couple that with intense cultural and societal pressure, and a previous experience during the SARS outbreak in 2003, and it is noticeable that not only Asian countries but even pockets of Asian communities within the Western world seem to have better success containing the pandemic in their areas.

In our future post-COVID-19 era, humanity is more than ever in need of understanding and trust, empathy, cooperation, collaboration, connectivity, and less confrontation. The pandemic itself is proof of our interdependence, just as climate change is affecting people all around the world in a myriad of ways. These problems are just the beginning – future challenges will likely also be on a larger and more global scale, requiring humankind to think bigger and build bigger in order to meet those challenges. New ways of global governance are desperately needed as are new ways of engaging the masses to work together for a collective good. Throughout the course of history, there are many great examples of the power of the human spirit – seen in people from all walks of life and professions who have demonstrated resilience, effectiveness, and leadership in the face of adversity. Each of us gets to choose how we contribute to the solutions rather than the problem.

THIRTEEN: CRAFT A NEW WORLD ORDER

Dr. Randall Forsberg, a famous leader of the "nuclear freeze" campaign of the 1980s, revealed in *Toward a Theory of Peace: The Role of Moral Beliefs*[78] the many ways that changing moral beliefs came to stigmatize forms of "socially sanctioned large scale group violence," such as human sacrifice, cannibalism, slavery, and lethal punishment. She believed that popular movements could transform people's moral beliefs and that we could apply that to war and weapons. But moral revolutions take many lifetimes to unfold, requiring centuries of dedication and struggle. And it is not until everyone understands what is crucial for world peace that the citizens of the world can begin to act upon it and our politicians can stop investing in weaponry and waging war. It is our duty to stop lies and misinformation, and spread the words of justice, fairness, and humanly peace on this planet.

After the free world triumphed over the Soviet Union when the Berlin wall crumbled, the United States was well positioned to provide global leadership according to their neoliberal ideology. It was the "End of History," as declared by Francis Fukuyama. But more than thirty years later, at the

---

78 Randall Caroline Watson Forsberg, *Toward a Theory of Peace: The Role of Moral Beliefs* (Cornell University Press, 2019).

beginning of the third decade in the twenty-first century, global society is again searching for a new direction and leader to follow and develop.

Three competing versions of a future world order clashed at the World Economic Forum's gathering at Davos in 2018. There was the one pushed by US President Donald Trump, calling for "economic nationalism" and his country's retreat from the current order. Another was advanced by Chinese President Xi Jinping who proposed a "new global economic system" built upon a paradigm of mutual respect, global collaboration, and win-win. And finally there was Canadian Prime Minister Justin Trudeau and French President Emmanuel Macron who urged Western leaders to double down on the current liberal order installed by the US and its allies in order to prevent the recurrence of world war and the economic nationalism giving rise to it. All three versions addressed current economic predicaments as perceived by each of the leaders.

It would be a mistake to dismiss their speeches as spectacle alone. Their debate is enormously consequential. The issue of global governance arises as a product of a neoliberal paradigm shift in international political relations. The prioritization of capital and market mechanisms over state authority-created governance gaps have enabled actors from private and civil society sectors to assume authoritative roles previously considered the purview of the State. This reinforces the divergence of views on global governance, issues that are of the utmost importance and priority in our globally connected world. Most political analysts, however, have ignored obvious cultural considerations such as a contrasting desire for competition versus cooperation and finite versus infinite thinking. If viewed from a Eurocentric point of view, without understanding Chinese culture and history, Xi's vision sounds like communist propaganda that should be dismissed or downplayed. But our world has changed, and ideology should no longer be a reason to discriminate against people or countries. If you look at Xi's vision more seriously, and assuming best intent, his words are a sincere reflection of Chinese and Confucian values, and a rallying cry for working together to build a better future for humanity.

STATE OF THE WORLD

As a result of increasing connectivity and transformational technologies, our world is becoming very different from that of past generations and is rapidly becoming ungovernable if we consider only our past experiences in government armed with outdated ideologies. The US became the only superpower in the world after the Cold War and has provided leadership since. But since the financial crisis of 2008, the G7 countries can no longer solve critical problems in our world without the cooperation of the developing countries, and the G20 was formed to facilitate collaboration. However, only a year later, President Obama initiated the Pivot to East Asia Strategy (2009-2017) which represented a significant shift in the United States' focus from the Atlantic/Middle East to the Pacific. Since then, US foreign policy has become increasingly hostile towards China, countering every step to its rapid economic rise, fighting to maintain American hegemony at all costs. Obama designed the Trans-Pacific Partnership (TPP) as the key economic pillar of the Asian pivot, aimed at excluding the largest developing country, China, in the play. According to Secretary Clinton, the "pivot" strategy was designed along six courses of action: strengthening bilateral security alliances; deepening America's relationships with rising powers, including China; engaging with regional multilateral institutions; expanding trade and investment; forging a broad-based military presence; and advancing democracy and human rights. It was clear that the design was to contain China. Even though China has no intention to become a hegemonic challenge to the US, such a strategy creates a self-fulfilling prophecy that is counterproductive to cooperation and world peace.

Although President Trump withdrew from the TPP, he expanded the "pivot" to include the Indian Ocean, which is now called the "Indo-Pacific Strategy" or the "Quad," which includes Japan, Australia, and India, forming a powerful alliance. The US uses trade embargoes, long-arm jurisdiction, and wars of every kind to try to slow down China's development. China and Chinese companies have been under attack by America's demonizing tactics, including outright lies and heresies, where no evidence is even needed because the West controls the global narrative. Adding insult to injury, China is further blamed for threatening American security and the global order and this could end in military confrontation. It appears that China was naive to assume that the government of the most powerful country in the world would not, without presenting any evidence, use security as a pretext to break a private company such as Huawei (along with 100 Chinese companies on the American list), even though the outcomes can only be lose-lose for both China and America. Even worse, Asians, and Chinese in particular, have become targets of American hate crimes.

Newly-elected President Joe Biden's administration, fearing Trump's accusation of being too soft on China, has refused to reverse Trump's America First strategy. Biden has made support for democracy at home and abroad the centerpiece of his presidency, so China continues to be enemy #1. Both the US and China talk about a multi-polar world, but there are major differences. China wants a multi-polar world where every country follows the rules defined under the charter of the United Nations, with every country treating each other equally and not interfering in each other's domestic affairs, which all nations agreed to after the two world wars. In contrast, the US wants to continue leading the liberal international order by seeking to dominate every region of the world permanently and promoting democracy everywhere. It looks like these two conflicting visions of a multi-polar world will be on full display throughout Biden's term. Washington will continue to do anything it can to uproot and bedevil Beijing, and Beijing will respond just like water flowing around obstacles. China also will not be afraid of going to war if they need to defend Chinese sovereignty.

The ultimate irony as the US tries to decouple from and undermine China, is that considering how ingrained China has become in the global supply chain, it is debatable whether the US's actions will have anywhere near the effect they want—in fact, it might very well hurt the US more than it hurts China. Increased interconnection between nations and city states has advanced the exchange of knowledge by bringing people, cultures, communities, and states closer together, but information flow is much more organic and increasingly difficult to manage and navigate. National economies are now intertwined in complex global networks with supply chains that governments have increasingly little control over. Additionally, pressing issues such as bio-security, cyber-security, and ecosystem and climate change all need immediate global attention, but national governments are not equipped to handle problems that are global in scope. New regulations, rules, and guidelines are required for future innovation in science and technology because ethical considerations are increasingly important. In this phase of globalization, we are and will be confronted with many cultural, social, and political issues in addition to the economic issues of the past. But our current global institutions have already proven inadequate to provide the guidance and leadership that is much needed to advance. So people and governments must work in tandem to find new ways going forward.

There is no doubt that global connectivity brings greater complexity and uncertainty if national self-interest is the only measure. Regional wars, terrorist threats, refugee problems, and widening income disparities are worldwide problems that are breeding populism and extremism in the developed world and in some developing countries, further undermining global balance and security, as we know it. Whichever way the global order turns, it will shape global stability, security, and prosperity for *all people* in our future world. What is needed now, more than ever, are new ideas, leadership, institutions, and scientific expertise for global governance in our ever-changing, increasingly diverse but more inclusive, technologically advanced international community, capable of leading and navigating us through future challenges, and weathering storms such as the 2020 global pandemic. Further, humanity needs to develop a global conscience capable of solidifying our common values and collective will.

According to Parag Khanna, connectivity is a major driver of the deep shift towards a more complex global system. Connectivity has increasingly replaced division as the new paradigm of global organization in this century. When established institutions such as the United Nations, the International Monetary Fund (IMF), or the World Bank failed to meet the needs of the rising developing countries, power in the current system of global governance became more diffused. The power shift accompanying the rise of Brazil, Russia, India, China, South Africa (BRICS), and others pose questions about the possible reordering of the current global structure. Under China's Silk Road initiatives, the Asia Infrastructure Investment Bank (AIIB) was established, now fully operational, with over 100 members, a list from which the US is noticeably absent. It is open, clean, green, win-win, and sustainable. Western ideas of privatization, autonomous markets, and open capital accounts are further challenged by the state-controlled approaches of rising nations in the developing South. Mutual respect, collaborative development, and multilateralism has become a trend in the second decade of the twenty-first century.

In Chapter Five, which described the inception of Chinese civilization in the first millennium BC, we discussed how the great success of the Zhou was due to their ability to integrate multiple beliefs into a grand, centralized schema that later generations of Chinese still share, and how Chinese rate other people by their degree of civilization and relationships with fellow human beings. It was the Chinese foundational precepts of diversity, tolerance, benevolence, inclusiveness, balance, harmony, flexibility, long term sustainability, and *Tianxia* that made the final unification of China possible in 221 BC. Other than a few short intervals of disunity, China has remained a unified political entity up to this day. There are many similarities between the Warring States period before Chinese unification by King Zheng of the Qin and the global multistate environment we have today. Wouldn't it be amazing if we could somehow apply their learnings and experience to our current context in crafting a more unified world for all of humankind?

COMMUNITY WITH A SHARED FUTURE

In 2013, Chinese President Xi Jinping first raised the concept of "a community with a shared future for mankind," which in essence, is connecting the prospects and destinies of every nation and country in the world, sharing good days and bad, and turning global society into a harmonious family. The concept of a community with a shared future for mankind is consistent with the traditional Chinese precept of *Tianxia*, which in fact overrides any differences in ideology, values, civilization models, and political systems, while offering an alternative for fair and reasonable global democracy and governance. In 2017, at the 55th UN Commission for Social Development (CSocD), a resolution was approved by consensus; it called for more support for Africa's economic and social development by embracing the spirit of building "a human community with shared destiny." Since then, Xi has repeated many times China's commitment: "Building a community with a shared future is an exciting goal, and it requires efforts from generation after generation; China is ready to work with all the other UN member states as well as international organizations and agencies to advance the great cause of building a community [for the] shared future for mankind." The CSocD resolution also welcomes further world efforts to carry out China's Belt and Road Initiative, a network connecting Asia, Europe, and Africa through more than sixty countries and regions, affecting more than 4.4 billion people.

Of course, China's Belt-Road initiative and the UN resolution are a good start, but insufficient for fully realizing this dream. The future of global connectivity, governance, and human welfare will need genuine trust and collaboration from all people, societies, and nations. But without contextual understanding and trust, some Westerners are very skeptical of Xi's intentions. It just sounds too good to be true. For these people, Khanna's research provides additional insights: Latin Americans, Africans, Arabs, Indians, and Asians all want a world in which they can multi-align and trade in all directions, not subject to either Chinese or American dictates. They will play the great powers off each other more willingly than they will accept unilateral impositions. They all believe—correctly—that connectivity rather than hegemony is the path to global stability. Supply and demand will shape how regions and powers interact. If America offers military support and technology, China provides infrastructure and export markets, Europe sends aid and governance advisers, and corporate supply chains smooth the flow of connections, this is the closest geopolitics can come to the stars aligning. Historical models of order have been built on spheres of influence, but a stable global society must be based on co-creation across civilizations.

Due to the need for industrial and technological development of the developing world, more of society is undergoing a fundamental transformation in which competitive connectivity takes place through infrastructure alliances: connecting physically across borders and oceans through tight supply chain partnerships. China's relentless pursuit of this strategy has elevated infrastructure to the status of a global good on par with America's provision of security. Geopolitics in our connected world will be played out less on a game board of territorial conquest and more in the matrix of physical and digital infrastructure. As Khanna further describes:

> Seeing the world through the lens of connectivity generates new visions of how we organize ourselves as a species. Global infrastructures are morphing our world system from divisions to connections and from nations to nodes. Infrastructure is like

a nervous system connecting all parts of the planetary body; capital and code are the blood cells flowing through it. More connectivity creates a world beyond states, a global society greater than the sum of its parts. Much as the world evolved from vertically integrated empires to horizontally interdependent states, now it is graduating toward a global network civilization whose map of connective corridors will supersede traditional maps of national borders. Each continental zone is already becoming an internally integrated mega-region (North America, South America, Europe, Africa, Arabia, South Asia, East Asia) with increasingly free trade coupled with intense connectivity across their thrivingcity-states.

At the same time, maps of connectivity are *also* better at revealing geopolitical dynamics among superpowers, city-states, stateless companies, and virtual communities of all kinds as they compete to capture resources, markets, and mind share. We are moving into an era where cities will matter more than states and supply chains will be a more important source of power than militaries—whose main purpose will be to protect supply chains rather than borders. *Comparative connectivity* is the arms race of the twenty-first century... Connectivity is nothing less than our path to collective salvation.

From Khanna's observations, devolution is the most powerful political force of our age: everywhere, central authorities are splintering and dissipating away from central capitals toward provinces and cities that seek autonomy in their financial and diplomatic affairs. But devolution has an important counterpart: aggregation. The smaller our political units get, the more they must fuse into larger commonwealths of shared resources in order to survive. This trend is playing out around the world, from East Africa to Southeast Asia, as new regional federations take shape while building new shared infrastructures and institutions. A perfect example of this is the Regional Comprehensive Economic Partnership (RCEP) mentioned earlier (established on November 15, 2020 after eight years of intense negotiation among fifteen very diverse Asia-Pacific nations). This agreement is expected to eliminate about 90% of tariffs on imports between its signatories within twenty years of coming into effect, as well as establish new rules for things like e-commerce, trade, and intellectual property.

Indeed, if we look around the world, devolution and aggregation are simultaneously taking place in every country. Intense economic activities are increasingly concentrated in super-aggregated areas around metropolises such as Tokyo Bay, New York, San Francisco Bay, the Yangtze and Pearl River deltas, and around Beijing and Tianjin, mostly away from political capitals. Regional free trade is increasingly popular and in fashion. The real world is competing over connectivity, global supply chains, energy markets, industrial production, and the valuable flows of finance, technology, knowledge, and talent—not capitalism versus communism, or any other ideology. And the global value chain (GVC) concept has gained popularity as a way to analyze the international expansion and geographical fragmentation of contemporary supply chains, and value creation and capture therein. Global supply chains themselves are a dynamic creative process transforming the world. Production sharing has linked cross-border flow of goods, investments, services, people, ideas, and know-how in novel ways. With a culture conducive to combining innovation, markets, production efficiency, collaborative planning, security, management, and crafting win-win scenarios, China excels in the world of global supply chains.

Khanna also advocates that we should view our ecosystem as a natural infrastructure—directly linked to the physical counterpart we have built to harvest it. Almost half of China's GDP is generated from eleven provinces where intense urbanization to meet growth targets has led to resource stresses as severe as that in Middle Eastern countries. In response, China's water infrastructure has been extended to build three water canals that bring water from the abundant Yangtze river in the south to quench the thirst of the drier Yellow river regions in the north, including Beijing. Low-loss long-distance grids were also built to transmit electricity from power-rich provinces in the western regions to the power-hungry populations in the eastern regions. Electric cars will be the future. Currency will all be digital. China is also exploring a polar silk route to transport natural gas from the Arctic ocean, and is investigating the feasibility of producing natural gas from permafrost on the eastern ocean floor. Renewable energy sources such as hydroelectric, solar, wind, tidal, and geothermal are increasingly being used. In 2020, President Xi pledged that China would achieve carbon neutrality before 2060 with a clear road map. These are just some of the environmental innovations and actions that China has been exploring, similar to much of the creative work conducted by environmentally conscious Europeans and people around the world. Over just the past few decades, the average global temperature has already risen by one degree Celsius and the effects are already visible, no matter where you live. Since we must share this planet and its natural resources, each and every effort must be made to protect our planet, and international efforts such as the Paris Accord, especially, must be defended before it is too late.

LESSON THREE: PROMOTE HARMONY IN DIVERSITY

With more and more countries in the Global South joining the ranks of the middle-income group, the gap between the developing world and the developed world is narrowing. Our global society is increasingly more diverse, plural, creative, and culturally rich and colorful. Moreover, with improved connectivity, diffusion of technology is widely taking place, improving the quality of education, skills, and lives in general for people in many developing countries. Together, our seven-billion-strong-humanity (projected to be nine billion by 2050) should be able to rationally find its direction, finding creative ways to overcome any man-made or natural challenges presented, as long as it can act in solidarity.

Karl Jasper called the Axial Age "the most creative period in human history." In about the same span of several centuries, intellectuals around the world generated various classical systems of ideas and values; for example, the One Hundred Schools period of China's Warring States, Greece's Classical Golden Age, and the Upanishads and Buddhism in India. Although some critics disagree with the term "Axial Age," it was indeed a period of immense creativity coincident with a broad diversity of technological, cultural, social, economic, and political achievements. The creativity of this era has remained unmatched by any other time, with only the industrial and contemporary knowledge and information revolutions potentially approaching similar profundity. Indeed, the dynamism unleashed during the Axial Age continues to this day, influencing many of our traditions and thinking.

Creativity and diversity are inherently connected, as we described in Lesson from History #3 from our previous book:

> *Lesson Three: Human creativity is the basis for technological, social, economic, and political advancement, as well as fulfillment and happiness. Because cultural, social, and political diversity, built on a foundation of harmonious human values, is a prerequisite for such creativity, plurality is therefore a basic foundational requirement for human existence and a way to maintain creativity and spontaneity, which opens the path to fulfillment and happiness for all people.*

Diversity does not preclude commonality and shared values. Between friends and among families, societies, and states, it is an innate characteristic that we enjoy human commonality and shared values, such as mutual affection for each other, love, loyalty, happiness, and a dislike of alienation, hatred, betrayal, and misery. Thus, pluralism refers both to the infinite variety of individual values, personalities, goals, aspirations, and dreams, and the complexities and fellowship of social belonging, which is essential for fulfillment and happiness for all humankind, not just a chosen few. But we must be vigilant, not allowing any person, institution, ideal, or religion to privatize collective ownership.

Diversity, however, is also a double-edged sword because it can trigger potentially volatile human emotions and values. On one hand, diversity empowers innovation and creativity. Cultural and political diversity, built on a foundation of common values, are essential for human progress, just as biodiversity is important to bio-evolution. On the other hand, diversity can generate conflict, which can lead to destruction if not handled properly. This is demonstrated by the numerous religious wars of the past in Europe and the Middle East, and in the last two world wars. As our world is becoming increasingly diverse, it is becoming even more imperative to understand the precept of harmony in diversity and integrate it as part of our global conscience.

To grasp this concept, we need to first understand and apply the concept of interdependence as a foundation for positive relationship building. To start with, each person must be at peace with themselves, feeling securely rooted and embedded. Once they've successfully reached a reasonable level of cultivation, they can then grow themselves outwards, practicing tolerance and understanding, first with another individual, and gradually building that mutual understanding and interdependence within their family, community, and then nation, such that eventually it influences the relationships between diverse global states under *Tianxia*. Sustainability is attained by striking a proper balance, not going to the extremes, and encouraging collaboration and sharing with others. Harmony requires dignity, trust, respect, and community. The feeling must be mutual or multilateral, not unilateral. It also demands the development of clear rules determined by common consensus and derived from shared values, and a rigorous policing of those rules in order to control emotion and greed, thus binding the participants together. The right rules and institutions are needed to enable us to make decisions, express our collective judgment of right or wrong, and protect harmony in diversity. Once set in place, these rules and institutions must then be allowed to evolve according to our collective moral sense. If any single party begins to believe it has a monopoly on truth or wisdom, evil will germinate.

Quoting again from Parag Khanna:

> Connectivity has also sparked a cognitive revolution by which we come to appreciate globality as a new baseline condition: there is a global dimension to everything. Neither Western nor Eastern ideas dominate, but wisdom flows in both directions, between Western tunnel vision and Eastern holism, between humanism and scientific materialism, between democracy and technocracy.

Daniel Bell, a Canadian political theorist at Tsinghua University, argues that harmony is a viable bridge between East and West because in Confucian thought, harmony seeks peaceful order, but also respect for diversity in social relationships. It is not premised on uniformity, as commonly portrayed. Choosing a seemingly "Eastern" concept such as harmony to drive new metrics would hardly privilege Asia: it is small Western countries such as Norway, Sweden, Switzerland, and New Zealand that rank highest on the Harmony Index. The emergent global culture deepens as the two real global languages—English and code—further connect the world through real-time communication and software.

LESSON FOUR: LEARN FROM EACH OTHER CONTINUOUSLY

In our daily lives and scientific endeavors, we build on our knowledge, a mass of theories that have held up to testing over extended periods of time. Because these theories have not been falsified by repeated testing, they become part of our store of human knowledge. Certain knowledge accumulates through time and becomes the basis of customs or traditions. Most traditions, past or present, are forged in association with the activities by which human beings meet their needs for existence, and through which, they ultimately aspire for happiness or fulfillment. Accordingly, traditions or cultural norms are not some abstract contrivance that eschews change and development. As the world becomes increasingly interconnected, invariably cultures and traditions should interact with each other and use their mutual influence to form new cultures and traditions. And at the personal level, we should continuously learn and self-cultivate based on our own and other people's traditions and cultures.

According to historian Robbie Robertson, the history of humanity, especially over the past five hundred years, is marked by a process of ever-developing interconnectedness. This interdependence has extended opportunities for human empowerment and promoted social transformation via the influence of varying human conditions and environments, population sizes and movements, technologies, economies, and cultures. Differences between these factors have always ensured that no one society or state became identical to another. The uniqueness of individuals, societies, and states is therefore presupposed, and should be fully respected, bringing us to Lesson from History #4 from our previous book:

> *Lesson Four: Every person, culture, society, and state is unique, yet each shares some essential attributes with others. In order for a person, culture, society, or state to survive and flourish, it must absorb nutrients both from its own tradition*

and the traditions of others. But it cannot simply copy. Traditional and external political, religious, and economic ideas and concepts are applicable to current situations only after they are properly digested, synthesized, internalized, and integrated under local conditions and contexts.

The record of human existence is a narrative of understanding, overcoming, and recreating our own assumptions, traditions, received wisdom, and culturally conditioned viewpoints in order to appreciate and accommodate the viewpoints and the resulting actions of others, past and present. In the face of the ever-changing conditions and problems that humankind faces, ideals, traditions, and established institutions must be dynamically transformed and renewed.

We first wrote this lesson of history more than a decade ago. We have since observed and interpreted global affairs by applying this lesson frequently, particularly in the context of contrasting Chinese and Western cultures. Before its historical decline, Chinese culture embraced change, was flexible, evolutionary, contingent upon conditions, and not principle-based. It was a cultural narrative, a secular and humanistic religion, in a sense, but without commitment to any deity or supernatural beings. As stated by contemporary Confucian Tu Wei-Ming: "Just as the self must overcome egoism to become authentically human, the family must overcome parochialism, the state must overcome ethnocentrism, the world must overcome anthrop-centrism to become authentically human." Traditional Chinese culture believes that any human can achieve evolutionary transcendence through education and self-cultivation. That is why, especially after the humiliation of the Opium Wars, Chinese intellectuals learned so quickly from the rest of the world, and continue to today, particularly in Western humanities, customs, science, and technology.

In fact, the advancement of humankind's cultural, social, and political states can be measured by degrees of self-transcendence. The Renaissance and the Industrial Revolution are excellent examples of how traditions can be transformed and renewed when new conditions are introduced into the sphere of human existence. We have gleaned from Chinese history that at the personal level, the individual achievements of a historical figure have always been measured by the degree to which he or she was self-cultivated and able to self-transcend, with the ultimate goal of serving the family, society, and state. Similarly, at the state level, the most prosperous times in Chinese history have always been the periods when China was open to foreign influence, and capable emperors listened to the advice of their officials—for example, during the early Tang Dynasty. The worst times occurred when China was closed to foreign influence and emperors and their officials were unreceptive to advice such, as in the Ming Dynasty. One of the best examples for successful cross-cultural synthesis, the fruit of the former, more open, stance was the sinicization of Buddhism from India during the Sui and Tang Dynasties, and perhaps China's current drive towards modernization, learning and synthesizing essential aspects of Western civilization to become part of a renewed Chinese tradition.

Traditional Western culture is monotheistic and principle-based and believes in the universality of applications. Its religious tradition, political constitutions and institutions, analytical, logical, and deductive thinking, and metaphysics, all resist real change. In recent years, society has been held back by egoism, parochialism, Eurocentric thinking, and anthropocentrism. Yet, with its cultural, social, political, economic, and military prowess and domination, it is still controlling global narratives. If the world is to have a paradigm shift from finite to infinite, embracing and sharing a common destiny, the Western world needs to put aside its pride and its biases, and start appreciating and learning from other cultures. It may take a revolution, or a global crisis such as a pandemic, for this realization to really happen. Western culture has been so dominant that everybody has had to learn the Western ways and there has been no impetus for that to change. But in this new age of high interconnectivity, when the world needs to globalize, work, and collaborate to create a peaceful shared future destiny, it will be the Western world that needs to adapt to the change for us to go forward in solidarity.

Respecting diversity and learning from others does not mean that we cease to recognize and acknowledge strengths and weaknesses. Some cultural values are more suited to our present human needs than others. Some economic systems are more productive. Some political structures are better able to mobilize the creative energies for the benefit and security of their people. We must be honest and courageous enough to concede that others' ways may be superior to ours in a particular area, and it is in our best interest to learn from them, or at least allow them to help or teach us. No individual or collective should force its views on another. We cannot impose ideological, religious, political, or economic systems on societies whose histories and traditions differ from our own. But we do need to create an open environment that encourages mutual learning and healthy competition, as in an infinite game. Human connectivity, productivity, prosperity, and personal fulfillment are all inextricably related.

In an age of increasing specialization, there is a growing need for integration and governance to supplement and manage specialization, especially in growing fields such as artificial intelligence, big data, ecology, biomedical sciences, brain development, or genetic engineering. In all of these, a holistic approach with an ethical dimension needs to be considered for further development, not only for a few people, but for the future of all humankind. No complex, non-linear system can be adequately described by dividing it into subsystems or various predefined aspects. That is why our understanding of human connectivity is so important. As best said by Nicholas Christakis and James Fowler[79] in their book, *Connected*, "The great project of the 21st century—understanding how the whole of humanity comes to be greater than the sum of its parts—is just beginning." We need to think not only in minute, detailed specificities, but also about macroscopic future consequences such as human survival, before it is too late. The qualifications, capability, and virtuosity of such leadership is becoming critical, especially at these early stages in the development of a global world order. Ultimately, people need to foster a more global conscience, seeking what is right for humanity, our planet, and our future generations.

At the global level, the world today is enjoying unprecedented prosperity, evident since the latter part of the twentieth century, when information, knowledge, and connectivity began to transform the way we communicate, think, live, and learn from each other, with the result that we

---

79 Nicholas A. Christakis and James H. Fowler, *Connected: The Surprising Power of Our Social Networks and How They Shape Our Lives—How Your Friends' Friends' Friends Affect Everything You Feel, Think, and Do* (Little, Brown Spark, 2011).

have overcome and transcended some of our histories, traditions, and prejudices. With increasing globalization, connectivity, and advances in technology, the global community is already becoming more mature and organized, and hopefully becoming more human, just, peaceful, open, harmonious, and green. We dream of a future where our planet will be free of nuclear or any other kind of lethal weapons, where war will be a distant memory, a small part of our growing pains; where it is no longer "us versus them," but all of us working together collaboratively and harmoniously. Our world will be even more diverse, individualistic, and colorful, and there will be no need for identities and borders, national or otherwise. Every member of humanity will be free to pursue their own dreams, using technology like robots to perform undesirable chores. Even the dream of a classless and stateless society according to individual needs can be realized. Capitalism will no longer be considered necessary. It will be truly democratic, free, and reflective as crucial decisions can be made instantaneously with the help of technology. We believe this is not just a dream, but that humanity will eventually embrace our shared destiny and work hard towards building this beautiful new world. It starts with each of us, opening our minds to new ways of thinking, learning from the history and cultures of humankind, and not just our own, and actively seeking ways to bring the best ideas and experiences to the forefront to be shared.

INDEX